ALIENATION

NEW DIRECTIONS IN CRITICAL THEORY

NEW DIRECTIONS IN CRITICAL THEORY
Amy Allen, General Editor

New Directions in Critical Theory presents outstanding classic and contemporary texts in the tradition of critical social theory, broadly construed. The series aims to renew and advance the program of critical social theory, with a particular focus on theorizing contemporary struggles around gender, race, sexuality, class, and globalization and their complex interconnections.

Narrating Evil: A Postmetaphysical Theory of Reflective Judgment, María Pía Lara

The Politics of Our Selves: Power, Autonomy, and Gender in Contemporary Critical Theory, Amy Allen

Democracy and the Political Unconscious, Noëlle McAfee

The Force of the Example: Explorations in the Paradigm of Judgment, Alessandro Ferrara

Horrorism: Naming Contemporary Violence, Adriana Cavarero

Scales of Justice: Reimagining Political Space in a Globalizing World, Nancy Fraser

Pathologies of Reason: On the Legacy of Critical Theory, Axel Honneth

States Without Nations: Citizenship for Mortals, Jacqueline Stevens

The Racial Discourses of Life Philosophy: Négritude, Vitalism, and Modernity, Donna V. Jones

Democracy in What State? Giorgio Agamben, Alain Badiou, Daniel Bensaïd, Wendy Brown, Jean-Luc Nancy, Jacques Rancière, Kristin Ross, Slavoj Žižek

Politics of Culture and the Spirit of Critique: Dialogues, edited by Gabriel Rockhill and Alfredo Gomez-Muller

Mute Speech: Literature, Critical Theory, and Politics, Jacques Rancière

The Right to Justification: Elements of Constructivist Theory of Justice, Rainer Forst

The Scandal of Reason: A Critical Theory of Political Judgment, Albena Azmanova

The Wrath of Capital: Neoliberalism and Climate Change Politics, Adrian Parr

Media of Reason: A Theory of Rationality, Matthias Vogel

Social Acceleration: The Transformation of Time in Modernity, Hartmut Rosa

The Disclosure of Politics: Struggles Over the Semantics of Secularization, María Pía Lara

Radical Cosmopolitics: The Ethics and Politics of Democratic Universalism, James Ingram

Freedom's Right: The Social Foundations of Democratic Life, Axel Honneth

Imaginal Politics: Images Beyond Imagination and the Imaginary, Chiara Bottici

ALIENATION

RAHEL JAEGGI

Translated by Frederick Neuhouser and Alan E. Smith

Edited by Frederick Neuhouser

COLUMBIA UNIVERSITY PRESS   NEW YORK

COLUMBIA UNIVERSITY PRESS
Publishers Since 1893
New York Chichester, West Sussex

cup.columbia.edu
Copyright © 2014 Campus Verlag GmbH
English edition copyright © 2014 Columbia University Press
Paperback edition, 2016

The translation of this work was funded by Geisteswissenschaften International — Translation Funding for Work in the Humanities and Social Sciences from Germany, a joint initiative of the Fritz Thyssen Foundation, the German Federal Foreign Office, the collecting society VG WORT, and the Börsenverein des Deutschen Buchhandels (German Publishers and Booksellers Association).

Library of Congress Cataloging-in-Publication Data
Jaeggi, Rahel.
  [Entfremdung. English]
  Alienation / Rahel Jaeggi; translated by Frederick Neuhouser and Alan E. Smith; edited by Frederick Neuhouser.
      pages cm. — (New directions in critical theory)
  Includes bibliographical references and index.
  ISBN 978-0-231-15198-6 (cloth : alk. paper) — ISBN 978-0-231-15199-3 (pbk. : alk. paper) — ISBN 978-0-231-53759-9 (e-book)
  1. Alienation (Social psychology)   2. Self psychology.   I. Title.
HM1131.J3413 2014
302.5′44 — dc23

2013044698

Columbia University Press books are printed on permanent and durable acid-free paper.
Printed in the United States of America
c 10 9 8 7 6 5 4 3 2 1
p 10 9 8 7 6 5 4 3 2 1

Cover Design: Jason Alejandro

.

CONTENTS

FOREWORD

Axel Honneth

NO CONCEPT HAS BEEN MORE powerful in defining the character of early Critical Theory than that of alienation. For the first members of this tradition the content of the concept was taken to be so self-evident that it needed no definition or justification; it served as the more or less self-evident starting point of all social analysis and critique. Regardless of how untransparent and complicated social relations might be, Adorno, Marcuse, and Horkheimer regarded the alienated nature of social relations as a fact beyond all doubt. Today this shared assumption strikes us as strange, for it seems as though these authors, above all Adorno, should have realized that the concept rested on premises that contradicted their own insight into the danger of overly hasty generalizations and hypostatizations. For the concept of alienation—a product of modernity through and through—presupposes, for Rousseau no less than for Marx and his heirs, a conception of the human essence: whatever is diagnosed as alienated must have become distanced from, and hence alien to, something that counts as the human being's true nature or essence. Philosophical developments of the past decades on both sides of the Atlantic have put an end to such essentialist conceptions; we now know that even if we do not doubt the existence of certain universal features of human nature, we can no longer speak objectively of a human "essence," of our "species powers," or of humankind's defining and fundamental aims. One consequence of this theoretical development is that the category of alienation has disappeared from philosophy's lexicon. And nothing signals more clearly the danger that Critical Theory might become obsolete than the death of what was once its fundamental concept.

Yet in recent years it has seemed to more than a few philosophers that our philosophical vocabulary lacks something important if it no longer has the concept of alienation at its disposal. It is often the case that we can hardly avoid describing individual forms of life as alienated; not infrequently we tend to regard social conditions as failed or "false," not because they violate principles of justice but because they conflict with the conditions of willing and of executing what we will. In such reactions to the conditions of our social world we inevitably find ourselves falling back on the concept of alienation, even if we are aware of its essentialist dangers; as antiquated as the talk of alienation may be, it apparently cannot simply be eliminated from our diagnostic and critical vocabulary. This book can be understood as a philosophical defense of the legitimacy of the category of alienation. Its aim is to revive for us today the social-philosophical content of this reviled concept.

The author, Rahel Jaeggi, is completely aware of the difficulties that such an undertaking entails. Updating the category of alienation requires not only the conceptual skills necessary for explicating its meaning in such a way that, without losing its critical force, it avoids essentialist presuppositions; beyond this, it must also be shown that it is truly indispensable for a critical diagnosis of the conditions of social life. In tackling the first task the author is helped by the fact that she is equally well versed in the classical history of the concept of alienation and in recent, analytically oriented debates concerning the nature of personhood and freedom. This familiarity with two philosophical traditions that until now have been split off from each other enables her to identify precisely those places in the classical concept of alienation where essentialist consequences can be avoided by relying on more formal accounts of human capacities. With respect to the second task, the author benefits from a considerable talent for the phenomenological description of everyday life. This talent enables her to depict human phenomena such as rigidity, the loss of self, and indifference so vividly that the reader is virtually compelled to look for ways of recovering the concept of alienation. These two philosophical sources define the strategy and landscape of the present investigation: it begins with a historical sketch of the concept of alienation that makes clear both the conceptual strengths and the essentialist presuppositions of the concept; in its main section it brings to light, through descriptions of types of individual self-alienation, the analytic potential of recent accounts of human freedom, which it then uses to establish a concept of alienation free from the defects of essentialism.

Her historical treatment shows with masterful lucidity how clearly Rahel Jaeggi grasps the difficulties that plague the classical concept of alienation. With precision and boldness she sketches the two traditions, deriving from

Rousseau, that analyze the pathologies of modern life more or less explicitly in terms of processes of alienation: first, the tradition of Marx and his heirs, who, following Hegel, understand alienation primarily as a disruption in human beings' appropriation of their species powers due to the structure, especially the economic structure, of their societies; second, the existentialist tradition of Kierkegaard and Heidegger, who understand alienation in terms of the increasing impossibility of returning from the universal into self-chosen, authentic individuality. In both cases the conceptual core of alienation is, as Rahel Jaeggi succinctly puts it, a "relation of relationlessness," namely, a defective, disturbed relation to that relation—whether it be cooperation with others or a relation to self—that constitutes the human being's authentic nature. From this it is easy to see the extent to which, for both Marxist and existentialist traditions, an objectivistic conception of the human essence serves as the normative foundation of alienation critique. For both, alienation consists in a prior human relation (in the former case, a relation of labor, in the second case, a specific form of inwardness) that has been lost sight of to such an extent that it can no longer be brought back into our own life practices.

On the basis of this insight into the architectonic of the classical concept of alienation, Rahel Jaeggi develops in the main section of her study, with the help of brilliantly portrayed individual cases, an alternative model of alienation that refrains from characterizing human nature in terms of a single, distinctive aspiration. She sees the possibility for such a parsimonious foundation for the concept in elements of a conception of freedom that looks to the functional conditions of human willing and of executing what we will. In constructing a foundation for her concept of alienation, Rahel Jaeggi appropriates the fruits of a comprehensive, in-depth discussion of freedom that has taken place in the past two decades among Harry Frankfurt, Ernst Tugendhat, Thomas Nagel, and Charles Taylor. The result of this extraordinarily productive reappropriation, which runs through this book as a second level of argumentation, is the thesis that alienation is an impairment of willing that results from a disappearance of the possibility of appropriating—of making one's own—one's self or the world. Once the weight of the concept of alienation has been shifted to the dimension of the individual relation to self, Rahel Jaeggi shows in the final step of her work how the necessary transition to social analysis is to be taken from here: impairments in processes of appropriation, as manifested in indifference to one's acquired social roles or in the failure to identify with one's own desires, often have their cause in social relationships that fail to satisfy the necessary conditions for such processes of appropriation.

In this manner the present book marks out the paths by which it is possible to reclaim a contentful concept of alienation by formalizing the normative framework of alienation critique. Whoever follows the signposts provided will discover that future talk of alienation by social critics and diagnosticians of society need not signify a falling back into a musty essentialism. For the Institute for Social Research it is at once satisfying and encouraging to be able to receive Rahel Jaeggi's work into its own ranks.

Frankfurt, September 1, 2005

TRANSLATOR'S INTRODUCTION

Frederick Neuhouser

RAHEL JAEGGI'S *ALIENATION* IS ONE of the most exciting books to have appeared on the German philosophical scene in the last decade.[1] It has two significant strengths that are rarely joined in a single book: it presents a rigorous and enlightening analysis of an important but now neglected philosophical concept (alienation), and it illuminates, far better than any purely historical study could do, fundamental ideas of one of the most obscure figures in the history of philosophy (G. W. F. Hegel). That the latter is one of the book's chief achievements may not be apparent to many of its readers, for Hegel is rarely mentioned by name, and the book does not present itself as a study of his thought. Nevertheless, the philosophical resources that Jaeggi brings to bear on the problem of alienation are thoroughly Hegelian in inspiration. Her book not only rejuvenates a lagging discourse on the topic of alienation; it also shows how an account of subjectivity elaborated two centuries ago can be employed in the service of new philosophical insights.

The main aim of *Alienation* is to resurrect the concept of alienation for contemporary philosophy. Renewed attention to this concept is called for, so the book's central premise, because without it philosophers are deprived of an important resource for social critique. For the concept of justice—the main focus of liberal social philosophers—is insufficient to comprehend an array of social pathologies that are widespread in contemporary life and best understood as various forms of estrangement from self: meaninglessness, indifference to the world, the inability to identify with one's own desires and actions, bifurcation of the self. The reason a resurrection is necessary is that traditional conceptions of alienation generally depend on substantive, essentialist pictures of human nature—accounts of "the human essence"—that are no longer compelling. Marx's, for example, relies on a version of the Aristotelian notion of *ergon*—an account of the distinctive species powers of human beings—while Rousseau's relies on the assumption of certain "truly human" ends—freedom, happiness, and the full development of human faculties— that nature supposedly sets for the human species. Jaeggi's ambitious book aims not only at reconstructing the concept of alienation such that it is freed from its essentialist underpinnings but also at showing how such a reconstructed concept brings to light and clarifies ethically significant phenomena that liberal social theories are powerless to detect. This dual task corresponds to the two quite different levels at which the book operates so marvelously: the abstract analysis of an obscure but indispensable philosophical concept and the phenomenologically rich consideration of various forms of what, under Jaeggi's adept analysis, reveals itself as alienation.

In part 1 Jaeggi introduces readers to the object of her study by sketching a brief history of theories of alienation that includes concise but illuminating discussions of Rousseau, Hegel, Marx, Kierkegaard, and Heidegger. The philosophical upshot of this survey is an initial formulation of what Jaeggi takes to constitute the core of alienation: "a relation of relationlessness," a condition marked not by the absence of a relation to self and world but by a deficient relation—a lack of proper connection—to the same. More precisely, alienation is said to consist in a distorted relation to oneself and to one's world that can be characterized as the failure to adequately *appropriate* oneself or the world, to make oneself or the world *one's own*. Alienation, then, stems from a disruption in one or more of the various processes of appropriation (of oneself or one's world), the successful carrying out of which is the mark of a healthy, integrated, self-affirming subjectivity. The possible consequences of such failure, depending on the particular way in which the process of appropriation is interrupted, include a sense of meaninglessness or estrangement, loss of power in relation to self and world, and subjugation to the products of one's own activity. The ways in which these various effects of failing to make oneself or one's world "one's own" constitute constraints on one's will point to the ethical significance of alienation, which resides in the connection between alienation and freedom: "only a world that I can make 'my own'—only a world that I can identify with (by appropriating it)—is a world in which I can act in a self-determined manner. Understood in this way, the concept of alienation attempts to identify the conditions under which one can understand oneself . . . as the master of one's own actions."

It is the centrality of appropriation to Jaeggi's conception of alienation that accounts for its Hegelian character. For both philosophers the mark of human subjectivity is, abstractly formulated, an activity or process in which consciousness confronts what initially presents itself as given or "other" and then endeavors in some way to make it its own—to strip its object of its alien, merely given character. Moreover, it is in such interactions with its "other" that the subject constitutes both itself and its world as something determinate. Successful appropriation of this sort not only gives specific content to subject and object (and, so, makes them "real"); it is also the subject's characteristic aim, or aspiration, and hence the source of a fundamental satisfaction, the absence of which manifests itself as alienation. For both Hegel and Jaeggi, self and world emerge out of a single activity in which the subject integrates what is first alien or "other" to it and, in doing so, transforms itself and the world.

Despite this fundamental agreement regarding the nature of subjectivity—or, as it is called here, the structure of human existence—Jaeggi's view diverges from Hegel's in two important respects. First, Jaeggi attempts to avoid all suggestion that the subject's activity of appropriation is in essence *reappropriation*. For her, what initially confronts the subject as a foreign reality genuinely is foreign in that it is not the product of a prior subjective act that has remained unrecognized as such: "the preconditions to which one—if not alienated—should be able to relate . . . are . . . neither invented nor made." This implies that overcoming alienation consists not in recovering an original subject-object relation that has become obscured or forgotten—even less in recovering some primordial differenceless harmony between the two—but in taking possession of the world in a way that first establishes a mutually constituting relation between self and world. Jaeggi's second major divergence from Hegel can be understood as a consequence of the first: if what the unalienated subject is ultimately to take itself to be is not already determined by the results of a prior but still unself-conscious act of self-expression, then a theory of unalienated selfhood will focus not on the content or results of the subject's appropriative activity but on its process or form: the presence or absence of alienation depends not on *what* the self takes itself (or strives) to be but on *how* it determines what it is.

This largely formal analysis becomes significantly more concrete in part 2 of the book, where Jaeggi discusses in admirable detail four examples of alienation, each of which illustrates a different way in which the self's appropriation of itself and world is disturbed or incomplete: an academic who experiences a loss of control over the course and dynamic of his life; a young professional who fails to identify with the social roles he occupies; a feminist who, because her desires and impulses conflict with her self-conception, cannot recognize them as her own; and, finally, the protagonist of Pascal Mercier's *Perlmann's Silence*, who suffers an enduring and paralyzing indifference to himself and his world. Jaeggi's phenomenological approach in part 2 is noteworthy for several reasons. Most obviously, in its imaginative and nuanced depictions of specific cases of alienation it ascribes a much greater philosophical importance to concrete examples and narratives than philosophers typically do. Instead of constructing highly artificial cases that generate counterexamples or help to fine-tune an abstract moral principle, Jaeggi relies on compelling examples derived from (what could be) real experience that serve to bring into relief the complex and often diffuse phenomenon of alienation and to refine our conceptual grasp of it.

Yet Jaeggi's examples serve a deeper purpose as well: they are the true starting point of her philosophical project in the strictest sense of the term. In contrast to the largely historical work of part 1, Jaeggi's phenomenological discussion plays a crucial role in establishing the validity of the normative vision of subjectivity that her historical predecessors implicitly or explicitly presuppose. It is in part 2, in other words, that the philosophical structure of the book's project comes into view: it begins with a consideration of examples of real-life phenomena whose pathological nature can be grasped only with the help of conceptual resources provided by the idea of self-alienation. Then, once the specific pathologies of the various examples have been identified and diagnosed, Jaeggi proceeds from the negative phenomenon (alienation) to reconstruct the positive vision of successfully realized subjectivity that implicitly underlies the diagnosis of those examples as instances of subjectivity gone awry. In taking this step, Jaeggi arrives at her own answer to a question that, at least since Fichte, has been a dominating concern of German philosophy: how are we to conceive of the essential nature (or "structure") of human subjectivity? The method Jaeggi employs to answer this question can be summed up in the question, What must subjectivity be like—what structure must it manifest—if alienation in its various guises is a possible and not infrequent feature of human existence? In attempting to uncover what the possibility of alienation reveals about the nature of subjectivity in general, Jaeggi adopts the same method—the *via negativis*—that Kierkegaard famously employs in his treatment of despair.

In part 3 Jaeggi returns to more abstract philosophical terrain, where she employs the conceptual resources won through her phenomenological analyses to refine her account of alienation, to fill out and defend her "appropriation model" of the self, and to situate alienation in relation to more familiar objects of ethical reflection such as freedom, self-realization and agency. Here, too, Jaeggi shows herself to be an imaginative philosopher thoroughly at home in both the Continental and Anglo-American traditions. Indeed, one of the book's features that makes it especially interesting to readers outside Germany is that throughout its pages it draws on and responds to the work of many contemporary English-speaking philosophers whose work is relevant to her concerns, among them Frankfurt, Nagel, MacIntyre, Williams, and Taylor.

I would be remiss in introducing Jaeggi's book to an English-reading public if I failed to mention the one noteworthy respect in which it fails to deliver what it originally promised. The book's original subtitle (omitted in this translation)—"A Contemporary Problem of Social Philosophy"—led its readers to expect a work that investigates the social causes of alienation rather than what one in fact finds: a philosophical account of, broadly speaking, an *ethical* phenomenon, together with an underlying "theory of the self" (or theory of human subjectivity). At the very beginning of the book, Jaeggi suggests a connection between her project and critical social theory: once the phenomenon of alienation has been adequately clarified, a path is opened up for criticizing institutions insofar as they fail to furnish the social conditions individuals need to live a life free of alienation. Yet this thought remains mostly undeveloped here. It would be foolish, however, to criticize Jaeggi for not having said more about this social-theoretical project; her failure to do so stems no doubt from the realization that completing this task would require (at least) a separate book-length treatment of its own (and her newest book, *Kritik von Lebensformen*, can be read as making important progress toward this goal). The project she has carried out in this first book is important and masterfully executed, and it is sure to reinvigorate philosophical discussion of alienation in all of its forms. *Alienation* is an astonishingly good representative of the work of an impressive new generation of German philosophers who, with roots in both of its major traditions, seem well positioned to reanimate Western philosophy, as well as to mend the internal cleavage that has for too long been its fate.

For the most part I have attempted to avoid including references to original German terms and cumbersome explanations of technical expressions. Nevertheless, three important expressions present translation problems that demand special mention. The most important of these is "having oneself at one's command" (*über sich verfügen können*), an expression Jaeggi borrows from Ernst Tugendhat to capture the central feature of unalienated selfhood. To be unalienated, this terminology suggests, is to have oneself at one's command, to have a handle on oneself, or, more literally, to have oneself at one's disposal. Talk of having oneself at one's "command" or "disposal" should not suggest, however, that the unalienated subject has an instrumental, objectifying, or dominating relation to itself that calls to mind self-control or self-mastery—as in "Get control of yourself (or of your feelings)!" or "Good character requires mastering one's impulses"—or that an unalienated subject has itself at its disposal in the same way that one might have a sum of money or a set of resources at one's disposal. Perhaps these misleading connotations—some of which are also possible misreadings of the original *verfügen*—can be avoided by bearing in mind that two near synonyms of *über sich verfügen können* are "being freely accessible to oneself," used in chapter 7, and *mit sich umgehen können*, translated here by the admittedly cumbersome locution "being familiar with and able to deal with oneself." The latter term, used less frequently in the text than "having oneself at one's command," makes use of the common expression *mit etwas umgehen können*, which means "knowing how to handle (or to deal with, or to navigate) something" or "knowing one's way around something." (*Ich kann mit meinen Gefühlen umgehen* means something like "I'm familiar with my emotional responses, and I'm adept at dealing with them in appropriate ways"). This implies that unalienated selfhood involves "knowing one's way around oneself"—being familiar with oneself and knowing how to deal appropriately with who and what one is. Consistent with this, a principal characteristic of an alienated self is what I have translated here as "intractability" (*Unverfügbarkeit*).

Another term central to Jaeggi's account of unalienated selfhood is "obstinacy" (*Eigensinn*). This expression initially strikes readers as strange because its most common meaning in both English and German is "stubbornness," which is not normally regarded as a positive attribute, let alone a central feature of successfully achieved subjectivity. But *Eigensinn* suggests a further meaning that "obstinacy" does not. *Eigen* ("one's own"), joined with *Sinn* ("meaning"), suggests that the obstinate person gives her own meaning to things, that she interprets them independently, rather than merely taking over customary, socially accepted interpretations of the world. Viewed in this way, obstinacy is a positive characteristic, a requirement of unalienated selfhood, although, as the term also suggests, obstinacy can slip into mere stubbornness when an individual simply rejects, for no good reason, or is completely impervious to, the meanings other individuals give to the elements of their shared world. This dual potential of obstinacy reflects the fact that unalienated selfhood, as Jaeggi construes it, requires finding the appropriate balance between individual self-assertiveness and immersion in society rather than embracing one of these poles at the expense of the other. (This use of *Eigensinn* originates with Hegel, who counts the capacity for it—a kind of freedom—among the subjective attributes the bondsman acquires from laboring for his lord (while noting as well that, in the absence of "absolute fear" of death, obstinacy can amount to a "servile" form of mere stubbornness).[2] In *The Philosophy of Right* Hegel approvingly characterizes subjective freedom—the claim to be bound by no principles other than those one has rational insight into—as a form of obstinacy that does honor to the human subject.[3]

I have translated *Verselbständigung* using locutions that include the expression "independent existence," as when I refer to something's taking on, or having taken on, an independent existence (of its own). *Verselbständigung* is closely related to the idea of reification (*Verdinglichung*), which has played a major role in Continental philosophy since Fichte and Hegel. Given the close connection between alienation and reification, it is no surprise that *Verselbständigung* plays a prominent role in Jaeggi's book. It refers to processes that are distinctive of subjectivity—knowledge, consciousness, or action—whose effects in the world come to appear as though they were not the products of subjects' activities but instead objective, "given" conditions. An aspect of my life that is a result of some decision I am responsible for but that appears to me merely as "my lot in life" is a paradigmatic example of a subjective activity that has taken on, for the subject who is in fact responsible for it, an independent, "thinglike" existence. Many of the phenomena of alienation examined in this book exhibit some version of this property.

Both Rahel Jaeggi and I would like to express our deep gratitude to Susan Morrow, who provided invaluable assistance in preparing the footnotes, quotations, and bibliography for English readers, as well as to Mathias Böhm and Eva von Redecker, who helped track down English versions of many of the texts cited here. The translation could not have been completed without their diligence and helpful advice.

Am Kleinen Müggelsee

PREFACE AND ACKNOWLEDGMENTS

"YET ANOTHER WORK ON ALIENATION?"[1] This is how many books on alienation began, even into the early 1980s, in the face of an overwhelmingly large body of secondary literature on the topic. The situation today looks different. The concept of alienation appears problematic and in some respects outmoded. It was for a long time the central concept of left (but also of conservative) social critique and the decisive theme of Marxist social philosophy (and thus of great importance for Western Marxism and Critical Theory). At the same time, it was influential in various versions of existentialist-inspired cultural critique. Yet not only has alienation nearly disappeared from today's philosophical literature, it also has hardly any place any longer in the vocabulary of contemporary cultural critique. The concept of alienation was too inflationary in the period at which it was at its height; its philosophical foundations look outmoded in the age of postmodernity; its political implications seem questionable in the period of political liberalism; and the aspirations of alienation critique can easily strike us as futile in the context of what looks like capitalism's decisive victory.

Yet the *problem* of alienation is still (or perhaps once again) of contemporary interest. In the face of recent economic and social developments, one sees signs of an increasing discontent that, if not in name then in substance, has to do with the phenomenon of alienation. The wide reception enjoyed by Richard Sennett's *The Culture of the New Capitalism*, with its thesis that "flexible capitalism" threatens the individual's identity and social coherence; the increasingly audible questioning of tendencies that produce a growing influence of markets and a greater commodification of ever larger areas of life;[2] and the newly emerging protest movements against powerlessness and loss of control in the face of a globalizing economy[3]—all are signs of a reawakening sensibility with respect to phenomena that the theories mentioned heretofore analyzed in terms of alienation or reification. And even if the "new spirit of capitalism"[4] appears to have transcended alienation critique in a cynical way—aren't the various demands on the flexibly creative modern "labor-power entrepreneur," for whom there no longer exists a boundary between work and leisure, a realization of the Marxist utopia of the "all-sided development" of the human being who can "fish in the morning, hunt in the afternoon, criticize in the evening"?—the ambivalences of such a development point more to the problem's stubborn persistence than to its disappearance.[5]

Is it that alienation no longer exists or merely that we no longer have the concept at our disposal? In view of the constantly renewed tension between aspiration and reality, between the social promise of self-determination and self-realization and the failures in realizing this promise, the topic of alienation—according to Robert Misik's diagnosis[6]—remains relevant and important, even if a firm foundation for alienation critique appears to have been lost.

The present investigation aims at resurrecting alienation as a foundational concept of social philosophy. My starting point is twofold: on the one hand, I am convinced that alienation is a philosophically contentful and productive concept capable of opening up domains of phenomena that can be ignored only at the expense of impoverishing the possibilities of theoretical expression and interpretation. On the other hand, the tradition with which the concept of alienation is associated cannot simply be taken up unreflectively, given that its assumptions have been, rightly, called into question. For this reason any further discussion of alienation requires a critical reconstruction of its conceptual foundations.

This book is an attempt at such a reconstruction. It is a *reconstruction* in two respects: on the one hand, it attempts to *articulate* the meaning of the concept of alienation in general. On the other hand, this concept must be systematically reinterpreted and conceptually *transformed* in light of the problems I have mentioned. The book's project, in other words, is a philosophical reappropriation of a view that for various reasons has become problematic as well as an attempt to recover its experiential content.[7]

My aim, then, is neither to update the problem of alienation by looking at its contemporary manifestations nor to discuss alienation in a way that remains within the confines of an already defined theoretical framework. What I want to attempt, rather, is *a conceptual analysis of the fundamental concepts* and assumptions that underlie the interpretive model that characterizes the concept of alienation in its various manifestations. Thus a diagnosis of alienation presupposes views about the structure of human relations to self and world and about the relations agents have to themselves, to their own actions, and to the social and natural worlds; it presupposes, in other words, a dense and complex picture of the person in her relations to the world. It is these assumptions—and with them the philosophical foundations of the concept of alienation, including its foundations in a theory of human nature—that need conceptual clarification, and for this reason I take them as my starting point here.

What does it mean to say that one can be "internally divided" or at odds with oneself in various ways? How are we to understand the possibility that some of one's own actions can confront oneself as alien? And how is the subject constituted if it is connected to the world in such a way that it becomes alienated from itself when it loses this connection? These are the questions that concern me in this book. Already here, however, a clarification is necessary: although the various ways in which individuals can become alienated from themselves stand at the center of my analysis, this does *not* mean that alienation is to be understood as a subjective problem that can simply be reduced to a relation to self. A misunderstanding that underlies Hannah Arendt's critique of Marx is instructive here: Arendt's remark in *Vita Activa* that alienation from the world, and not, as Marx thought, alienation from oneself, is the real problem of modern societies is a flat-out—if also in some ways a productive—misinterpretation:[8] for Marx (as well as for Arendt) alienation from oneself is inseparably bound up with alienation from the material and social world; it is precisely the impossibility of appropriating the world as the product of one's own activity that constitutes alienation. Thus alienation from the world implies alienation from oneself, and, conversely, the subject is alienated from itself because it is alienated from the world; moreover, it is precisely this interrelation that makes the concept interesting. For this reason the starting point of self-alienation always includes the relation a subject has to various dimensions of the world. The distinction, then, is a matter of perspective rather than one that belongs to the phenomenon itself.

Since, as we shall see, the central thesis of the theory of alienation is that living one's own life means identifying in a certain way with oneself and the world—being able to "appropriate" the world—it is importantly different from standard, usually Kantian conceptions of autonomy, according to which autonomy is unaffected by the world in either a positive or a negative sense. The approach that is crucial for alienation critique, in contrast—focusing on the qualities of individuals' relations to self and world, and distinguishing between successful and disturbed or deficient relations to self and world—opens the way for a critique of the social institutions in which individuals lead their lives. This form of critique goes beyond the perspective of liberal theories of justice, which legally regulate individuals' "passing by one another" without relying on substantial conceptions of self and community.[9] Thus the theory of alienation entails the idea of a "qualitatively different society" (Herbert Marcuse); alienation critique is always already bound up with the question of how we want to live. In its "negativistic" approach, the concept of alienation investigates not only what prevents us from living well but also, and more important, what prevents us from posing the question of how we want to live in an appropriate way.

Already before entering into a more detailed discussion, several dimensions of the problem of alienation can be distinguished:

As an *ethical* problem, alienation points to ways in which individuals' lives can go wrong. In this case the feeling of apathy and indifference toward life that is bound up with alienation threatens to undermine the question of the good life in general.[10] The internal division associated with alienation and the feeling of powerlessness, so the diagnosis, affect the conditions of personal autonomy at its core.

Alienation is a key concept of *social philosophy* (ever since Rousseau), insofar as it can be used to diagnose social pathologies—that is, deficiencies in the social conditions of individual self-realization.[11] From this perspective a social form of life is alienated (or alienating) when individuals cannot identify with it, when they cannot realize themselves in it, when they cannot make it "their own."

As a foundational concept of *social theory*, alienation functions not only as a diagnostic but also as a descriptive and explanatory category, the key to understanding the workings of capitalist societies. Marx, for example, even after he gave up the appeal to human nature that marks his early writings, describes the "bourgeois economy" in terms of a process of alienation.[12]

In taking up the social-philosophical dimension of the concept of alienation here, I will focus on the social relations within which individuals lead their lives as opposed to the concept's merely ethical dimension (which, as will become evident, is nevertheless intertwined with these social relations). Alienation is, in this sense, a concept of social philosophy par excellence, insofar as its interpretive scheme implies a perspective for which the relations to self and world—the individual's relations to self and social forms of life—are conceptually intertwined. It is this feature of the discussion of alienation—together with its implications for the analysis of social pathologies—that I believe to be worthy of our attention today. As an analytic concept that aims to explain the workings of society, the concept of alienation is too thin; moreover, in its traditional forms it combines descriptive and normative aspects without explaining how the two are related. Yet, despite these shortcomings, focusing on the social-philosophical meaning of the concept makes it possible to arrive at standards for diagnosing social pathologies. At the same time, it is obvious that the social-philosophical aspects of the concept are intimately bound up with its ethical significance: what is at issue in the concept of alienation are the conditions of a good human life, and success in living such a life is the standard by which social pathologies are to be judged.

Because alienation concerns itself with the just *and* the good society, with freedom *and* happiness, with self-determination *and* self-realization—precisely the mix of themes found in traditional Critical Theory—the fruitfulness of the concept lies in the fact that it calls into question some of the dichotomies that dominate contemporary philosophical debates and brings into view dimensions of social phenomena that would otherwise remain obscured. It is precisely this that makes exploring the potential of those traditions oriented around the concept of alienation still alluring today.

My inquiry is divided into three main parts. The first, "The Relation of Relationlessness," articulates the problem domain associated with the concept of alienation from a historical-systematic perspective. By attending both to everyday and philosophical uses of the concept, I explore its content as well as the problems it points to and I make some initial suggestions concerning how the concept should be reconstructed. The second, "Living One's Life as an Alien Life," carries out these suggestions for reconstruction with respect to the idea of self-alienation. Each of the four chapters of this part is based on a description of a concrete situation with the help of which various dimensions of alienation can be illustrated and analyzed. These examples—which can be understood as a kind of phenomenology of alienation (or as a microanalysis of phenomena of alienation)—are intended to provide the starting point for reconstructing the concept.[13]

The third part, "Alienation as a Disturbed Appropriation of Self and World," elaborates the systematic implications of these analyses and integrates them into a comprehensive account of the problem of alienation by situating them in relation to concepts such as freedom, emancipation, self-realization, and self-determination in order then, as a final step, to discuss in greater detail the relation between self-alienation and social alienation.

This book can be read in a variety of ways. Readers who want to jump directly into the problem can begin with the second, phenomena-oriented part and after that turn to the first part's reconstruction and account of the history of the concept. The third part is intended to stand on its own as an evaluation and systematization of the analyses of phenomena that can, but do not have to be, read in conjunction with the discussion of the theory of alienation in the first part.

This book is a revised version of my dissertation, which I submitted in July 2001 to the Faculty of Philosophy and Historical Sciences of the Johann Wolfgang Goethe-Universität in Frankfurt.

I would like to thank above all Axel Honneth, who encouraged me from the beginning in this undertaking and provided motivation and support throughout the various and sometimes difficult phases of its development. My work with him stimulated me in this project in more ways than I could recount individually. Gustav Falke was probably my most important interlocutor while the work was being conceived; Martin Löw-Beer played the same role in a difficult moment that proved to be crucial for its completion. During this period Rainer Forst, Martin Saar, and Stefan Gosepath were colleagues on whose collaboration, help, and friendship I could always rely. For years I have had conversations with Werner Konitzer about topics relevant to the problem of alienation. I would like to thank Undine Eberlein and Helmuth Fallschessl for reading the first draft and for their many skeptical comments in both the left- and right-hand margins of the manuscript. Martin Frank and Arnd Pollmann also performed the thankless task of commenting on the project's still very fragmentary outline. In addition, I would like to thank Martin Saar, Ina Kerner, and Carolin Emcke for their resolute rescue action during the extraordinary night before the submission of the work to the Doctoral Commission in Frankfurt as well as Emmanuel Renault for his interest and helpful suggestions at the very end.

I would like to thank Christoph Menke for his willingness to serve as an examiner of the dissertation and Seyla Benhabib for the invitation to visit Yale in the academic year 2002–3, as well as for the suggestions for reworking the manuscript that emerged from the seminar we cotaught on contemporary Critical Theory. I owe thanks to Jan-Phillip Reemtsma and the Hamburg Foundation for Science and Culture for a generous stipend for the completion of the project and to the members of the Frankfurt Institute for Social Research for accepting the book into the institute's series.

Without Robin Celikates's help in revising the manuscript I would have been lost. I would like to thank Sandra Beaufaÿs and the staff at the IfS for proofreading and editing. The friendly staff of Berlin's Staatsbibliothek probably have no idea how helpful their constant encouragement during particularly difficult periods of work can be. Finally, Jakob Wohlgemuth's increasingly vivid presence contributed decisively to completing the process of submitting the manuscript. My most personal thanks go to Andreas Fischer. But that does not belong here.

PART ONE

THE RELATION OF RELATIONLESSNESS: RECONSTRUCTING A CONCEPT OF SOCIAL PHILOSOPHY

ALIENATION IS A *RELATION OF relationlessness.* This, condensed into a very brief and abstract formulation, is the starting point of my reflections here. According to this formulation, alienation does not indicate the absence of a relation but is itself a relation, if a deficient one. Conversely, overcoming alienation does not mean returning to an undifferentiated state of oneness with oneself and the world; it too is a relation: a *relation of appropriation.* The principal idea underlying my reconstruction of the concept of alienation is the following: in order to make the concept of alienation fruitful once again, we must give a *formal* account of it. In contrast to providing a substantial definition of what one is alienated from in relations of alienation, it is the character of this relation itself that must be defined; what the concept of alienation allows us to diagnose is various ways in which relations of appropriation are disturbed. These relations of appropriation must be understood as productive relations, as open processes in which appropriation always means both the integration and transformation of what is given. Alienation is a failure to apprehend, and a halting of, the movement of appropriation. It is possible, using these ideas, to give a consistent account of processes of alienation without recourse to an Archimedean point beyond alienation.

With this approach, I will argue, it is possible to overcome two problems the theory of alienation frequently confronts: on the one hand, its essentialism and its perfectionist orientation around a conception of the essence or nature of human beings (or an objectivistically conceived ideal of the good life); on the other hand, the ideal of reconciliation—the ideal of a unity free of tension—that seems to be bound up with alienation critique when it takes the form of social theory or of a theory of identity. Regarding alienation as a relation of disturbed or inhibited appropriation of world and self brings into view an illuminating connection between freedom and alienation. Insofar as freedom presupposes that one can make what one does, and the conditions under which one does it, *one's own*, overcoming alienation is a necessary condition of realizing freedom.

The first part of this study seeks to introduce the problem domain marked off by the concept of alienation. It first goes into (1) the various dimensions of the *concept* and of the *phenomenon* of alienation—into how alienation reveals itself both in everyday language and in philosophical treatment of the concept. This will be deepened with the help of (2) a more precise consideration of alienation's theoretical starting points and of how they are arrived at both in Marx's theory and in Heidegger's existential ontology. Against this background, after the concept's potential as a foundational concept of social philosophy has been revealed, (3) its structure as well as the *problems* associated with it will be discussed. Finally, I will outline (4) my *suggestions for reconstructing* the concept as carried out in the remainder of the book.

1

"A STRANGER IN THE WORLD THAT HE HIMSELF HAS MADE": THE CONCEPT AND PHENOMENON OF ALIENATION

THE CONCEPT OF ALIENATION REFERS to an entire bundle of intertwined topics. Alienation means indifference and internal division, but also powerlessness and relationlessness with respect to oneself and to a world experienced as indifferent and alien. Alienation is the inability to establish a relation to other human beings, to things, to social institutions and thereby also—so the fundamental intuition of the theory of alienation—to oneself. An alienated world presents itself to individuals as insignificant and meaningless, as rigidified or impoverished, as a world that is not one's own, which is to say, a world in which one is not "at home" and over which one can have no influence. The alienated subject becomes a stranger to itself; it no longer experiences itself as an "actively effective subject" but a "passive object" at the mercy of unknown forces.[1] One can speak of alienation "wherever individuals do not find themselves in their own actions"[2] or wherever we cannot be master over the being that we ourselves are (as Heidegger might have put it). The alienated person, according to the early Alasdair MacIntyre, is "a stranger in the world that he himself has made."[3]

PHENOMENA OF ALIENATION

Even in our first encounters with the topic we can see that alienation is a concept with "fuzzy edges." The family resemblances and overlaps with other concepts such as reification, inauthenticity, and anomie say as much about the domain within which the concept operates as do the complicated relations among the various meanings it has taken on in both everyday and philosophical language. If the "experiential content" of the concept feeds off of the historical and social experiences that have found expression in it,[4] it is also the case that, as a philosophical concept, alienation has influenced the interpretations of self and world held by individuals and social movements. These "impure" mixes make for a diverse field of phenomena that can be associated with the concept of alienation.[5]

* As linguistic usage would have it, one is alienated from oneself insofar as one does not behave as one "genuinely" is but instead "artificially" and "inauthentically" or insofar as one is guided by desires that in a certain respect are not "one's own" or are not experienced as such. One lives then (already according to Rousseau's critical diagnosis) "in the opinions of others" rather than "in oneself." According to this conception, role behavior and conformism count, for example, as alienated or inauthentic; but talk of "false needs" by critics of consumerism also belongs to the domain of phenomena that can be theorized as alienation.

* "Alienated" describes relations that are not entered into for their own sake, as well as activities with which one cannot "identify." The worker who thinks only of quitting time, the academic who publishes solely with a view toward the citation index, the doctor who cannot for a moment forget her fee scale—all are alienated from what they do. And someone who cultivates a friendship only because it serves her own interests has an alienated relation to the person she takes to be her friend.

* Talk of alienation can also refer to detachment from one's social involvements. In this sense one can become alienated from one's life partner or from one's family, from one's place of origin, or from a community or a cultural milieu. More specifically, we speak of alienation when someone cannot identify with—grasp as "her own"—the social or political institutions in which she lives. Social isolation or excessive demands for privacy can also be regarded as symptoms of alienation. Slightly romanticized, alienation is sometimes understood as an expression of "rootlessness" and "homelessness," which conservative cultural critics trace back to the complexity or anonymity of modern life or to the "artificiality" of a world that is experienced only through the lens of public media.

* The depersonalization and reification of relations among humans, as well as of their relations to the world, counts as alienated insofar as these relations are no longer immediate but are instead (for example) mediated by money, insofar as they are not "concrete" but "abstract," insofar as they are not inalienable but objects of exchange. The commodification of goods or

domains that were previously not objects of market exchange is an example of alienation in this sense. The claim that bourgeois society, dominated by relations of equivalence (as Adorno might have put it), destroys the uniqueness of things and of human beings, destroys their particularity and nonfungibility, is a critique of alienation that one encounters even beyond the boundaries of Marxism.

■ Alienation means—a dominant theme already in Goethe's time—the loss of the "whole human being," the fragmentation and narrowing of activities produced by a specialized division of labor as well as the failure to realize human capacities and expressive possibilities that arise from it. As a mere "cog in the machine," the alienated worker is deindividualized and carries out a narrow, partial function within a larger process he cannot see in its entirety and over which he has no control.

■ Relationships can be described as alienated in which institutions appear as all-powerful or where systemic constraints appear to provide no place for free action. In this sense alienation or reification refers to a condition in which relations take on an independent existence (*Verselbständigung*) that stand over and against those who constitute them.[6] The "dead marriage" is in this sense just as much a phenomenon of alienation as certain administrative boards in modern democracies; the same holds for the "iron cage" of welfare state bureaucracy or when economic constraints eliminate possibilities for free action.

■ The "absurd" can also be regarded as belonging to the family of phenomena covered by the term *alienation*. The characters created by Franz Kafka, Samuel Beckett, and Albert Camus are only the most well-known literary examples of individuals who experience utter detachment and meaninglessness.

THEORIES OF ALIENATION: "A CRISIS IN THE CONSCIOUSNESS OF THE TIME"

What then is alienation? "It seems that whenever he feels that something is not as it should be, he characterizes it in terms of alienation."[7] This remark of Richard Schacht's about Erich Fromm seems an apt description of how the concept is often used (and not only by Fromm). However, as varied as the aforementioned phenomena might be, they provide an initial sketch of the concept of alienation. An *alienated* relation is a *deficient* relation one has to oneself, to the world, and to others. Indifference, instrumentalization, reification, absurdity, artificiality, isolation, meaninglessness, impotence—all

these ways of characterizing the relations in question are forms of this deficiency. A distinctive feature of the concept of alienation is that it refers not
only to powerlessness and a lack of freedom but also to a characteristic impoverishment of the relation to self and world. (This is how we should understand
the dual meaning Marx means to convey when he describes alienation in
terms of the "double loss of reality" of the world and the human being: having become unreal, the individual fails to experience herself as "effective,"
and the world, having become unreal, is meaningless and indifferent.) It is
the complexity of these interrelations that has made alienation into the key
concept of diagnoses of the crisis of modernity and one of the foundational
concepts of social philosophy.

As an expression of a crisis in contemporary consciousness (as Hegel might
have regarded it), the modern discussion of alienation stretches from Rousseau and Schiller, via Hegel, to Kierkegaard and Marx. Elevated to the "sickness of civilization *par excellence*,"[8] alienation became, from the eighteenth
century onward, a cipher used to communicate the "uncertainty, fragmentation, and internal division" in humans' relations to themselves and to the
world that accompanied the growth of industrialization. It was this diagnosis
that Marx captured in his theory of alienation and put to work in his critique
of capitalism. And the "modern human's loss of an essential definition or calling" shapes the existentialist question,[9] deriving from Kierkegaard, of what it
means both to be oneself and to lose oneself. To this tradition, experiences of
indifference and radical foreignness appear as nothing less than an ontologically situated misapprehension of the world and the human's relation to self
and world, which, despite all divergences from the Marxian diagnosis, also has
something in common with it. Diagnoses of alienation in their modern form
always concern (for example) freedom and self-determination and the failure
to realize them. Understood in this way, alienation is not simply a problem of
modernity but also a modern problem.

A SHORT HISTORY OF THE THEORY OF ALIENATION

One could give a (very) short history of the modern theory of alienation
as follows:

1. Even if the term itself is absent, Rousseau's works contain all the key
ideas that theories of alienation (in the social-philosophical sense), both past

and present, have relied on.[10] Rousseau begins his "Discourse on the Origin of Inequality Among Men" (1755) with a striking image: "Like the statue of Glaucus, which time, sea, and storms had so disfigured that it less resembled a God than a ferocious Beast, the human soul, the human soul altered in the lap of society by a thousand forever recurring causes, by the acquisition of a mass of knowledge and errors, by the changes that have taken place in the constitution of Bodies, and by the continual impact of the passions, has, so to speak, changed in appearance, to the point of being almost unrecognizable."[11] The disfigurement Rousseau speaks of here is the deformation of human beings by society: with his nature divided, alienated from his own needs, subjected to the conformist dictates of society, in his need for recognition and with his sense of self-worth dependent on the opinions of others, the social human being is artificial and disfigured. The mutual dependence of civilized humans, their unlimited needs produced by social contact, and their finding their orientation in others give rise at once, according to Rousseau, to domination and enslavement as well as to a loss of authenticity and (self-) alienation—to a condition, in other words, directly opposed to the autonomy and authenticity of the state of nature, conceived as a condition of self-sufficiency.

There are two apparently opposed ideas that have made Rousseau's thought influential as a theory of alienation: first, the development of the modern ideal of *authenticity* as an undisturbed agreement with oneself and one's own nature and, second, the idea of *social freedom*, as expressed in Rousseau's formulation of the principal task of the *Social Contract*. If in the Second Discourse Rousseau vividly describes the alienated character of (as he sees it there) the exclusively negative effects of socialization, he also, in the *Social Contract*, invents the normative ideal of an unalienated form of socialization. Without wanting to deny the tensions internal to Rousseau's work, one could describe the connection between the two ideas as follows: the gap between authentic selfhood and society that Rousseau so eloquently articulated gives rise, in accordance with his own presuppositions, to an aporia that can be resolved only by establishing a condition in which individuals live within social institutions that they can experience as their own. On the one hand, the alienated human described by Rousseau loses herself insofar as she establishes relations to others: the natural human "lives within himself; sociable man always outside himself."[12] On the other hand, the human being can regain herself only through society. Since restoring the self-sufficiency of the state of nature—and with it a freedom that requires independence and detachment from others—comes at too high a price (the price of losing such specifically human qualities as reason and the capacity for reflection),[13] the solution to the problem of alienation cannot lie in dissolving social bonds but only in transforming them. The mutual dependence of socialized individuals, experienced as alienating, must be reconfigured in accordance with the idea, set out in the *Social Contract*, of an association in which each individual alienates all her rights to society and thereby becomes "as free as before." What was once alienating heteronomy becomes subjection to "one's own law." Rousseau's thought, then, led his followers in two directions. On the one hand, Rousseau (and especially "Rousseaueanism") represents the continually recurring form of alienation critique that turns away from the "universal" and, embracing an ideal of unfalsified nature or primitive self-sufficiency, regards sociality and social institutions as inherently alienated. On the other hand, he is the inspiration not only for the Kantian idea of autonomy but also for Hegel's conception of the social character of freedom.

2. It is left to Hegel, though, to develop the concept of "self-realization in the universal." Although for him, too, modernity is characterized by alienation — the fragmentation of modern consciousness, the coming apart of "particular" and "universal" in relationships within a civil society threatened by disintegration — he locates the core of the problem in the *cleavage* between individual and society rather than in the individual's loss of self *through* society. For Hegel alienation (or internal division) is a *deficiency in social life* (*Sittlichkeit*), the "loss of ethical universality in social life" (*sittlicher Allgemeinheit*). In this context the idea of an ethically satisfying social life refers not to the substantial ethical integration typical of premodern communities (the integrated ethical life of the premodern *polis*) but to a form of social integration that does justice to the "individual's right to particularity." Hegel's rejection of atomism rests on the idea that individuals always find themselves already *in relations*,[14] the "realization" of which (in multiple senses) constitutes the conditions of their freedom.

Where Hegel takes up the set of problems outlined by Rousseau, he transforms the latter's starting point by conceiving of freedom *as* ethical social life (*Sittlichkeit*) and ethical social life *as* freedom: we become free in and through the social institutions that first make it possible for us to realize ourselves as individuals. Rousseau's still atomistic ideal of authenticity is replaced by a view that locates self-realization in individuals' identification with the institutions of ethical social life. Although Hegel's theory strives to overcome the ideal of freedom as self-sufficiency, it also aims to incorporate the (Kantian) idea of autonomy: its goal is to articulate the conditions that make it possible to "refind oneself" in social institutions. Hegel's conception of *Bildung* gives an account of the process through which individuals work their way out of the relations of dependence they initially find themselves in and then make their social relations—the conditions of "themselves"—*their own.*[15]

3. The two post-Hegelian strands of the theory of alienation meet in Kierkegaard and Marx, each of whom undertakes versions of Hegel's project that start from a specific conception of human nature.[16] To be sure, the late nineteenth-century emphasis on "real existence" and the "real, active human being" leads them in different directions: Marx's turn toward economics stands in contrast to Kierkegaard's concern for the ethical dimensions of human existence. The attention the theory of alienation pays to the problems of internal division, indifference, and loss of relation to self and world leads both philosophers to the theme of practical *appropriation*. Just as Kierkegaard understands "becoming oneself" in terms of appropriating one's own actions and one's own history—as a process of "taking hold of oneself in practice," of actively taking possession of what alien forces have brought about—so, too, for Marx the idea of a productive appropriation of world and self functions as the model for unalienated existence.

Kierkegaard's ethical ideal consists in becoming a "singular human being" in the face of the conformist tendencies of contemporary bourgeois society, whereas Marx's approach is characterized by his understanding the appropriation of one's own human essence in terms of an appropriation of "species-being" (where species-being, Feuerbach's concept, can be understood as a naturalized version of Hegel's vision of an ethically satisfying social life [*Sittlichkeit*]). Thus, both the starting and end points of the existentialist critique of alienation diverge importantly from those of the Hegel-Marx line of development insofar as alienation is understood in the latter case as alienation *from* the social world, whereas in the former case the condition of being immersed in a public world is itself regarded as the source of alienation, understood as the subject's loss of authenticity in the face of a public world defined by leveling (Kierkegaard) or by the rule of "the They" [*das Man*]" (Heidegger). Nevertheless, there are multiple points of overlap between these two strands of the theory of alienation (and not only with respect to their historical reception): Hegel's diagnosis of internal division focuses on the fact that individuals cannot refind themselves in social and political institutions; Marx's analysis of alienation in the 1844 manuscripts argues that in alienated labor we are unable to appropriate our own activity, its products, and the conditions of communal production; the existentialist-inspired conception of alienation points to the structural obstacles to individuals' ability to understand the world as their own and to understand themselves as subjects that shape that world.

4. In the twentieth century the discussion of alienation (and therefore the social-philosophical legacy of Marx's thought) played a prominent role in various strands of Western Marxism. This created the possibility for a normative dimension of social critique that was of fundamental importance for the development of a critical theory of advanced capitalism. Already in the 1920s, without yet knowing the 1844 manuscripts' account of alienation,[17] Georg Lukács extended Marx's analysis of commodity fetishism into a theory of alienation, or reification, in his well-known essay "Reification and the Consciousness of the Proletariat."[18] Here, with his central thesis of the "universality of the commodity form" as the distinctive feature of modern society, the theory of reification became a theory of modern capitalist society in all its manifestations. The influence of Max Weber's theory of rationalization and Georg Simmel's diagnosis of objectification (*Versachlichung*) led Lukács to a view slightly different from Marx's that regarded as salient the phenomena of indifference, objectification, quantification, and abstraction, which, with the spread of the capitalist market economy, come to characterize all relations and forms of expression of modern bourgeois society. Weber's image of the iron cage, in which humans are imprisoned by a bureaucratized capitalist society; Simmel's description of the "tragedy of culture," in which the products of human freedom take on an independent existence as something objective over and against the human being; his analysis of how, with the spread of the money economy, freedom is turned into a loss of meaning—all fruitfully captured the phenomena that Lukács saw as "in the air" at the time. The intersection of Marxist and existentialist themes was a distinctive characteristic of Lukács's thought,[19] and it is easy to see both that this theoretical mix was crucial for the further development of Critical Theory and that even today it remains crucial for the concept of alienation in its various guises.[20]

2

MARX AND HEIDEGGER: TWO VERSIONS OF ALIENATION CRITIQUE

IN WHAT FOLLOWS I WILL discuss Marx and Heidegger in further detail, viewing them as the sources of two historically important versions of alienation critique that overlap in multiple ways with respect to their influence. Directed against the "pseudo-ontology of the given world,"[1] Marx's and Heidegger's critiques of alienation—despite different conceptual foundations—thematize the dominance of modern individuals' reified relations to world and self and the "transformation of the human being into a thing" that accompanies it,[2] a situation in which individuals mistakenly view the world as given rather than as the result of their own world-creating acts. Examining the important differences between the two positions—which can be traced back to (among other things) the difference between Marx's focus on a paradigm of production expressively conceived and Heidegger's understanding of "being-in-the-world"—will provide us with valuable resources for reconstructing the concept of alienation.

MARX: LABOR AND ALIENATION

In the "Economic and Philosophical Manuscripts" of 1844 Marx distinguishes four results of the "national-economic fact" of alienated labor: alienated labor alienates the worker, first, from the product of his labor; second, from his own activity; third, from what Marx, following Feuerbach, calls species-being; and fourth, from other human beings.[3] Alienation, then, can be understood as a disturbance of the relations one has, or should have, to oneself and to the world (whether the social or natural world). Conversely, unalienated labor, as a specific way of appropriating the world through production, is a condition of being able to develop an appropriate relation to oneself, to the objective world, and to others.

Already in this brief account we can see the two most important aspects of Marx's conception of alienation. First, the contrast between appropriation and alienness posits a connection between two problems that is far from obvious: the loss of meaning, the impoverishment and meaninglessness of the world, on the one hand, and impotence, or powerlessness in relation to the world, on the other. Second, in this central text we can see the specific twist Marx gives to the problem of a relationlessness between human being and world: the scandal of alienation is that it is alienation from something the self has made. It is our *own* activities and products—social institutions and relations that we *ourselves* have produced—that have turned into an *alien power*. One can call this, following Charles Taylor, a "Promethean-expressivist" twist that Marx, borrowing from Hegel's "externalization-model" of Spirit and from Feuerbach's concept of projection, brings to his own interpretation of the problem of externalization.[4]

In what follows I will first examine the dimensions of alienation discussed by Marx, together with the content and richness of his concept of alienation. After that I will articulate the concept of labor in relation to Marx's anthropology, or theory of human nature, which will provide the background for a discussion of the productivist turn in Marx's concept of alienation.

DIMENSIONS OF ALIENATION

We can identify two dimensions of the deficit in the relation to self and world that Marx theorizes as alienation: first, the inability meaningfully to *identify* with what one does and with those with whom one does it; second, the inability to exert *control* over what one does—that is, the inability to be, individually or collectively, the subject of one's actions. Alienation from the object—from the product of one's own activity—means at once *loss of control* and *dispossession*: the alienated worker (as the seller of her labor power) no longer has *at her disposal* what she herself has produced; it does not *belong* to her. Her product is exchanged on a market she does not control and under conditions she does not control. Alienation also means that the object must appear to her as *fragmented*: laboring under conditions of specialization and the division of labor, the worker has no relation to the product of her work as a whole. As someone who is involved in one of the many specialized acts that make up the production of Adam Smith's famous pin, she has no relation to the pin as a finished product, as small as the pin might be. Put differently, the product of her specific labor—her specific contribution to the production of the pin—does not fit for her into a *meaningful* whole, a unity with significance.

The same pairing of powerlessness and loss of meaning (or impoverishment) marks the worker's alienation from her own activity. Alienated labor is, on the one hand, unfree activity, labor *in which* and *into which* one is forced. In her labor the alienated worker is not the master of what she does. Standing under foreign command, her labor is *determined by an other*, or *heteronomous*. "If he relates to his own activity as to an unfree activity, then he relates to it as an activity performed in the service, under the domination, the coercion, and the yoke of another human being."[5] And, being powerless, the worker can neither comprehend nor control the process as a whole of which she is a part but that remains untransparent to her. At the same time, alienated labor is also characterized by—as a counterpart to the product's fragmentation—the *fragmentation and impoverishment* of laboring activity. Thus Marx also regards as alienated the dullness and limited character of the labor itself, "which make the human being into as abstract a being as possible, a lathe, etc., and transforms her into a spiritual and physical monstrosity" (as he says in his "Comments on James Mill"). Alienation from others, from the world of social relations of cooperation, also reflects these two dimensions: in alienated labor the worker has no control over what she, together with others, does. And in alienated labor others are for her, one could say, "structurally indifferent."[6]

It is interesting and of great importance for his theory that Marx denounces not only the instrumentalization of the worker by the owner of her labor power but also the instrumental relation to herself that the worker acquires through it. From Marx's perspective, the instrumental relation that the worker develops (or is forced to develop) to herself and to her labor under conditions of alienation also appears problematic—or, more forcefully, "inhuman." What is alienating about alienated labor is that it has no intrinsic purpose, that it is not (at least also) performed for its own sake. Activities performed in an alienated way are understood by those who carry them out not as ends but only as means. In the same way, one regards the capacities one acquires from or brings to the activity—and therefore also oneself—as means rather than ends. In other words, one does not *identify* with what one does. Instrumentalization, in turn, intensifies into utter *meaninglessness*: When Marx says that under conditions of alienation life itself becomes a means ("life itself appears only as a *means to life*")[7]—what should be an end takes on the character of a means—he is describing a completely meaningless event, or, as one could say, the structure of meaninglessness itself. Formulated differently, for Marx the infinite regress of ends *is* meaninglessness. In this respect Marx is an Aristotelian: there must be an end that is not itself in turn a means.[8]

Here we see the concept's many layers: as alienated one does not *possess* what one has oneself produced (and is therefore exploited and dispossessed);[9] one *has no control* over, or power to *determine*, what one does and is therefore powerless and unfree; at the same time, one is unable to *realize* oneself in one's own activities and is therefore exposed to meaningless, impoverished, and instrumental relations with which one cannot identify and in which one experiences oneself as internally divided. Conversely, the "real appropriation" that Marx contrasts with this type of alienation represents a form of wealth that goes beyond the mere distribution of property.[10] Appropriation in this sense includes taking possession of, gaining power over, and finding meaning in something. Thus the content of what could one could call Marx's conception of the good life is an idea of self-realization understood as an identificatory, appropriative relation to oneself and to the world.[11]

MARX'S ANTHROPOLOGY OF LABOR

The foundations of this conception of appropriation and alienation are found in Marx's philosophical concept of labor—for him the paradigmatic human relation to the world—in which labor is conceived as the externalization and objectification of essential human powers. Put very briefly, "essential human powers"—the will, goals, and capacities of humans—become objective, are made material, only by being externalized in the world through labor. The capacity for labor, conceived as a process of metabolic exchange with nature, simultaneously transforms both the world and the human being. The human being produces *herself* and her *world* in a single act. In producing her world, the human being produces herself and vice versa. And, insofar as this process is successful, she makes both the objective world and herself her own. That is, she recognizes *herself* (her will and capacities) in her own activities and products and finds herself through this relation to her own products; she realizes herself, therefore, in her appropriative relation to the world as the product of her activities. In this sense, labor—unalienated labor—counts for Marx as the human being's essential characteristic.[12] What makes someone into a human being is that, in distinction to an animal, she is capable of consciously forming herself and her world through social cooperation; moreover, she realizes herself in this process and also produces herself in the very concrete sense that she develops her own capacities, her senses, and her needs to the degree that she labors on and forms the world.

Of great importance for the concept of alienation is the following twist: if a successful relation to self and world, via labor, is viewed as a process of the externalization, objectification, and appropriation of these essential human powers—as an appropriative relation to one's own objectified labor power— then alienation can be seen as a failure of this process, as an impeded return out of this externalization. The failure, strictly speaking, is the failure of a kind of process of "retrieval" that is supposed to "give back" what has been external- ized to the subject that has externalized it. Someone who produces something externalizes herself in the world, objectifies herself and her essential powers in it, and then reappropriates them through the product. This is precisely what is expressed in the well-known metaphor of industry as the mirror of human species activity. In this metaphor reconciliation—the overcoming of alienation—refers to a perfect correspondence between the image reflected in the mirror and the source of that reflection. Conversely, alienation is an im- peded appropriation of one's own externalized essential powers—the inability to recognize oneself in the mirror or, in other words, the distortion of the mir- ror image.[13] Now this model of labor and externalization, together with the idea that accompanies it—that an internal plan is materialized externally—is problematic for a number of reasons.[14] Most important in the present context is that, according to this conception, appropriation is always to be understood as a *re*appropriation of something that already exists. The conceptual frame- work implicit in this model of labor does not allow for the possibility that, even when not distorted by alienation, actions can have consequences that develop their own dynamic and that relationships, even those made by us, do not always appear as fully transparent and subject to our control.

If the Promethean interpretation of alienation assumes that it is the pro- ducer's own activities that confront her as an *alien power*, then what is *alien* is something that was once *one's own*, and alienation is the problem of no longer having at one's command something that was once, and ought still to be, at our command (because it results from our own activity). What is alienated or reified is something that has been *made* but that appears as *given* (by nature, as it were, and in such a way that it appears not subject to our will). This model for conceiving of alienation, influenced both by Feuerbach's critique of reli- gious projection and by Hegel's conception of Spirit, can already be found in Marx's writings prior to the 1844 "Economic and Philosophical Manuscripts" (for example, in "On the Jewish Question" and the "Critique of the Hegelian

Philosophy of Right") in his recurring references to the "idol-like character" of social relations that, having been produced by us, take on an independent existence of their own and turn against us, a motif that reappears in *Capital* in the metaphor of the fetish character of commodities. This motif—where something that is one's own takes on an alien form—continues in the "Critique of Political Economy" as a "denaturalizing" critique that reveals the social character of what presents itself as a natural relation.

It is here that it is easiest to identify the parallels between the existentialist and the Marxian-Hegelian critiques of alienation: pointing out the "objectivation mistake"[15]—in which something that has been made is mistakenly taken as given—is also the core of what one could call Heidegger's critique of alienation. In contrast to Marx, Heidegger does not conceive of the human's relation to the world as a process of production. Rather than starting from the idea of the world's being *produced* through labor, Heidegger begins with an analysis of a prior "being-in-the-world," which leads him to what can be regarded as an existentialist version of Marx's thesis of the priority of praxis.

HEIDEGGER: WORLD AND REIFICATION

In Heidegger's framework, alienating reification can be understood as an *objectifying relation* to the world or, in Heidegger's terminology, as a failure to apprehend what is "ready-to-hand" as "present-at-hand," along with a failure to apprehend the world as the totality of what is given rather than as a practical context.[16]

Heidegger's analysis of being-in-the-world serves as the background for his critique of objectification or reification. One can summarize Heidegger's basic intuition as follows: the world is not given to us as something that exists prior to our relating to it—after the fact, as it were—in knowledge or action. As beings that "lead a life," we always already move within the world; we find ourselves always already acting within it; we are always already related to it practically.[17] On this conception, the world is not a set of relations among objects, nor the totality of those objects; it is not, as Heidegger says, the "totality of entities." The world for existentialist ontology is a context that emerges in our practical dealings with it, in our practical "creations" of the world. Heidegger elucidates his idea of the environment (*Umwelt*) with his famous analysis of "equipment" (*das Zeug*): we use the hammer for hammering. This hammering serves us in the making of a chair, which in turn serves us (or someone else) for sitting. As the context of such interrelations, a world opens up, in this case a life-world marked by craftsmanship in which we are immersed whenever we deal with it (when we use the hammer for hammering, the chair for sitting). The world that emerges in this way is made up of meaningful relations: only in the context of this world does the hammer exist as something "for hammering," and only in that context is it comprehensible as such.

Heidegger's distinction between the present-at-hand and the ready-to-hand—which is crucial for the problems of objectification and alienation—can be understood as a distinction between two ways of relating to the world. Things as they confront us in the context of a world exist for us as ready-to-hand (in the previously described sense of their function and significance) in the performance of actions. Something that is ready-to-hand "is good for something and is used in order to do one thing or another."[18] In contrast to this, things in the world appear to us as present-at-hand when we detach them from these practical contexts or when we regard the world as a whole as something separate from us, as something that appears to stand over and against us as objective (as given or unaffected by us).[19] Thus Heidegger espouses the (to a certain extent) pragmatist thesis that things are not simply objects; they are not simply "there" in the sense of being purely present-at-hand. They are ready-to-hand in the activities of life; they acquire significance through their use and in the context of a world. Present-at-hand and ready-to-hand, then, are not properties that belong to different types of objects, nor do they refer to two possible attitudes to the world or to things in the world. (And it would also be a misunderstanding to think, for example, that the hammer exists ready-to-hand only when I use it and that when it lies in the corner it becomes merely present-at-hand. Even when I consider it only passively, I understand it on the basis of its being ready-to-hand, as something that can exist for me in some specific way as ready-to-hand or that I can use in some specific way.) A view that understands something ready-to-hand as something present-at-hand and that conceives of the world as a collection of the present-at-hand is false or, more precisely, reifying. And one can read *Being and Time*, as well as Heidegger's later work, as an attempt to criticize this very consequential misapprehension.

The misapprehension here has two aspects. First, the character of both the objects we deal with and the world we live in is misapprehended (as if they were simply given, independently of the fact that the latter is our world, that we first make it into a world).[20] The *practical character* of the world as the "totality of practical contexts of action" (Ernst Tugendhat) is "masked" by this objectifying misapprehension. Second, we fail to apprehend our relation to the world and what one could call our *entanglement* in it: as if we were able to act outside the practical context that constitutes the world, as if we were in a position to consider the world from the outside without already being involved in it, as if we were able to detach ourselves—as "naked" subjects—from the structure of being-in-the-world. As Heidegger writes: "It is not the case that man 'is' and then has, by way of an extra, a relationship-of-Being towards the 'world'—a world with which he provides himself occasionally. Dasein is never 'proximally' an entity which is, so to speak, free from Being-in, but which sometimes has the inclination to take up a 'relationship' towards the world. Taking up relationships towards the world is possible only *because* Dasein, as Being-in-the-world, is as it is."[21] Thus our relations to self and to world are equally primordial.

Both points—antidualism and the priority of praxis—are important for the diagnosis of alienation. The world, in Heidegger's interpretation, is a structure that overarches and includes within it subject and object.[22] The separation of the two sides—ontologically considered—is alienation, the separation of what belongs together.

Alienation as inauthenticity. The second dimension of alienation that is articulated against the backdrop of Heidegger's existential ontology concerns the self's relation to itself, understood as its relation to its own existence (*Existenz*). Here, too, there can be a kind of misapprehension, namely, falsely objectifying attitudes (to self and world). Loosely formulated, someone who does not relate to herself as to someone who has her own life to lead reifies herself insofar as she denies the character of her life activities as praxis, as activities that she must decide on. This failure of apprehension—the "systematic blinding of inauthenticity"[23]—rests, in turn, on the flattening out of a conceptual distinction that is of crucial importance for existential philosophy: the distinction between existence (*Existenz*) and being present-at-hand or, as Sartre puts it, between essence and existence.

This distinction differentiates *Dasein*, or our existence (*Existenz*), from the kind of being that ordinary things in the world have. When Heidegger says that *Dasein* is "not just one entity (*ein Seiendes*) among other entities" but is rather "totally different from all other entities," the distinctive characteristic of *Dasein* to which he means to draw our attention (a point already anticipated by Kierkegaard) is that *Dasein* is "an entity" for whom "in its very Being, that Being is an issue for it." It is not the case that *Dasein* simply "is;" it has, as Heidegger puts it, "its Being to be." That humans exist means that they do not simply live; they have their lives to lead, and they relate to their lives by understanding and valuing. They do not merely do this or that; rather they (implicitly or explicitly) relate to what they do. The aspect of this account of an individual's self-relation that is crucial for the critique of reification lies in the opposition between the concepts of existence (*Existenz*) and being present-at-hand. When we relate to ourselves existentially (*existierend*), we do not relate to ourselves as to an object that is simply present in the world. We relate to ourselves in our life activities—that is, in what we will and do. That I have "my own Being to be" means that I do not simply exist as any object could be (present-at-hand); rather, I must lead my life, carry it out myself. This means, among other things, being confronted with the fact that my own life must be decided on by me—or, as Tugendhat puts it, it means being confronted with "practical questions."

Against this backdrop it is possible to characterize more precisely two aspects of self-alienation that can be formulated in Heidegger's vocabulary: alienation means both making oneself into a thing and adapting oneself to others in what one does. In the one case someone fails to apprehend that she *leads* her life; in the other, that she *herself* has to lead it.

▪ The flattening out of the distinction between existence (*Existenz*) and being present-at-hand leads to a "fallenness" that consists in taking thinghood as the paradigm for Being—or, as one could also say, to an "essentialization of existence." In this case *Dasein* identifies "its own Being with the Being of things."[24] Sartre (1991) has provided an illuminating (if chauvinistic) example of what it is to make oneself into a thing in his famous analysis of bad faith:[25] a young woman responds to a suitor's overtures by allowing her hand, which he has taken hold of, to remain in his grasp, but she does so passively and indifferently, as if she has not noticed the attempted overture. Her hand is no longer a part of herself; she is not in what she does, that is, she takes no part in her own action. That she, as Sartre puts it, "inertly" makes herself into a thing means that she denies her responsibility for what she does and for her reactions to what happens to her. In this context fallenness refers to a failure to apprehend the fact that in what we do we (always already) act or conduct ourselves practically, which is to say that we have options and, in choosing among them, we decide. Accordingly, self-alienation (in the sense of Heidegger's inauthenticity or Sartre's bad faith) refers to a failure to apprehend the fact that one has one's own life to lead and that one is unavoidably always already leading it.

⁂   Self-alienation in a second sense refers to a failure to apprehend not only that one leads one's own life but also that one leads it oneself or that one is called on to live it oneself.[26] What Heidegger means when he refers to failing to apprehend the "impossibility of having one's life represented by someone else"—one dimension of our relation to ourselves in leading our lives—can be understood as a version of Kierkegaard's project of "becoming an individual." In Heidegger's account this dimension of (self-)alienation— inauthenticity—results from "fallenness into others," from a fallenness into the "public we-world,"[27] from the "way things have been interpreted" by the "They" (*das Man*). To be sure, the existence of the "with-world" (*Mitwelt*), the social world that is shared with others, is just as fundamental to Heidegger's analysis as being-in-the-world in general: one necessarily understands one's own existence from within the world, and in the present context this means in relation to a public interpretation of the world. On the other hand, the social world is the cause of inauthenticity and self-alienation. Heidegger traces the circumstance that "proximally and for the most part, *Dasein* is not itself"[28] back to the fact that we always already exist publicly, that we are forced to understand ourselves from within a public interpretation.

These ideas capture the idea of inauthenticity and a subtle form of heteronomy that consists (according to this interpretation) in a conformist orientation to others. The "mode of being of the 'They'" (*Seinsweise des Man*) is the source of the loss of self that Heidegger calls inauthenticity. Insofar as this can be understood as a pejorative description of the sphere of sociality in general,[29] it refers to a social interrelatedness characterized by, at once, conformity and anonymity—that is, a situation in which decisions and evaluations are not made explicitly but as if it were simply self-evident how one should decide and evaluate. "In *Dasein*'s everydayness the agency through which most things come about is one of which we must say that 'it was no one.'"[30] This, too, describes a kind of domination: we have fallen under "subjection to the other," but there is also a strange oscillation here between domination by others and self-"domination" (or self-rule), which is explained by the anonymous and fleeting character of the subject of this domination (by the "They"). The "They" is "not this one, not that one, not oneself, not some people, and not the sum of them all."[31] Thus this description, too, contains an element of alienation critique: what we ourselves have created turns back on us and affects us as something alien; "we ourselves" become an anonymous "no one" who can neither *take responsibility* for nor *be made responsible* for the world we ourselves have created: "it was no one." At the same time, however, relations appear reified, as if they could not be any other way. For this reason the "They"—"rule by nobody," as Arendt calls it—could be read as a description of precisely that structure we are attempting to find in connection with the topic of alienation: the "They" as a social power that has taken on an independent existence and is responsible for the fact that individuals cannot "re-find themselves in their own actions."[32]

3

THE STRUCTURE AND PROBLEMS OF ALIENATION CRITIQUE

ALIENATION, AS SKETCHED THUS FAR, is an interpretive schema, a concept with whose help one (individually or collectively) understands and articulates one's relation to oneself and to the world. An interpretive schema of this kind is productive when it puts us in a position to perceive, judge, or understand aspects of the world that would remain unknown without it. The merit of concepts like alienation lies also in their ability to enable us to see certain phenomena "together" (or to think them together)—that is, to make visible connections among phenomena that would otherwise remain hidden. And in some respects alienation critique does in fact describe phenomena in ways that run against the grain of how they are normally described.

- Alienation is tied to the problem of a *loss of meaning*; an alienated life is one that has become impoverished or meaningless, but it is a meaninglessness that is intertwined with *powerlessness* and impotence.
- Alienation is (therefore) a *relation of domination*, but of a kind that is not captured by standard descriptions of unfreedom and heteronomy.
- Alienation means disconnectedness or *alienness*, but an alienness that differs from simple relationlessness.

In what follows I discuss some implications of the concept of alienation as I have articulated it thus far.

LOSS OF MEANING AND LOSS OF POWER

First, the idea of alienation contain two different but intertwined diagnoses. On the one hand, the diagnosis of a *loss of power*, which we experience, when alienated, in relation both to ourselves and to a world that has become alien to us: alienated relations are those in which we are disempowered as subjects; on the other hand, the diagnosis of a *loss of meaning*, which characterizes a world that appears alien to us, as well as our relation to that world and to ourselves. An alienated world is a meaningless world, one that is not experienced by us as a meaningful whole. Thus alienation refers at once to both heteronomy—having one's properties determined by an other—and the complete absence of essential properties or purposes; moreover, it seems to be one of the main points of the phenomenon described as alienation that in it these two problems—power's being turned into impotence and the loss of meaningful involvement in the world—are intertwined.

Now the connection between these two themes is not self-evident. Is it not possible to be immersed in a meaningful world without having power or control over what one does? Is it not possible, more generally, to be unalienated in a relation that is determined by something or someone other than oneself? These are questions about the relation between freedom and meaning and about whether *self-determination* and *self-realization* stand in a constitutive relationship to each another. The underlying thesis could be formulated as follows: only a world that I can make "my own"—only a world that I can identify with (by appropriating it)—is a world in which I can act in a self-determined manner. (And, by the same token, only identification that takes place in a self-determined manner counts as successful identification.) Understood in this way, the concept of alienation attempts to identify the conditions under which one can understand oneself as a subject, as the master of one's own actions.

This thesis has implications. One could even understand what distinguishes emancipatory from conservative diagnoses of alienation in the following way: the former focus on the expressive and creative power of individuals as acting beings, whereas the latter emphasize the loss of connection to a given meaningful order. My understanding of how the problem should be framed, however, rules out a nostalgic longing for premodern unalienated conditions—for the meaningful order of feudal relationships, for example; it also means that the conservative view, which traces alienation back to the overly demanding requirements of modern freedom and its lack of social bonds, is no longer plausible. In other words, the conservative critique of alienation conceives of (modern) freedom as the cause of alienation, whereas the emancipatory critique views alienation as a *form* of unfreedom.

AT ONCE ALIEN AND ONE'S OWN:
STRUCTURAL HETERONOMY

Second, if alienation is a form of powerlessness and impotence, then the theory of alienation concerns itself with both more and something other than straightforward relations of domination. What we are alienated from is always *at once alien and our own*. In alienated relations we appear to be, in a complicated manner, both victims and perpetrators. Someone who becomes alienated in or through a role at the same time plays this role *herself*; someone who is led by alien desires at the same time *has* those desires—and we would fail to recognize the complexity of the situation if we were to speak here simply of internalized compulsion or psychological manipulation. Social institutions that confront us as rigid and alien are at the same time created by us. In such a case we are not—and this is what is specific to the diagnosis of alienation— master over what we (collectively) do. As Erich Fromm vividly puts it:

> [The bourgeois human being] produces a world of the greatest and most wonderful things; but these, his own creations, confront him as alien and threatening; although they have been created, he no longer feels himself to be their master but their servant. The whole material world becomes the monstrosity of a giant machine that prescribes the direction and tempo of his life. The work of his hands, intended to serve him and make him happy, becomes a world he is alienated from, a world he humbly and impotently obeys.[1]

In relations of alienation the feeling of impotence does not necessarily imply the existence of an actual power—an agent—that creates a condition of impotence. Typically the theory of alienation—whether in the form of Heidegger's "They" or Marx's analysis of capitalism—concerns itself with subtle forms of structural heteronomy or with the anonymous, dominating character of objectified relationships that appear to take on a life of their own over and against individual agents. Formulated differently, the concept of alienation posits a connection between *indifference and domination* that calls for interpretation. The things, situations, facts, to which we have no relation when alienated do not seem indifferent to us without consequence. They dominate us in and through this relation of indifference.[2]

THE RELATION OF RELATIONLESSNESS

Third, alienation is not simply foreignness or strangeness. As the etymological structure of the concept indicates, alienation does not mean simply disassociation; it is not the mere *absence* of a relation. Alienation is itself a relation, even if a deficient one. The things we are capable of becoming alienated from are not merely alien to us in the sense of being unfamiliar, unrelated, or indifferent. As Daniel Brudney aptly notes in his study of Marx: "One might find Mars and the Martians and the objects on Mars opaque and alien, but it would be odd to describe oneself as *alienated* from these things unless one either had or perhaps ought to have a relation to them in which they were not opaque and alien."[3] Thus alienation denotes relationlessness of a particular kind: a detachment or separation from something that in fact belongs together, the loss of a connection between two things that nevertheless stand in relation to one another. Being alienated from something means having become distanced from something in which one is in fact involved or to which one is in fact related—or in any case ought to be.

The terms *Entfremdung* and *Entäußerung* themselves evoke images: they suggest the separation of things which naturally belong together, or the establishment of some relation of indifference or hostility between things which are properly in harmony.[4] Only if one presupposes a logically, ontologically, or historically *prior relation* is it possible to understand alienation as the loss of a relation. It is crucial for the structure of the concept that the relation or connection underlying alienation *ought* to exist, even if it ostensibly no longer does. When we speak, for example, of someone having become alienated from his family, we not only presuppose that she was not always foreign to it; it is also suggested that she in some way still belongs to her family or even that she belongs to it regardless of whatever real (actually lived) relation she has to it. Thus things or relationships from which someone has become alienated make a claim, enigmatically, to being also still "one's own" even though they have become alien: "They are yours, *faute de mieux*, but no longer truly yours: they are yours, but you are alienated from them."[5] These considerations bring to light a fundamental characteristic of the concept of alienation: alienation is a specific form of relation, not a nonrelation or the mere absence of a relation. Alienation describes not the absence but the *quality* of a relation. Formulated paradoxically, alienation is a *relation of relationlessness*.

ALIENATION AS A DIAGNOSTIC CONCEPT

Precisely this last point, however, raises a problem: if alienation as a relation of relationlessness refers to a dissolution of, or a becoming indifferent to, a relation that nevertheless exists, does that mean that the connection actually still exists, that it *factically* continues to exist? Or does it mean that, despite the appearance of being alien, it *ought* to continue to exist, because (for instance) families simply belong together? When we characterize a situation as alienated, are we describing or criticizing it? Are we describing a condition or establishing a norm? It is a peculiarity of the concept of alienation that it claims to do both—or, perhaps, that it undermines this distinction.[6] As a *diagnostic* concept, alienation is at once normative and descriptive. Similar to how a term like *sickness* functions (as Richard Schacht suggests), classifying diagnostic findings as phenomena of a particular type, alienation is an interpretive scheme with whose help we can simultaneously discover, interpret, and evaluate certain phenomena in the world. The concept of alienation is, to borrow an expression from Bernard Williams, a "thick ethical concept."[7] Describing a situation as alienating implies an evaluation of it, or, put differently, the evaluation is not merely added on to the description but is inextricably bound up with it. Of course, this does not mean that a description or evaluation of this kind is presuppositionless. While the remark "you look sick" does not need to be followed by "and being sick is bad (for you)," the self-evident character of this connection rests on (shared) background assumptions: for example, a certain conception of health and sickness, as well as the idea that health is preferable to sickness. One might ask whether the concept of alienation does not depend in a similar way on ethical background assumptions—on a conception of what is destroyed or unachieved in the alienated condition, of what is absent but nevertheless desirable. To return to the example of the family: why should the fact that I *was* once tied to my family and am indisputably descended from it imply in any way that I *ought* to be further tied to it? Does not the claim that there "really" is a relationship there already have a normative character? Is not an appeal to the original bond—"but those are your parents"—compelling only if it appeals to already shared assumptions of what it means to be a family? Or put differently: if one can appeal to that original bond without further argumentation, it is because the description of the *relationship* (that I have or do not have to my family) is normatively tinged through and through.

If the relational character of an alienated relation is itself up for debate in each case, then the problematic character of the concept of alienation as well as the possibility of its reconstruction depend crucially on how the normative background assumptions mentioned here are to be understood and justified.

If one looks more closely at the previous examples of alienation, it becomes clear that each depends on ideas that are far from self-evident: from whom or what is one alienated when one becomes alienated from oneself? By what standard do we recognize genuine needs? How precisely are we to understand the unity that is contrasted with internal division, and what capacities would one have to develop in order to be a whole human being or a fully developed personality? Does not the ideal of personality and immediacy on which the critique of objectification relies ignore the emancipatory potential contained in depersonalized relations and the indifference that characterizes them? Is not the ideal of transparency and creative power that underlies a critique of social relations as alienating and reifying illusory in a society marked by complex social and economic organization? Thus the essentialism that haunts the concept of alienation appears just as problematic as the ideal of transparency and reconciliation bound up with the idea of the unalienated human being and the unalienated society.

CRITIQUE OF THE CRITIQUE OF ALIENATION

If, beginning with Rousseau, alienation is conceived of as a mismatch between the nature of human beings and their social life, then the return from an alienated condition back to an unalienated one obviously means a return to this essence, to the human being's purpose or nature. In this case the critique of alienation would always presuppose an (objectively grounded) shape or purpose of true human existence from which one has become distanced in the alienated condition. Saying that something is alienated or that one becomes alienated from something suggests that there is something essentially "one's own" from which one has become alienated. If alienation consists in the "contradiction between human beings' existence and essence" (according to a formulation of the young Marx), then alienation is not merely something that *ought* not to be but rather something that in a certain sense *is* not. "Appearance"—the alienated condition—is then, in a manner of speaking, already logically and ontologically "wrong." And once alienation is conceived as a contradiction that manifests itself as an intermediary historical stage, history (as the arena of alienation's progress) pushes toward reconciliation and an overcoming of the alienated condition. This is, in any case, how one can understand the Hegelian strategy of finding a solution for alienation in a philosophy of history, traces of which are easily found also in Marx. Thinking of alienation as "being outside oneself" and of the overcoming of alienation as "coming to oneself" is tantamount to ascribing to it something like a "built-in mechanism for self-overcoming."[8]

Hence, there are various points of criticism to which the theory of alienation is vulnerable. Ever since Althusser criticized Marx's "humanism" and its ideal of the subject's self-transparency and self-directed powers—thereby disavowing the conception of alienation from a perspective internal to Marxism—the critique of essentialism has become part of philosophical "common sense."[9] Moreover, no one today would endorse the kind of justification offered by a Hegelian philosophy of history, with its normatively teleological view of historical development. And even paring the philosophy of history down to a view that makes alienation into one constituent of a theory of the good life is frequently met with the charge of paternalism.

There are essentially two contemporary positions that stand in conflict with theories of alienation: the Rawlsian tradition of philosophical liberalism, which eschews objective conceptions of the good life, and the poststructuralist critique of the subject, which calls into question the conception of the subject that the theory of alienation appears to presuppose.

OBJECTIVISM, PERFECTIONISM, PATERNALISM

From the perspective of liberal theory one aspect of the critique of alienation appears problematic above all others: theories of alienation appear to appeal to objective criteria that lie beyond the "sovereignty" of individuals to interpret for themselves what the good life consists in. Herbert Marcuse exemplifies this tendency of many theories of alienation in *One Dimensional Man*—a book that provided a crucial impulse for the New Left's critique of alienation in the 1960s and 1970s—when, unconcerned with the liberal objection, he defends the validity of diagnoses of alienation with respect to the increased integration and identification with social relations that characterize the members of affluent industrial societies: "I have just suggested that the concept of alienation seems to become questionable when the individuals identify themselves with

the existence which is imposed upon them and have in it their own development and satisfaction. This identification is not illusion, but reality. However,
the reality constitutes *a more progressive stage of alienation*. The latter has
become entirely objective; the subject which is alienated is swallowed up by
its alienated existence."[10] The subjective satisfaction of those who are integrated into objectively alienated relations is, according to Marcuse, "a false
consciousness which is immune against its falsehood."[11] Here, however, the
theory of alienation appears to have made *itself* immune to refutation.

It would seem, then, that the concept of alienation belongs to a perfectionist ethical theory that presupposes, broadly speaking, that it is possible to determine what is objectively good for humans by identifying a set of properties
or a set of functions inherent in human nature—a "purpose"—that ought to
be realized. But if the foundation of modern morality and the fundamental
conviction of liberal conceptions of society is the idea "that it should be left
to each individual how he lives his own life"[12]—that individuals are sovereign
with respect to interpreting their own lives—then a theory of alienation that
relies on objective perfectionist ideals appears to reject this idea in favor of
a paternalist perspective that claims to "know better." For the latter (and as
seems to be the case for Marcuse), it is possible for something to count as objectively good for someone without him subjectively valuing it as such. By the
same token, it is possible to criticize a form of life as alienated or false without
there being any subjective perception of suffering. But can someone be alienated from herself in the sense outlined here if she herself fails to perceive it?
Can we claim of someone that she is alienated from her own desires or driven
by false (alienated) needs or that she pursues an alienated way of life if she
claims to be living precisely the life she wants to lead? In diagnoses of alienation the question arises, then, whether there can be objective evidence of
pathology that contradicts individuals' subjective assessments or preferences.

This is a dilemma that is difficult to resolve. On the one hand, the concept of alienation (this is what distinguishes it from weaker forms of critique)
claims to be able to bring to individuals' prima facie evaluations and preferences a deeper dimension of critique—a critical authority—that functions as
a corrective to their own assertions. On the other hand, it is not easy to justify
the position of such a critical corrective. What could the objective criteria
that overrule the assessments and preferences of individuals be in this case?[13]

The arguments from human nature frequently appealed to in this context
demonstrate, even in their most methodologically sophisticated, "thin" vari-
ants, the problems that plague attempts to derive normative standards from

some conception of human nature.[14] Even if there is—in a banal sense—something humans share on the basis of their natural, biological constitution, and even if—in a banal sense—certain functional needs can be derived from these basic presuppositions of human life (all humans need nourishment or certain climatic conditions in order to survive), these basic conditions imply very little when it comes to evaluating how humans, in relation to issues beyond mere survival, *lead their lives*. On the other hand, the more human nature is given a specific content such that it becomes relevant to (culturally specific) forms of life, the more controversial and contestable the claims become. How are we to define human nature when its extraordinary variability and malleability appear to be part of human nature itself?[15] And how are we to pick out among diverse forms of human life those that really correspond to human nature, given that even forms of life criticized as alienated have been in some way developed, advanced, and lived by human beings?[16]

ALIENATION AND THE CRITIQUE OF THE SUBJECT

The second position that calls into question the viability of alienation critique or rejects it outright is—broadly speaking—poststructuralism with its critique of the subject. Michel Foucault directly takes aim at conceptions of alienation and emancipation when he comments in an interview:

> I have always been somewhat suspicious of the notion of liberation, because if it is not treated with precautions and within certain limits, one runs the risk of falling back on the idea that there exists a human nature or base that, as a consequence of certain historical, economic, and social processes, has been concealed, alienated, or imprisoned in and by mechanisms of repression. According to this hypothesis, all that is required is to break these repressive deadlocks and man will be reconciled with himself, rediscover his nature or regain contact with his origin, and reestablish a full and positive relationship with himself.[17]

Here Foucault not only attacks essentialist appeals to human nature; he also rejects the very idea of subjectivity that appears to underlie the critique of alienation. Directing himself specifically against theories of alienation, Foucault claims that the repression hypothesis (as he calls it) presupposes the idea of a subject "beyond power," a subject that exists "for itself" in an unalienated manner somewhere beyond the social powers that form and oppress it. The thesis that Foucault opposes to this view—the "productivity of power"—radically calls into question the possibility of distinguishing inner from outer, "one's own" from alien, and social formation from individual uniqueness. Influenced by Althusser's theory of "subjectivization," he conceives of the subject as the result or effect of an "interpellation" on the part of "power" (which is no longer understood on the model of sovereign power). If the subject, as this view would have it, is both *subjected* to the rules of power and at the same time *constituted* by them (as a desiring and acting subject), then the distinction that alienation critique requires between self and what is alien, between an unrepressed (or undistorted) subject and a repressive (or distorting) power, is no longer tenable. The normative standard of the autonomous subject, which is capable of being transparent to itself as the author of its actions, is then called into question. Alienation critique appears to have lost its standard or, expressed differently, alienation becomes constitutive and unavoidable. Thus Judith Butler speaks (in a clearly melancholic tone) of an insuperable "primary and inaugurative alienation in sociality":

> The desire to persist in one's own being requires submitting to a world of others that is fundamentally not one's own (a submission that does not take place at a later date, but which frames and makes possible the desire to be). Only by persisting in alterity does one persist in one's "own being." Vulnerable to terms that one never made, one persists always, to some degree, through categories, names, terms, and classifications that mark a primary and inaugurative alienation in sociality.[18]

4

HAVING ONESELF AT ONE'S COMMAND: RECONSTRUCTING THE CONCEPT OF ALIENATION

MY CLAIM IS THAT ALIENATION critique today *cannot,* but also *need not* be grounded in strongly essentialist or metaphysical presuppositions;[1] moreover, it cannot but also need not rely on perfectionist or paternalistic arguments. The rich social and ethical dimension of alienation critique can be made accessible without the strongly objectivistic interpretive scheme that is frequently associated with it. And it is possible to avail ourselves of the critical import of the concept of alienation without relying on the certainty of a final harmony or reconciliation, on the idea of a fully self-transparent individual, or on the illusion of having oneself and the world completely at one's disposal or command.[2] The perspective from which the problem of alienation is approached ceases to be interesting precisely when it presupposes a pre-established harmony among relations or a seamless "oneness" of individuals with themselves or with the world; it becomes productive when it calls these relations into question without supposing that they can be completely free of conflict. Focusing on the sources of disturbances in living one's life, it points out the conditions of successfully relating to self and world, which can be normatively described in relatively sparing but still contentful terms.

It could then turn out that precisely the point of the concept of alienation is to mediate between unsatisfying alternatives—between ethical subjectivism and objectivism, between refraining from and espousing substantial moral conceptions of the good life, between abandoning the idea of autonomy and holding onto illusory conceptions of subjectivity. The concept's potential would then lie not in the possibility of providing a robustly substantial ethical theory but in being able to criticize the content of forms of life precisely without needing to appeal to ultimate, metaphysically grounded (substantial) ethical values. Its potential would also lie in the possibility of evaluating ways of relating to self and world without needing to presuppose a subject that is unified and in possession of all its powers from the outset. The unalienated life would then no longer be one that is reconciled; it would no longer be the happy life, perhaps not even the good life. Instead, not being alienated would refer to a certain way of *carrying out* one's own life and a certain way of *appropriating oneself*—that is, a way of *establishing relations* to oneself and to the relationships in which one lives (relationships that condition or shape who one is).

HOW, NOT WHAT—TUGENDHAT'S CONCEPTION OF THE FUNCTIONAL CAPACITY OF WILLING

I would now like to take up Ernst Tugendhat's reflections on the problem of grounding a modern ethical theory, which will prove to be useful for reconstructing a theory of alienation that overcomes the charges of essentialism and perfectionism.

In "The Ethics of Antiquity and Modernity" Tugendhat raises the problem of whether it is possible to reformulate antiquity's inquiry into the nature of happiness (or the good life) under modern conditions. A modern inquiry into the good life must, on the one hand, do justice to the view that its answer cannot "deny the autonomy and thus the interpretive sovereignty of those concerned," and its method must be such that it avoids committing itself to a "specific and unjustifiable picture of the human being."[3] On the other hand, if modern ethical theory is to recover the interpretive content of ancient ethics, it must be able to identify an objective criterion that allows us to say "whether it is going well or badly for a person independently of their actual perceptions of their present or future well-being." What is needed, then, is a criterion that, on the one hand, is not identical with the desires or preferences a person actually has and that, on the other hand, does not call into question the interpretive sovereignty of the person and with it the modern ideal of self-determination. Tugendhat's proposed solution is to develop a *formal* conception of psychological health. Starting from (what appears to him to be) an unproblematic definition of *physical* health in terms of "functional capacity," he develops for *psychological* health a conception of the "functional capacity of willing" and its possible impairment.[4] Tugendhat elaborates his criterion with the example of compulsive behavior: a volition that is compulsive in some sense would count as impaired and hence as being disturbed in its functional capacity.

This provides a standpoint that is immanent to the subject's will and, at the same time, not subjective in the sense in which contingent and unevaluated preferences are: "In this way we would attain precisely what is sought, a point of view that is independent of the respective subjective goals of our willing but that nevertheless derives its authority from the perspective of willing itself. As willing (freely choosing) beings, we always will to be unlimited in our free choosing."[5] With the standard of the "impairment of the functional capacity of willing," which asks whether we have ourselves at our command in what we will, Tugendhat has achieved a middle ground between subjectivistic and objectivistic positions of the sort he was looking for. One could call such a position a "qualified subjectivism."[6]

This provides us with a starting point for overcoming the opposition between modern antipaternalism and the paternalism of a more substantial ethical theory: whether something is good for me always depends (antipaternalistically) on my personal view, on whether I in fact want it. This view, however, must be *qualified* in the sense that the volition it expresses must be a "true volition" and therefore not subject to internal constraints. I must be free in what I will; I must have my will at my command if it is to count as my own. This criterion is, in the first place, *formal*: it concerns the *How*, not the *What*, of willing. That is, I need not will anything in particular; rather, I must be able to will what I will in a free or self-determined manner. It is not necessary, then, to identify a "true object of willing," but only a certain way of relating, in one's willing, to oneself and to what one wills. As Tugendhat puts it, "the question of what we truly will concerns *not the goals of our willing but the How of willing*."[7] Second, this criterion is *immanent*: the criterion is the functional capacity of willing itself, a claim posited by the act of willing itself. When I say, "I want to be able to do what I will," I must also mean, "I want to be able—freely—to will."

My account of the problem of alienation can be linked up with this conception of willing in the following way: instances of alienation can be understood as obstructions of volition and thereby—formulated more generally—as obstructions in the relations individuals have to themselves and the world. With the help of Tugendhat's conception of having oneself at one's command, instances of alienation can be reconstructed in terms of disturbed ways of establishing relations to oneself and to the world. In this way the problem of alienation is tied to that of freedom.

FREEDOM AND ALIENATION

My thesis is that alienation can be understood as a particular form of the loss of freedom, as an obstruction of what could be called, following Isaiah Berlin, positive freedom.[8] Formulating the notoriously controversial distinction as briefly as possible, freedom in this sense refers not (merely negatively) to the absence of external coercion but (positively) to the capacity to realize valuable ends. In the sense described (and criticized) by Berlin, positive freedom has a variety of implications:

> The "positive" sense of the word "liberty" derives from the wish on the part of the individual to be his own master. I wish my life and decisions to depend on myself, not on external forces of whatever kind. I wish to be the instrument of my own, not of other men's, acts of will. I wish to be a subject, not an object; to be moved by reasons, by conscious purposes, which are my own, not by causes which affect me, as it were, from outside. I wish to be somebody, not nobody; a doer—deciding, not being decided for, self-directed and not acted upon by external nature or by other men as if I were a thing, or an animal, or a slave incapable of playing a human role, that is, of conceiving goals and policies of my own and realizing them. . . . I wish, above all, to be conscious of myself as a thinking, willing, active being, bearing responsibility for my choices and able to explain them by references to my own ideas and purposes. I feel free to the degree that I believe this to be true, and enslaved to the degree that I am made to realize that it is not.[9]

As unsystematic and indeterminate the various dimensions of positive freedom might be, the important point is that conceptions of positive freedom always depict the free life as not alienated and vice versa.[10] As Robert Pippin puts it, only those acts and intentions that I can "link . . . with me such that they count as due to me or count as mine" are "instances of freedom."[11] Being a human being rather than a thing means, according to this view, ascribing to oneself what one wills and does, taking responsibility for it and (therefore) being able to identify with it.

Understood in this way, the concept of alienation concerns itself with the complex conditions of "linking" one's actions and desires (or, more generally, one's life) with oneself, "counting them as due to" oneself, or making them "one's own." It also concerns itself with the various obstructions and disturbances that can affect these relations. One is not always already "with oneself;" one's actions and desires are not always one's own from the start, and one's relation to the surrounding natural and social world is equally constitutive and threatened. Positively formulated, clarifying the various dimensions of alienation enables us to specify the conditions for being able to understand one's life as one's own (and therefore to lead one's life *freely*). An unalienated life, according to this view, is not one in which specific substantial values are realized but one that is lived in a specific—unalienated—manner. The belief that everyone should be able to live her own life no longer stands in opposition, then, to the project of alienation critique. Rather, the absence of alienating impediments and the possibility of appropriating self and world without such impediments is a condition of freedom and self-determination.

ALIENATION AS AN IMPEDED RELATION OF APPROPRIATION

Thus the problem domain of freedom and alienation is centrally concerned with ways of appropriating one's own life. The concept of appropriation refers to a way of establishing relations to oneself and to the world, a way of dealing with oneself and the world and of having oneself and the world at one's command. Alienation, as a disturbance in this relation, concerns the way these acts of relating to self and world are carried out, that is, whether processes of appropriation fail or are impeded. As in Tugendhat's attempt to formalize the good, the analysis of the phenomena of alienation focuses on *How* the relating to self and world is carried out rather than on *What* an act of willing strives to achieve. Alienation can then be understood as an *impairment of acts of appropriation* (or as a *deficient praxis* of appropriation). If the overcoming of alienation appears as a successful relation of appropriation, we can inquire into the conditions of its success without needing to conceive of that relation as teleologically guided or fully completable. Nor must this process be understood essentialistically, as the recovery of an essence that is already defined and set prior to the process itself.

Focusing on disturbances of acts of appropriation has important implications that can be seen by returning to our initial examples. Instead of defining the potentials the "whole human being" is supposed to develop in terms of their content, the analysis of alienation looks at disturbances in the development of interests and capacities; instead of getting caught up in the confusing paradoxes bound up with distinguishing genuine from inauthentic, alienated desires, the theory of alienation analyzes the circumstances of will formation

and the various ways in which desires are integrated. And instead of reconstructing social relations on the basis of a substantial model of ethical and
social life (*Sittlichkeit*), what matters is the conditions under which social
practices are carried out and structured.

The following points are important for an approach that focuses on relations of appropriation:

* The concept of appropriation refers to a comprehensive conception of
practical relations to self and world. It includes a broadly understood capacity of knowing and dealing with oneself: having access to or command over
oneself and the world. This can be explicated as the capacity to make the life
one leads, or what one wills and does, one's own; as the capacity to identify
with oneself and with what one does; in other words, as the ability to realize
oneself in what one does.

* The theory of alienation conceives of relations to self and world as
equally primordial. Therefore an impairment of the relation to self, not having
oneself at one's command, must also always be understood as an impairment
of one's relation to the world. Whether what is at issue is appropriating one's
own personal history. the "task of becoming oneself through one's own deed"
(as in Heidegger's concept of resoluteness), or the appropriation of one's own
activities in Marx's sense—what is of concern is always an appropriation of
the world and, at the same time, an appropriation of the (variously defined)
given preconditions of one's own actions. In this sense someone is alienated
when she cannot relate to herself and (thereby) to her own preconditions, that
is, when she cannot appropriate them as her own.

* While the model of appropriation sketched here is closely related to the
thick conception of appropriation found in Marx, my reconstruction does not
conceive of appropriation as the reappropriation of a given essence. Instead,
appropriation is productive; what is appropriated is, at the same time, a result
of the process of appropriation. Therefore the *preconditions* to which one—if
not alienated—should be able to relate and the *relation* that one—if not alienated—has to realize are primarily neither invented nor made.

APPROPRIATION

What does it mean to *appropriate* something?[12] If the concept of appropriation refers to a specific relation between self and world, between individuals
and objects (whether spiritual or material), what precisely does this relation

look like, what are its particular character and its specific structure? Various aspects come together here, and together they account for the concept's appeal and potential. As opposed to the mere *learning* of certain contents, talk of appropriation emphasizes that something is not merely passively taken up but actively worked through and independently assimilated. In contrast to merely theoretical *insight* into some issue, appropriation—comparable to the psychoanalytic process of "working through"—means that one can "deal with" what one knows, that it stands at one's disposal as knowledge and that one really and practically has command over it. And appropriating a role means more than being able to fill it: one is, we could say, identified with it. Something that we appropriate does not remain external to ourselves. In making something our own, it becomes a part of ourselves in a certain respect. This suggests a kind of introjection and a mixing of oneself with the objects of appropriation. It also evokes the idea of productively and formatively interacting with what one makes one's own. Appropriation does not leave what is appropriated unchanged. This is why the appropriation of public spaces, for example, means more than that one *uses* them. We make them our own by making a mark on them through what we do in and with them, by transforming them through appropriative use such that they first acquire a specific form through this use (though not necessarily in a material sense). Although it has one of its roots in an account of property relations, the concept of appropriation, in contrast to mere possession, emphasizes the particular quality of a process that first constitutes a real act of taking possession of something. Accordingly, appropriation is a particular mode of seizing possession.[13] Someone who appropriates something puts her individual mark on it, inserts her own ends and qualities into it. This means that sometimes we must still make something that we already possess *our own*.

Relations of appropriation, then, are characterized by several features: appropriation is a form of praxis, a way of relating practically to the world. It refers to a relation of penetration, assimilation, and internalization in which what is appropriated is at the same time altered, structured, and formed. The crucial point of this model (also of great importance for Marx) is a consequence of this structure of penetration and assimilation: appropriation always means a transformation of both poles of the relation. In a process of appropriation both what is appropriated and the appropriator are transformed. In the process of incorporation (appropriative assimilation) the incorporator does not remain the same. This point can be given a constructivist turn: what is appropriated is itself constituted in the process of appropriation; by the same token, what is appropriated does not exist in the absence of appropriation. (In some cases this is obvious: there is no public space as such without its being publicly appropriated; but even social roles exist only insofar as they are constantly reappropriated.)

One now sees the potential and the peculiar character of the concept: the possibility of appropriating something refers, on the one hand, to a subject's power to act and form and to impose its own meaningful mark on the world it appropriates. (A successful appropriation of social roles or activities and, by extension, the appropriating relation one can take to one's life in general constitute something like self-determination and being the author of one's own life.) On the other hand, a process of appropriation is always bound to a given, previously existing content and thereby also to an independent meaning and dynamic over which one does not have complete command. (Thus a role, for example, in order to be appropriated, must always be "found" as an already existing model and complex of rules; it can be reinterpreted but not invented from scratch. Skills that we appropriate are constrained by success conditions; leading our own life depends on circumstances over which we do not have complete command.) There is, then, an interesting tension in the idea of appropriation between what is previously given and what is formable, between taking over and creating, between the subject's sovereignty and its dependence. The crucial relation here is that between something's being alien and its accessibility: objects of appropriation are neither exclusively alien nor exclusively one's own. As Michael Theunissen puts it, "I do not *need* to appropriate what is exclusively my own, and what is exclusively alien I am *unable* to appropriate."[14] In contrast to Marx, then, for whom appropriation is conceived of according to a model of *re*appropriation, the account of the dynamic of appropriation and alienation that I am proposing reconceives the very concept of appropriation. This involves rehabilitating what is *alien* in the model of appropriation and radicalizing that model in the direction of a nonessentialist conception of appropriation. Appropriation would then be a permanent process of transformation in which what is appropriated first comes to be through its appropriation, without one needing to fall back into the myth of a *creatio ex nihilo*. Understanding appropriation as a relation in which we are simultaneously bound to something and separated from it, and in which what is appropriated always remains both alien and our own, has important implications for the ideas of emancipation and alienation bound up with the concept of appropriation. The aspiration of a successful appropriation of self and world would be, then, to make the world one's own without it having been already one's own and in wanting to give structure to the world and to one's own life without beginning from a position of already having complete command over them.

THE PROJECT AND THE METHOD OF RECONSTRUCTION

On the basis of what I have sketched thus far it is possible briefly to outline the project of reconstructing the concept of alienation as I aim to carry it out in what follows.

1. The break with objectivistic ethical theory follows from the procedural or formal orientation of my approach, namely, its focus on the *How* of the process of appropriation. Instead of relying on a strongly objectivistic theory of the good life, my reconstruction is based on what could be called a qualified subjectivism. Whereas the individual (her subjective states and desires) remains the final reference point for the diagnosis of alienation, it is also possible to call into question her prima facie evaluations.

2. Replacing essentialist conceptions of self and community with a focus on how acts of willing are carried out and how they can be disturbed represents a break with strong forms of essentialism that depend on the idea of realizing human nature. The objects to be examined are existential acts or human beings in what they do and will, not as they are "in essence."

3. Since the diagnosis of alienation, thus conceived, starts from the sources of disturbances of successful relations to self and world, it is open-ended and not dependent on a closed, harmonistic model of reconciliation. And although it can be said that the talk of disturbances presupposes conditions of successful functioning, the (in this respect "negativistic") approach pursued here is, in crucial respects, quite modest in its positive appeal to the idea of a successful human existence.

4. Because of its emphasis on concepts like experience and experiment, alienation critique is part of an open-ended process in the carrying out of which it is possible to identify and modify criteria for failure and success. So considered, alienation is less a "fall" from a successful, reconciled state than a breakdown and halting of experiential processes that are to be understood as experimental. Understood in this way, the concept of alienation *problematizes* what is "one's own" rather than presupposing it, or, put differently, both the relation and relationlessness of alienation are always contested.

IMMANENT CRITIQUE AND CULTURAL SELF-UNDERSTANDING

In what kind of critique, though, are we engaging when we carry out alienation critique? And from where does it acquire its standards?

Alienation critique can be understood as a form of *immanent critique*, a critique that, put very briefly, judges the subject or form of life in question according to criteria that the objects of critique themselves have posited or that are implicit in them. Two kinds of tension between critique and the object of critique are possible here. On the level of relations to the material and social world and its institutions, alienation critique points out discrepancies between the claims of modern ideals of freedom and their actual realization or, in other words, discrepancies between the ideal of control or command and actual impotence with respect to (self-created) relations. On the level of the individual's relations to self, on the other hand, a tension exists between the qualities we (it could be claimed necessarily) impute to subjects when we regard them — whether ourselves or others — as responsible agents and the obstructions of responsible agency that accompany alienated relations to self. To return to Berlin's description of positive freedom: what underlies this tension is a distinction between the qualities of (responsible, acting) human beings and those of (passive, "driven") things. This distinction does not derive from external criteria (external to an agent's self-conception) or from criteria that rely on a certain picture of human nature; it is, rather — in the sense previously discussed — internal to what it means to understand oneself as a person in a certain sense.

These methodological reflections on the concept of alienation raise the question of the status and scope of the dimension of critique that I want to explore in this study. If, as I have claimed, a diagnosis of alienation can be understood as immanent critique, how far can such a critique extend if, as it appears, immanence always requires shared premises? How universal can alienation critique be if it proceeds immanently? If what alienation critique — regarded both historically and systematically — points out are contradictions internal to modernity (to the modern idea of freedom) or possible tensions within personhood, is it not then based on a specific ethically and culturally shaped conception of the person and a specific, culturally influenced interpretation of freedom? Alienation critique would then be an element of the critical, evaluative self-interpretation of a modern culture that has made freedom and self-determination its core values.

The objection that this conception of critique (and with it the diagnosis of alienation) is culturally relative is not without merit. In comparison to the universalistic content of a theory that takes a view of human nature as its starting point, the scope of alienation critique, as I reconstruct it, is limited. Even when it relies on methods of deep interpretation to point out internal contradictions or failings, its domain is always limited to a specific shared form of life; its reach does not extend beyond its immediate context. It is not immediately clear, though, how much weight this objection carries. One might be tempted here to follow Joseph Raz, who, untroubled by such an objection, makes the following claim about the value of personal autonomy: "The value of personal autonomy is a *fact of life*. Since we live in a society whose social forms are to a considerable extent based on individual choice, and since our options are limited by what is available in our society, we can prosper only if we can be successfully autonomous."[15]

The validity of a critique that is oriented around such immanent values depends on how far the sphere of influence of a specific form of life in fact extends. And that will always be larger than where there is actual, explicit endorsement of those values. Thus a critique that is immanent in this sense can also be understood as laying out the implications and consequences of the practices bound up with specific forms of life, without it being the case that those who share a certain form of life are necessarily conscious of those implications, or immanent critique can also be understood as laying out contradictions internal to a form of life that point beyond the form of life in question.

PART TWO

LIVING ONE'S LIFE AS AN ALIEN LIFE: FOUR CASES

Someone lives my life. But it is not me.

AN EVERYDAY THEME. **SOMEONE SUDDENLY** becomes aware that her own life has become alien to her in crucial respects. She is now indifferent to people who once meant something to her; things that once excited her now leave her cold; projects she earlier pursued with dedication now seem pointless to her. In her job she merely gets by. She lives, as it were, *her own life as an alien life*. When a social role forces us to behave in ways that make us feel uneasy, when we suddenly become aware that in everything we do we are only attempting to satisfy others' demands, or when we are helplessly at the mercy of certain emotional reactions, we also sometimes speak of not being ourselves or of being alienated from ourselves. We observe with amusement the freshly styled junior editor who all too zealously imitates his boss's polite but superficial speech and we regard him as inauthentic. With less amusement we observe the existential crisis of an acquaintance who no longer feels "at home" in his own life or believes that his life is a failure. A person who is alienated from herself has (as a psychological description of a clinical symptom would have it) lost a relation to her own feelings, desires, and experiences and can no longer—even to the point of spatiotemporal disorientation—integrate them into the way she experiences her own life. She is alien to herself in what she wills and does. Incapable of experiencing herself as an actively structuring force, she feels unable to have any influence on what happens to her, which instead she experiences as something alien. These various phenomena point to the same idea: if one can be *alien to oneself*, then one can apparently also be more or less *oneself*, and the life one leads can be, for various reasons, more or less *one's own*.

But how can one become alien *to oneself*? Who becomes alienated here from whom? How are we to understand the claim that one can be *not* oneself, and in what nontrivial sense can my life be really *my own*?

Here the problems already encountered that are bound up with defining the human essence and the criteria of alienation critique resurface: if we speak of a *false self*, we are obviously presupposing a *true self*; if we can become alienated from ourselves, then it is also possible to be *with ourselves*. In each case we start from a gap or discrepancy and presuppose the possibility of eliminating it. In each case we think of the subject as internally divided, which can be interpreted in various ways: as a falling away from one's essence, as a failure to realize one's potential, or as falling short of one's true calling. We assume, in other words, a criterion for true, authentic selfhood against which to diagnose various types of deviation from it.

This becomes clear if we consider some of the everyday self-interpretations we encounter in conjunction with the aforementioned existential questions. The bank employee and father who says that "he is really an artist" believes that he has fallen short of his true calling. The young dynamic editor who, in a crisis, expresses a need finally to "find his way back to himself" suggests that somewhere underneath the behaviors he has merely passively adopted his true self lies dormant. We are presumably all familiar with people who interpret their lives in these ways and with life histories that seem to call for such interpretations. Nevertheless, it is not easy to understand what exactly could be meant here. Even if deeply embedded in the ways individuals understand themselves, these ideas are problematic. Where has the editor lost himself? And, when he searches, is he himself or not himself? How could the unlived life of the aspiring artist be his more real or more authentic life?

It is not that the idea of self-alienation merely has many meanings, but that it seems to be paradoxical at its core. The concept of alienation shares in the paradox of every essence-based critique: something that does not correspond to its own essence simultaneously partakes of it and does not partake of it.[1] The bank employee is *really* an artist, even if he is not currently one; and the junior editor, too, claims precisely not to be what he is.

The conception that underlies these ways of speaking seems to rest on several characteristic assumptions: the *authentic* or *true* self is something located somewhere *inside*. It exists independently of whether it is expressed, of whether it is realized in actions or externally manifested in other ways. The self we are capable of falling away from somehow has a substantial *essence* that exists prior to, and remains the same independently of, what it does. The thought that it must be possible to distinguish a true self from a false or alienated self, in the same way that we distinguish an inner core from its outer husk, is the metaphorical idea around which these everyday notions revolve. The true self is thought of as a kind of "proto-self" that can be distinguished from its falsified forms. We are, on this picture, "with ourselves" when we exist in conformity with this essential inner core and we are alienated or inauthentic, in contrast, when this core has been falsified by external factors or when we have distanced ourselves from it. Thus the authentic self — according to what is common to these ideas — would correspond to something that we can search for and find, but that we can also fall short of.[2]

This picture — which I treat for now as an idea of common sense — can be criticized from various perspectives, two of which are of crucial importance for my problem: on the one hand, one can point out the *reifying* consequences that go along with such a definition of essence; on the other hand, one can criticize the conception of *inwardness* bound up with the inner-outer metaphor, which Frederic Jameson refers to somewhat irreverently as "the container model of self."[3]

First, to make the criticism that this view relies on an essentialist and *reifying* conception of the self means, very briefly: it is not merely that the idea of an essential core hypostatizes the authentic self into a kind of person inside the person, where it remains unclear how the relation between these two creatures is to be conceived. It is also that this idea misrepresents the structure of human existence. For on this view we are forced to imagine a person as we do any object in the world, as a thing we can investigate in order to find out what essential properties it has, how it is constituted, and how it functions. But how am I to find out (with regard to myself) who I am beyond the things

I will and do? It is well known that I am already on shaky ground if I say, of the object that I use to hammer a nail, it is "really only a block of wood" and therefore not a hammer.[4] But when I say of the upstanding father that he is "really" a wild bohemian and artist, I fail to do justice to the fact that humans are beings that *lead their lives* and that become what they are only in doing so.

Second, implicit in the container model of the self is the idea that the self exists somewhere inside, waiting to be expressed, and that it has an existence independent of its expression. Thus, the bank employee thinks that his nature as an artist lies dormant in him, and the junior editor who has fallen into a crisis assumes that there is something there—inside—that he could fall back on if he were first freed from the falsifications the external world imposes on him. According to this model, there is a self that exists prior to and apart from its being realized, something that constitutes the innermost part of someone without it needing to be *realized* in any deed, activity, or other mode of expression. But this idea is highly dubious. It is unclear what the inside of a person is supposed to be such that, on the one hand, it does not require articulation but, on the other hand, it already exists as something determinate. In opposition to this, one could maintain that there is no truth of the self beyond its manifestations. What we *are* must be expressed and *externalized* in order to acquire reality. There is no self apart from its realization; it becomes determinate only as something realized.

As I have already suggested, though, it seems that we sometimes have reason to speak of losing or being untrue to ourselves or of being outside ourselves or not completely "with ourselves" in what we do. If we do not want to claim that these ways of speaking are completely empty, we must attempt to understand the problems they express. Put differently, what consequences would follow from giving up the vocabulary that such ways of speaking depend on? Are not the junior editor and the bank employee in some sense right in claiming that they are not fully identical with what they do, or how they present themselves at a particular moment, or with what is expected of them? Are not there in fact other talents lying dormant in the bank employee? Has not the editor in fact given up too many aspects of his personality? Utterances of this type, at the very least, reveal a current dissatisfaction with oneself, a hunch that something is not right with one's own life. The question: "Am I really *myself* in what I am doing here?" may be wrongly put, but it points to a problem that cannot be gotten rid of so easily. Such thoughts give expression to ways individuals interpret themselves that cannot simply be criticized away by conceptual arguments. They belong to the repertoire of self-understanding and self-interpretation of (at least) *modern* individuality and are therefore crucially bound up with reflection and self-examination.[5] In other words, they belong to the attempt to lead one's life as *one's own*.

If questions like these are bound up with a critical examination of our own lives, they have (one could claim) a critical, even emancipatory significance. The idea of a discrepancy between the authentic and inauthentic self, between the true and false self, functions as a kind of placeholder in individuals' practical relation to self. Understood in this manner, asking oneself who one really is and whether the life one leads is really one's own means that one does not identify with what one *factically* is, wills, and does or with what is demanded of one; it points to the fact that one can take up an attitude of critical *distance* to these things.

The reflections that follow take up the case, as it were, for these ways of thinking of oneself and one's life in the face of the critique of substantializing and essentializing conceptions of the self referred to earlier. In accordance with the strategy for reconstructing the theory of alienation set out in the introduction, I will undertake in-depth analyses of various cases of self-alienation with the intention of showing that it is possible to give the problems depicted in these self-descriptions a meaningful, nonparadoxical formulation. At the same time, the fruitfulness of the interpretive schema employed by alienation theory will be demonstrated by showing that it brings into view connections among phenomena, the analysis of which deepens our understanding of what it means "to live one's own life" in important ways. The various respects in which we experience our own life as an alien life, when traced back to various kinds of impediments to the *appropriation* of one's own life, reveal the internal relations between freedom, authenticity, and self-realization, as I noted in my earlier discussion of the theory of alienation. The change of perspective that my investigation must undertake in relation to the "essence" and "core" models of the self follows for the most part directly from the critique of those models I have sketched previously:

1. When the reifying conception of the self falsely hypostatizes potentials and unrealized possibilities into a "more authentic" reality, it searches for an essence and in doing so hypostatizes a "doing" into a "being." In contrast to this, I analyze the cases to follow by looking at the *actions* individuals find themselves performing and the ways they relate to themselves and to the world in what they do. Thus self-alienation will be conceived of—in accordance

with the conception of appropriation I have sketched earlier—not as a falling away from one's essence but as a disturbed relation to self, as a disturbed relation to our own actions, desires, projects, or beliefs.

2. Whereas the container model locates the true self somewhere *inside*— prior to and apart from its articulation—I start from the assumption that what constitutes us is developed and formed only in being *articulated*. Thus my analysis aims at distinguishing alienating from nonalienating—authentic from inauthentic—modes of *articulation* and finds in these distinctions the conditions for a successful appropriation of self and world.

3. As a consequence of these two points, a further theme (already indicated) becomes important: if self-alienation is also always alienation from the world—if it is to be understood as a relation to what I will and do (in the world)—then the self cannot be investigated apart from but only *in* its relations to the world.

On the assumption, then, that the concept of self-alienation is not necessarily bound up with an essentialist concept of the self, my investigation follows up on the suggestion that our relations to our own desires and activities are vulnerable to being disturbed. Self-alienation, so the thesis I will defend here, is a condition in which one is unable in crucial respects to *appropriate* the life one is leading and in which one does not *have oneself at one's command* in what one does, where the latter condition is understood such that it does not presuppose that complete transparency and command constitute the normal or ideal state of individuals.

A theory of self-alienation, then, investigates the structure of a relation that has the peculiar feature that it can also go wrong in various ways. The thought, derived from Lacan, that we are always already "strangers to ourselves" (as the title of one of Julia Kristeva's works puts it) is valid as an objection only against an unrealistic and all too harmonious conception of a subject's perfect self-transparency and its having itself completely at its command. Yet—contrary to its own rhetoric—this way of thinking cannot do without a certain idea of what it means to be oneself or to have oneself at one's command. The question, however, of how one can adequately relate to oneself becomes all the more urgent the less one is able to rely on a conception of the self in which one is always already "with oneself" and in which one possesses an original familiarity with oneself.

We again confront the question concerning the normative criterion of alienation critique. If, as indicated before, alienation is both a descriptive and a normative concept, where do we find the normative criterion that allows us to diagnose certain self-relations as alienating? As we will see, such standards are implicit in each of the various phenomena of alienation to be analyzed here. Being accessible rather than alien to oneself or being able to understand oneself as the author of one's own actions presupposes certain features of *personhood*. Peter Baumann's summary of the characteristic properties of persons captures the traits most important for this project: "Persons are beings that are not passively related to their environment but that are in a position to establish a relation to their environment actively. At the same time they have a relation to themselves. Both—relation to world and relation to self—are intimately bound up together: the particular characteristic of the person's relation to her environment lies in the fact that in that relation she at the same time relates to herself."[6] The self-conceptions of persons, according to this description, are characterized by three dimensions relevant to our undertaking here: persons develop opinions about themselves, they take up evaluative positions in relation to themselves, and they are capable of having the desire to change themselves. That is why they ask questions such as "What kind of human being am I?" and "What kind of human being do I want to be?"[7] It is against the backdrop of this understanding of the nature of persons that phenomena of self-alienation come into view and can be grasped as problematic. Being alienated from oneself refers to a disturbance of precisely this relation to self and world. It means not having oneself—one's own desires and actions—at one's command or not being at one with oneself in them. The diagnosis of self-alienation, then, relies on an internal reconstruction of the self-conception we develop and strive to realize when we understand ourselves as persons who *act*. For this reason it is, as already noted, less an essence-based critique than a version of immanent critique.

If, as I have claimed, alienation is a relation of relationlessness rather than the mere absence of a relation, then giving an account of this relation will be especially complicated: as clear as it is, on the one hand, that we are somehow antecedently connected to ourselves, it is, for precisely this reason, just as unclear how it is possible for this connection to break down. (That is the source of the air of paradox that surrounds this topic on all sides.) The thesis, then, is that a *relation* to *oneself* is a relation that can be disturbed in various ways. And in this relation, too, we find the feature mentioned previously: when alienated, we are alienated from something that is *simultaneously our own and alien*, we are involved in relations in which we alienate ourselves, we are in a certain sense *at once perpetrator and victim*.

STRUCTURE OF PART 2

As previously announced, I will proceed in what follows to analyze phenomena in which various dimensions of self-alienation are to be unpacked and analyzed. Various aspects of the relation between what is one's own and alien that is intrinsic to phenomena of alienation will be at the center of my discussion.

In chapter 5 the phenomenon of one's own actions taking on an independent existence and the resultant feeling of powerlessness will be in the foreground: when our life falls into a dynamic of its own we are just as alienated from ourselves as when our own actions ossify into structures over which we no longer have command. In these cases we can no longer understand ourselves as authors of our own actions. Chapter 6 deals with behavior in social roles as a form of inauthenticity and hence with the question of under what conditions being immersed in certain social relations manifests itself as self-alienation. Chapter 7 discusses cases of internal division, in which one's own impulses, desires, and actions appear alien to oneself and where one therefore appears to oneself as dominated by an alien power. Finally, chapter 8 addresses indifference as a case of alienation. Someone who is indifferent with respect to her (own) projects and plans, who cannot identify with anything, so the thesis goes, is not only alienated from the world but also from herself, since one "wins" oneself only through a meaningful relation to the world (and to one's projects and plans within it).

5

SEINESGLEICHEN GESCHIEHT OR "THE LIKE OF IT NOW HAPPENS": THE FEELING OF POWERLESSNESS AND THE INDEPENDENT EXISTENCE OF ONE'S OWN ACTIONS

They had managed it. There was a completely furnished apartment and they lived completely furnished together in it. On the one wall hung a large, colorful picture in a thin, white wooden frame; a modern lamp hung down from the ceiling into the room. One was now powerless against it all.

—ROLF DIETER BRINKMANN, *KEINER WEIß MEHR*

IN THIS CHAPTER I EXAMINE one aspect of self-alienation: the feeling of powerlessness or of loss of control over one's own life.[1] It involves the (not uncommon) impression that one's life confronts one as an independent event over which one has no influence without, however, being able to describe oneself as determined by alien causes, or heteronomous, in any straightforward sense. What explains how it can be that someone experiences her own life as determined by an alien power if, at first glance anyway, she herself is the agent? How are we to understand the relation here between what is *one's own* and what is *alien*? And what would it mean in the present context to be the master of one's own actions? My claim is that we can become alien to ourselves, or our lives alien to us, when processes that take on a dynamic of their own or conditions of rigidification hinder us in understanding ourselves as agents in what we do (as the "subjects" of our actions and our lives). This structure differs from straightforward coercion or manipulation. In examining it I will first (1) sketch a situation that illustrates the phenomenon in question. Then I will (2) elaborate my account of the specific problem of this form of self-alienation by distinguishing it from other possible interpretations. In the next step (3) I will interpret the phenomenon as a specific form of not being present in one's own actions, a condition characterized by what might be called the masking of practical questions. The discussion of objections (4) that can be brought against this interpretation will lead us finally (5) to a conception of self-alienation as a form of loss of control that does not, however, depend on an unrealistic ideal of self-mastery.

(1) A SUBURBAN EXISTENCE

A young academic takes up his first position. At the same time he and his girl-friend decide to marry. That makes sense "because of the taxes." A short time later his wife becomes pregnant. Since large apartments in the city are expensive and hard to find, they decide to move to a suburb. After all, life outside the city will be "better for the child." The man, a gifted mathematician, who until then has led a slightly chaotic life, oscillating between too much night life and an obsessive immersion in work, is now confronted with a completely new situation. All of a sudden, and without him having really noticed it, his life is now, as it were, "on track." One thing seems to follow ineluctably from another. And in a creeping, almost unnoticeable process his life acquires all the attributes of a completely normal suburban existence. Would he, who earlier ate fast food most of the time and relied on convenience stores for picking up milk and toilet paper as the need arose, ever have thought that he would one day drive every Saturday morning to the shopping mall to buy supplies for the week and fill the freezer? Could he ever have imagined that he would hurry home from work on Friday because the lawn needed to be mowed before the barbecue? At first he and his wife hardly notice that their conversations are increasingly limited to their child and the organization of household chores. Sometimes, however, he is overcome by a feeling of unreality. Something is wrong here. While many envy him for the beautiful suburban house he lives in, he is not really at home in this situation. The life he leads, which, as it seems to him, has so suddenly tightened around him—one could almost say "rearranged" him—seems, in a strange way, not to be his own life. Everything is as if it could not be any other way; everything happens with a certain inevitability. And in spite of this—or perhaps precisely because of it—it remains in a crucial respect alien to him. To what extent is this life "not really" his own? To what extent is he, in this life that he leads, *alienated from himself*?

(2) DEMARCATING THE PHENOMENON AND DEFINING ITS CHARACTERISTICS

I will now attempt to demarcate the phenomenon in question more precisely.

First, it cannot be the *change as such*—the circumstance that our young academic now lives a different life from the one he was used to—that can be described as alienating in this case. The circumstances of (almost) all humans go through decisive changes throughout the course of their lives. Yet, even in cases where these changes are painful and complicated, they are not usually experienced as alienation. Life can be painful, complicated, or unfamiliar for a time without there being any reason to regard it as a life that is not "one's own." For this reason it is also not merely a matter of what one is accustomed to. If it could be said of the young academic, "He must simply get accustomed to the new conditions of his life," then the problem would be a different one: not alienation but mere unfamiliarity. In our case, in contrast, the fact that his new situation becomes increasingly familiar to him has no effect on his feeling of foreignness—in fact, it is only strengthened by that familiarity. In this sense one can be completely *familiar* with a situation—one knows it well enough—and in spite of this feel *alien* in it.

Second, the phenomenon to be explained here is also not a simple problem of *external coercion* or heteronomy. No one has coerced or manipulated the young mathematician. He wanted his position, the wife, and his child. Nor is it the case that he regretted his decisions shortly after making them or wanted to reverse them and was prevented from doing so by external forces. He has therefore not simply made a wrong decision such that one could say that he is under the compulsion of his own decision, which, since he can no longer identify with it, now rules him as an alien power. Moreover, the feeling that his life is alien also does not mean that he rejects it outright and directly. He is not unhappy in his marriage; he is a proud father; and his position has brought him rewards beyond merely the advancement of his career.[2] It seems as if he and his wife have stumbled into a way of life that neither of them really wanted but that they nevertheless have entered into, developed, and created. If he has fallen into a trap, it is not one that someone set for him. In spite of this he is not, in a certain sense, the "master" of his own life; he feels himself to be the object, not the subject, of the course it has taken.

The situation appears as alienating to the extent that it seems to him as if an alien power were at work in his life and, in a certain sense, working through him. Yet the problem here is manifestly not one of manipulation or even of a feeling of being manipulated. When I am manipulated (however subtly), someone other than myself is (however anonymously) controlling me. It is not merely that no alien power can be identified here; it appears, instead, as if there were no power at work at all. Put differently, while the life he leads is not his own, it is also not someone else's. It seems to belong to no one. It is a situation, therefore, in which, to quote Robert Musil, "the like of it now happens."

Our protagonist, in contrast to someone who is manipulated, acts *himself*, but he acts without really acting. It is, in a certain sense, "defective" action. One could say that he is entirely or in part not really *present* in what he does. And it is this nonpresence in his own actions that makes his life in a crucial respect not his own, something that *has taken on an independent existence* and stands opposed to him. This requires further explanation.

(3) INTERPRETATIONS: A DYNAMIC OF ITS OWN AND RIGIDIFICATION

The following remarks shed light on two different aspects of the situation depicted here and two ways in which something can take on an independent existence. The life that one leads can (a) take on a dynamic of its own or (b) "rigidify" (be lived within a set of rigid relationships). In both cases, I will argue, one can speak of not really being present in one's life. My interpretation will trace both cases back to the fact that the aspects of actions and decisions that make one's life one's own have become unrecognizable.

A DYNAMIC OF ITS OWN

First, one can describe the development depicted here as a process that has *a dynamic of its own* and that has taken on an independent existence in which, as a result, its participants seem to be helplessly at its mercy. Things as they have developed in the life of the young couple have taken on a life of their own. The seeming ineluctability of events is part of this: both their marrying with an eye to taxes and their retreat to the suburbs seem to follow almost necessarily from the new situation created by the birth of their child. Once the lawn is there, the grass has to be mowed, and after acquaintances have been made at the playground come the first invitations that have to be reciprocated. What is of interest here is not the conventionality of this way of life but merely the fact that events appear to follow of themselves and to be already decided without anyone having made a decision about them. One stumbles, as it were, involuntarily into the life one leads. But what exactly does the metaphor of a "dynamic of its own" or of "things taking on a life of their own" mean? And to what extent can one speak of such a dynamic as a process of alienation?

Developments that have a dynamic of their own appear—like natural or biological processes—to follow of themselves. They take a course that is determined by an inner necessity without requiring help from without. This inner necessity can consist of different types of causal chains on which we have no influence. This is what distinguishes them from processes that qualify as *actions*. Developments that have a dynamic of their own are processes in which nothing is genuinely done or decided, if acting or doing is understood as an intervention that *steers* events—as an initiating of events or as the interruption of a causal chain.[3] This is how Ernst Tugendhat distinguishes happening from doing in relation to an agent's action and volition: "We speak properly of doing in all those cases in which we demarcate intentional and deliberate events from mere occurrences. It thereby follows that where something is done or enacted we are dealing with a process whose continuation into the next respective phase depends on whether the agent wants it."[4]

This opposition, between process and action, "blind" and "steered," unintentional and willfully intended happenings, helps to locate the problem in the case just given. While doing and acting are bound up with an agent's intention or will, something's having a dynamic of its own refers to a happening without an agent, one that takes place behind his back or that works through him. If developments in one's own life proceed according to the model of a dynamic of its own, this contradicts—keeping in mind the standards we have articulated in the account of persons as agents—the assumptions implicit in our talk of someone *leading* her life. When we speak in this way, we assume an active relation to—a "steering" of—what one does, even if some of the conditions under which one does it are not fully within one's command. In contrast, the part of my life that can legitimately be described as a mere happening (for example, biological processes of maturation or vegetative functions of the body) is precisely not what makes it *my life*, a life that is "in each case one's own"[5]—that is, it is not the part of life that allows me to identify it as my life in any robust sense. Being subjected to processes that have a dynamic of their own means a loss of responsibility and control that stands directly opposed to the idea that one can *lead* (steer and direct) one's own life. A person will regard her life as alien in this sense when her own development stands over and against her as a process she cannot affect. Crucial for our example, and for regarding it as a case of self-alienation, is the discrepancy alluded to earlier between the presumption that one has the power to act, on the one hand, and its actual absence, on the other. To be sure, it is also possible to lament one's powerlessness in the case of events that are not in fact subject to human discretion and control—one can, for example, experience bodily changes over which one has no control as alien to the point that one "no longer feels at home" in one's own body.[6] What is crucial for understanding processes such as these as alienating in a normative sense, however, is the discrepancy between one's own (perhaps only apparent) powerlessness and the nature of what one at least takes to be (or to be able to be) an *action*.[7] What is crucial, then, for the diagnosis of alienation I am developing here is that a person experiences a process that she can in principle influence (or should be able to influence) as beyond her influence—or that something that can in fact be decided on appears to her as if it could not be. If we were to take what seems here to be an automatic process beyond one's control and unpack it into its individual components, we would discover that every individual component could have been the object of a possible decision: just as much speaks in favor of moving to the suburbs with a small child as against it; a tax break is not a sufficient argument for marriage; and one can always let one's lawn run wild, rely on pizza delivery for food, ignore the neighbors, and satisfy one's need for communication via the Internet. (As we will see in what follows, the problem here is not only that the agent does not actively decide but also that the situation in which he finds himself appears to him as one in which his behavior is necessary and deciding is impossible.)

One can summarize our academic's situation as follows: that he experiences his own life as alien and does not feel "with himself" in his life is due to the fact that he is not really present in his life, where taking part in one's own life is understood as participating in it as an agent. His lack of presence can be traced back to a lack of awareness of the possibilities of action that are open to him. Each individual aspect of his life—the consequences it has, for example, for the next decision—has not really been decided on. Thus, his situation is in fact "out of control" in a certain sense, and—this is crucial—it is a situation for which no one can genuinely be held responsible.[8] This does not merely mean that he has not acted, or has not availed himself of his possibilities for acting, but that he has not even understood his situation as one in which action is called for or possible; it does not merely mean that he has not decided something for himself, or has not led his life *himself,* but that he has been incapable of understanding or regarding it as something he can or must *lead*. This is how we are to understand the sense in which someone like our academic is not the author of his life, is not the subject of what he does, even when there is no one else who acts in his stead. Thus the apparent paradox that one at once acts and does not act, that the life one leads is at once one's own and an alien life, can be resolved as follows: to be sure, one does something here oneself, but it is not, we could say, action in a full sense; it is one's own life, but one has not, in crucial respects, *made it one's own*.

Thus the dynamic described here fits into the domain of phenomena that includes reification or naturalization: something made turns into something given and outside one's command; the agent's own actions (or their results) confront her as an alien power. This theme, applied to our example, can be translated as follows: what is at issue when one lives a life that is reified in this sense is a masking of the fact that the life one leads is not given and that it cannot be understood (from an objectifying standpoint) as something that takes place without us. In contrast, as I noted in relation to Heidegger, it is something that takes place within a context of possibilities for action to which we must relate. To use a phrase coined by Ernst Tugendhat: *Leading* one's life means confronting the "practical question."[9] Practical questions are questions about what is to be done, what one ought to do, how one should act. Such questions, according to Tugendhat, can be posed at more or less fundamental levels. They can be merely instrumental questions about how to act appropriately in relation to a given goal and therefore questions about which means one should employ; however, they can also be about the final ends of one's actions themselves ("How should I live?" "What kind of human being do I want to be?"). But posing practical questions always presupposes a domain of possibilities within which action can be taken. Practical questions concern contexts within which I can act in this way or that—situations in which I am required to take a position. Taking up Tugendhat's account, I propose to call the structure of the reified or reifying dynamic described earlier—in which the individual steps of some development are not made the object of practical questions—a *masking of practical questions*. The thesis that such questions can be masked implies that it cannot be taken for granted that we generally perceive situations as the object of practical questions or that they "come into view for us" as such.[10] (At the same time, the concept of masking is supposed to indicate that what is at issue is not merely a subjective *misapprehension* but something that can be true of a situation as well as of the agent who finds herself in it.) If the existence of a domain of practical questions, along with the capacity to pose and answer them, is a constitutive condition of a self-determined life, then a structure that leads to such a masking—a life that, as described, takes on a dynamic of its own (or is experienced as such)—undermines the conditions of self-determination and the capacity for action.

HETERONOMY AND ALIENATION

We are now in a position to begin to answer the question of what distinguishes the kinds of alienation just described from simple cases of coercion or of being determined by alien forces (heteronomy), as well as from the more complex case of manipulation. The despair that grips our academic when he looks at his life a few years later is not the despair of someone who is manipulated or deceived, of someone who discovers that for the entire time he has been led to do things he did not really want to do. His despair results, to be sure, from realizing that in a certain respect he has not really been involved in conducting his life. But it is not simply that *he himself* did not decide the things that determined him—that he made decisions that were influenced or even coerced by others; what is important about his decision, rather, is that in fact *nothing at all* was decided. As distinct from even extremely subtle forms of heteronomy,[11] he does nothing contrary to his will, but instead fails to develop a will at all: there is, in a certain sense, no will at all in play. He is not forced, however subtly, to decide in one way or another or to do this or that. Nor is his will manipulated; no alien will is foisted on him. He merely does not see, or is prevented from seeing, that what he does could be the object of a decision. Of course, one can describe this as an anonymous and quasi-structural form of heteronomy. Someone who is driven by events instead of guiding them herself is not autonomous; she does not live according to her own law. Joseph Raz, in defining personal autonomy (understood in a thick sense, as being the author of one's life), helpfully captures the distinction between autonomy and being driven in what one does: personal autonomy "contrasts with a life of no choices, or with *drifting through life* without ever exercising one's capacity to choose."[12] It is important to note that, with respect to its content, this account of autonomy cannot be understood as the symmetrical opposite of most conceptions of heteronomy. When heteronomy is conceived of as the opposite of autonomy in this thick sense, its essential characteristic, namely, that a foreign law and a foreign will take the place of one's own, no longer strictly applies.[13] When "the like of it now happens," nothing at all is "posited as a law." Things happen in such a way that what is one's own has not yet been differentiated from what is alien. Or, put differently, the question of how something can become my own or is not my own is precisely the problem in the phenomena examined here, a problem that the label of heteronomy masks rather than resolves. It seems to me an advantage of a theory of alienation that it brings into view the preconditions of self-determination in a more differentiated way than the simple opposition between autonomy and heteronomy does. (I revisit the relation between self-determination and alienation in chapter 10.)

RIGIDIFICATION

An iron cage. A further feature marks the life of our academic who has ended up in the suburbs: a peculiar rigidification. Not only does everything simply take its course; the relations that come about in this way seem to determine how he lives, rather than vice versa. That is a mark of the rigidity or lifelessness of the way of life he finds himself in: "One was now powerless against it all." While it seemed as if there were no action whatsoever (drifting instead of acting), it becomes clear from this perspective that the results of actions can take on an independent existence over and against the agent who has done them. This solidifying and becoming independent of the results of our actions can also occur in relations that, at the beginning, we consciously decided to enter into. (In this respect the phenomenon of rigidification is different from things having a dynamic of their own. In our example both could be present, but these two aspects of the case should be considered independently.)

Rigidification, too, ultimately leads to what I have called the masking of practical questions. Even if someone has at some point posed such practical questions, she can at a later point stop posing them. Thus the process of rigidification described here also has the consequence that the things that determine a life no longer appear as things that can (still) be objects of decision. Ossified relations are those that are immune, or make themselves immune, to further questioning. The life one leads then consists of fixed, invariable components that one no longer has access to. Everything appears unalterable, "congealed."[14] When one's life takes on a life of its own in this way, the result is a life devoid of life.

Why, in such circumstances, is someone alienated from herself? This can be explained by referring to the masking of practical questions: rigidified relations give answers to such questions in advance of their being posed.[15] Here, too, one is no longer asked to make decisions, to act, or to pose practical questions. Everything appears as though it could not be different. Here, too, one is passive and no longer an active participant in the relations in which one lives; one is, instead, determined by them. And if everything appears as though it could not be different, then an acting subject is superfluous. The new and interesting point here is this: practical questions must be posed not just once but over and over, even with respect to familiar, longstanding practices.

Events that run their course automatically and situations that become rigid-ified are two examples of how a process can take on an independent existence over and against the agent involved in it, and each can be understood as an aspect of *reification*. In both cases a process that really ought to be a result of actions—or that by its nature *is* an action process—appears (or must appear) to the participants as taking place independently of human agency. In both cases breaking down this structure of reification means uncovering the possibilities for action: what is, could, as a result of actions, also have been different. It is not only a question of realizing that the relations in which one lives are in principle malleable but also of coming to see that decisions already made are fluid and open to revision. The existence of a field of possibilities for action means not merely that something could also be different from how it is; a field of possibilities for action exists precisely when something can (in principle) *always again become* different from how it is. That is, as we will see, not only a problem of individual agents but also one of how the relations are constituted in which individuals act (or do not).

(4) OBJECTIONS

Is it, then, that every process that takes on an independent existence or a dynamic of its own, or every state of rigidification that one's own life can fall into, is to be described as alienation? Are there not also such processes that are not experienced as alienating and that should not, even from an external standpoint, be described as such? This question leads to two kinds of prob-lems. The first concerns very generally the *normative status* of the analyses I have given here and the standard of evaluation that underlies them, according to which control or command over one's own life—or, more generally, having an actively structuring relation to it—is to be preferred over other options. Is it so obvious that control and command over one's life are what we should value? Why should we actively *lead* our life? When we do not, do we then have a false, unhappy, or bad life? What, for example, speaks against a fatalis-tic attitude of letting oneself drift in which one just goes along with the course of events and identifies with the direction that one's life, for whatever reasons, happens to take? Naturally, this is a question of degrees. And it could be claimed that various degrees of activism and fatalism ("being able to let things be") characterize something like different life*styles* within a form of life.[16] So understood, even letting oneself drift would still be a way of *leading* one's life. In determining how far one can go in this direction it will help to recall some aspects of what we have seen in reconstructing the self-conceptions we have as persons: the active, controlling model for leading one's life is intimately bound up with the fundamental possibility of understanding oneself as a person or agent, as the *subject* of one's life, which only then becomes *one's own* life in a genuine sense. And only insofar as we understand ourselves as agents can we be held responsible for what we do. Moreover, this status accounts for a significant part of what it means to be able to understand oneself as an independent person and to be respected by others as such. For this reason what we have here are not arbitrary options but attitudes with regard to which it is questionable whether *we* at any rate are capable of abandoning them (in a radical way) without becoming entangled in contradictions. (I return to these questions in part 3.)

The second group of objections is of a different kind. They concern the *internal* plausibility of the underlying conceptions of personhood. Even if we cannot in principle do without those conceptions, does not my analysis rely on overly strong assumptions about our capacity to act? There are two objections here: first, do we not need to take more seriously the *complexity* of decisions and their consequences? and, second, do we not need to take into account the fact that a certain fixity of relations is always necessary in order to frame the setting within which we live and that therefore we cannot make transparent *all* the conditions under which we live and regard them always as fluid and at our command?[17]

THE UNFORESEEABLE NATURE OF THE CONSEQUENCES OF ACTIONS

The concept of complexity points to the following problem: individual decisions not only produce consequences and effects that one failed to foresee but also consequences and effects that one could not have foreseen. (One could say that this is an inescapable consequence of the fact that the life one lives is not a life one has already lived.)

Not having the consequences of actions at one's command is a characteristic feature of acting itself: actions have consequences, and these in turn have their own consequences.[18] The unpredictable effects our own actions have on others, together with the repercussions their reactions in turn have on us, produces a complexity that makes it more difficult to form and pursue only predictable intentions and, so, only intentions that are (in this sense) one's own.

This problem, however, can be discussed in relation to the conception of action itself. Even if we accept the view, as I did earlier, that acting involves pursuing intentions, this does not imply that the result of an action could "mirror" this intention in an undistorted manner or that intention and result must coincide. On the contrary, the result of an action typically contains a certain "surplus" beyond what the agent takes his intention to be.[19] Helmuth Plessner even regards this phenomenon positively, referring to it as "the emancipatory power of our deeds." In a passage criticizing Marx's theory of alienation, he notes: "It is characteristic of human action to bring forth products that slip from its control and turn against it. This emancipatory power of our deeds (. . .) should not be understood as frustrating the realization of our intentions. On the contrary, it makes the realization of our intentions possible and develops its effect, unforeseen by intention, only on the basis of the realized product."[20] In all these respects (and for all these reasons) the life that one leads is not in all its facets the result of decisions, and it is never completely controllable or thoroughly self-chosen. A life, even a mostly not alienated "life of one's own," can never be attributed in its entirety to the person who leads it, as if it were nothing but the result of that person's own decisions. One never is, and never could be, the sole author of one's life history. This peculiar tension between making plans and pursuing intentions, on the one hand, and their effects (of which one can also always say "it was no one"),[21] on the other, is obviously *also* a characteristic feature of the way one leads one's life. What is important in the present context is that the presence of an independent dynamic, *to some degree*, and the fact that, *to a certain extent*, results of actions take on an independent existence are not usually experienced as alienating, and the same is true of the fact that one is affected by unforeseeable and uncontrollable events. Not everything that is not at our command makes our life alien to us in the sense under discussion here; to claim otherwise would be to rely on an overblown, overly robust conception of autonomy and of our power to act.

Moreover, in many cases we welcome being overpowered by events (for example, *falling* in love). Even when we are confronted with circumstances we could never have imagined—circumstances we could neither have foreseen or planned and with respect to which we are powerless—we do not necessarily feel alienated from ourselves. (Think of the state of "being outside oneself" when one is in love or when one takes uninhibited delight in something.) Such circumstances produce instead an uplifting feeling of "being in accord" with oneself. One is overpowered, but, in contrast to the condition described in the example, one is intensely present in what one does and in what happens to one.

It is possible, then, to be outside oneself without being alienated from oneself. How can this be? In these cases we identify with events, even when we have not initiated them or cannot control them. Clearly, we can be present in a situation without completely being in control of it (or of ourselves in it). There must be, then, a distinction between alienating and nonalienating situations where one has lost control or where the results of our actions take on an independent existence in relation to us. This distinction can be located, on the one hand, in one's later attitude to the events in question: one can reject or accept them; one can identify (or not) *after the fact* with events that had a dynamic of their own. On the other hand, we can also locate the distinction in different ways of participating in events that have taken on an independent existence. The idea of a self's being "present" (or "present to itself") at least hints at the relevant point here: there can be degrees of identification with events for which the self is not entirely responsible that depend not on the amount of control one has over them but on the greater or lesser extent to which one is present in them.[22] (One is then "taken in" by the situation, absorbed in it; one forgets oneself in it, in contrast to the distance that characterizes the young man of our example.)

According to this analysis, then, not every case in which the results of actions have taken on an independent existence and not every uncontrollable dynamic of life events is alienating per se. We have seen that the question of whether a life takes on an independent existence in an alienating manner is not decided by whether it is in every respect self-structured, controlled, or predictable but rather on whether the part of it that is *outside one's command* can be *appropriated* in a certain way. The theme of appropriation here (as set out in chapter 1) is supposed to bring out the point that having something at one's command, "putting oneself in relation to something," or being able to identify with something does not depend on understanding that something as—in Marx's sense—the product of one's own activity. Rather, it is a question of whether or not one can *appropriate* the events that determine our lives, especially when they are not steered or controlled by us, where they are not "placed into the world" by us. The process of externalization and reappropriation at issue here is perhaps best thought of as a process of "balancing out": every decision, every action sets processes in motion or produces results that may at first be alien and can be made our own only by (re)appropriating them. What is one's own, then, is not necessarily something one has produced or directed oneself; the result of an act of appropriation does not consist only of something that was *previously* one's own. Having an appropriating relation to the (uncontrollable) events of one's own life means that one must be able to bring oneself into an affirmative relation to what is alien or uncontrollable. Alienation is not the foreignness (or the becoming foreign) per se of the results of actions but rather an interruption or disturbance of the *process* in which actions produce (uncontrollable) results to which one then establishes a relation of reappropriation.

The concept of appropriation is well-suited for illustrating the practical character of this process. Appropriation is not a matter of making a choice from a disengaged or objective standpoint, nor is it a matter of merely rejecting or agreeing to the result of an action. What I have called balancing out does not depend on weighing things from an external perspective; it is a process in which one is *involved*. The process of appropriation is not made up only of cognitive elements, and it is not subject only to the will. Not everything one might like to be can actually be made one's own. Appropriation is a process of learning and experience in which the relation between freedom and uncontrollability is negotiated. Conversely, alienation is a halting of this process.

CONSTITUTIVE RIGIDIFICATION

What about the aspect of our actions taking on an independent existence that I have discussed under the name of *rigidification?* Is every form of rigidification alienating per se? It is not only the idea of controllability but also the accompanying ideas of transparency and fluidity that can seem to be illusory. It is, of course, never possible to make explicit all the implicit decisions on which a life depends, but it is also the case that not everything we tacitly take as self-evident can or should be made explicit. There is something eerie about the expectation that we do so and the result would presumably be a life that was in its own way "devoid of life." It is also unrealistic to think that one can make everything fluid in order to avoid the rigidification of one's life; it is therefore also unrealistic to believe that one can renew or renegotiate every detail of one's life. Routines, institutions, and rituals are not *in themselves* rigidified and lifeless; apart from their well-known ability to relieve us of the burdens of choice, they make us "at home" in our lives in a certain sense (as Arnold Gehlen's theory of social institutions famously suggests). Hence we must distinguish forms of routine action and ways in which relations take on an independent existence that are constitutive for us, on the one hand, from problematic forms of rigidification that result in alienation, on the other. What is crucial here is neither complete transparency nor a constant transformation of the relations of life but rather a basic consciousness of the possibility of choice.

The talk of rigidified relationships as reifying helps us to see certain aspects of the aims of alienation critique, namely: to reveal our actions to us as something "made" (by us) and to reveal to us the implicitly decidable character of what we do. In a situation of doubt—which is to say, in a situation of conflict—this stance enables us to make explicit what is implicit and hence to examine and revise decisions that have taken on an independent existence. This does not mean that we can structure and construct our whole lives from scratch, as if at a drawing board. Practical questions pose themselves in the context of practical problems. They never pose themselves completely outside or independently of a context and they seldom pose themselves fundamentally in the sense that, once posed, one's whole life suddenly hangs in the balance; in cases where they become fundamental in a meaningful sense, they become radical only gradually, out of the problem itself.[23] Thus, a nonreifying, unalienated stance, in opposition to a rigidified one, would consist, above all, in an openness to problems—an openness to revision and experimentation.

(5) RECAPITULATION

With respect to the aspect of self-alienation examined in this chapter—the problem of the loss of power and control—the following points have emerged: processes in which conditions of life take on an independent existence are not alienating per se, and it is not only when I have complete control over each of my actions that I can experience my life as my own. In contrast to this, I have described alienation as an interruption of the process of appropriating one's own actions. Relationships are reified and alienating when they cannot be understood as providing a field for possible action and experimentation. And, with respect to rigidification, it can be said that alienation does not consist in the solidifying of relationships per se—what is alienating is the halting of experimentation. (Experiment, however, is not to be understood as a haphazard, aesthetic life experiment but rather in a pragmatist sense that emphasizes the necessarily experimental character of every problem-solving activity. Thus alienation or reification—the processes described here as rigidification or as things taking on an independent existence—are impediments to experimentation that come to be perceived as problematic especially when they prevent problems from being perceived and solved.)[24]

Finally, some further comments are necessary regarding the subjective and objective conditions of alienated or unalienated life situations. Let us return to the narrative of our example: is it that our academic has simply not paid attention, has out of carelessness failed to perceive practical questions as such? Or was his situation constituted so that it could not even come into view as one in which action was possible? Put differently, was it he who concealed the practical questions (as practical questions), or were these questions structurally concealed and therefore not even recognizable as such? The concept of alienation—and this is an advantage of this approach—allows us to address both sides of this problem. On the subjective side it is a question of the subject's accessibility to itself; on the objective side the question concerns the accessibility of situations.

On the one hand, an awareness of fields of possible action presupposes a certain accessibility of the self.[25] For example, one must be perceptive, to some extent, in order to be able to identify cases of conflict and phenomena of rigidification,[26] as well as to notice when something is not quite right; moreover, one must be internally flexible, to a certain extent, in how one reacts to such observations. There must be options available; possibilities for action must be present. That means being accessible to oneself in what one experiences and does. And this suggests the diagnosis that our mathematician was not accessible to himself in the situation sketched earlier.

Alongside these subjective conditions, there are also objective conditions, those that have to do with how the circumstances of life themselves are constituted. We said of our protagonist that he was not able to see his life as a series of actions; this should lead us to ask what conditions made this impossible or, conversely, under which conditions it would be possible to grasp the situation as one that calls for the raising of practical questions. This question concerns not the (internal or external) impediments to an individual's freedom to decide but rather the phenomenon underlying it: whether, independently of individuals' subjective attitudes, a situation can in principle even be grasped as a field of possible action, whether it is at all accessible as such. The crucial point here concerns the opening up (or, conversely, the constitutive limitations) of the horizon of possibility that is given within a particular life situation or in a particular form of life.

My thesis is that there is a multitude of causes for the failure of situations encountered in life to appear as belonging to the sphere of possible actions or decisions. I cannot treat these causes exhaustively here, but I will briefly indicate some relevant aspects of them. Conventions, for example, can be understood as a subtle way of structuring forms of life, the essential feature of which is that they do not coerce individuals to do anything or prescribe a particular way of life for them. Of course, they do this too, but the main respect in which they limit us is that they succeed in presenting certain alternatives as unavoidable. That is, they narrow the horizon of possibility—the domain within which decisions can be made—and it is here that their effects unfold (sometimes almost unnoticed). The power of convention means not only that "everyone" has to act in some way or another; it also affects the possibility of whether certain desires and ideas, and thereby certain ways of life, are even thinkable. We understand ourselves on the basis of models given by convention; we interpret our own scope of action against their background—and we depend for this reason on those interpretations in order to understand ourselves and our lives. The idea that it is "better for the children" to live in the suburbs, or that one "will finally be a grown-up" once one leads a well-ordered married life, belongs to this type of (normalizing) influence. (Yet, and we will return to this later, the reason they are potentially alienating is not because they imply a way of life shared with others.)

Thus conventions limit the spectrum of the imaginable; they shape and limit possibilities of experience.[27] Even when a life's taking on a dynamic of its own, as already discussed, is not *caused* by the conventionality of a certain way of life, it could nevertheless be claimed that conventional ways of life *encourage* the masking of practical questions, if only because in a conventional way of life so much is taken to be self-evident (with help from the social environment) and because the pressure to engage in reflection appears to be greater in unconventional forms of life. As long as unconventional forms of life have not themselves become conventional (as may happen in a subculture), it is not so easy to regard them as self-evident or "natural."

6

"A PALE, INCOMPLETE, STRANGE, ARTIFICIAL MAN": SOCIAL ROLES AND THE LOSS OF AUTHENTICITY

LaCroix: And Collot screamed as if possessed: one must rip off the masks.
Danton: And the faces will go along with them.

—GEORG BÜCHNER, DANTONS TOD

ROLE BEHAVIOR, A FIXED PATTERN of behavior imposed on individuals by social roles, is often taken to be the paradigmatic manifestation of self-alienation. Thus Helmuth Plessner remarks in 1960: "With the figure of the alienated human being contemporary literature gives expression to the idea of the solitary individual in social roles dictated to him by an administered world: the human being as the bearer of a function."[1] In everyday usage, as well as in sociology and social philosophy, *role* functions as a code word under which sociality in general is discussed as well as the relationship between the authenticity of individuals and the ways society shapes them.

In what follows I will discuss the extent to which certain forms of role behavior represent cases of self-alienation, even if, according to my thesis, the absence of alienation cannot be understood as a condition existing prior to or outside sociality—as a condition in which one is a "human being in general" behind all social roles. Proceeding from the view that it is in roles that we are, in certain respects, first *formed* into persons, I will interpret self-alienation as a symptom that emerges in the absence of (the possibility of) appropriating roles. What is *alienating*, I claim, is not roles per se but the impossibility of adequately articulating oneself *in them*.

I will again (1) begin with some examples in order (2) more precisely to demarcate the problem and contrast it with other phenomena. This will require (3) a short explanation of the concept of a role as it is used both in sociological theory and in everyday usage, which will enable us to understand why it is so frequently assumed that roles are inherently alienating. Proceeding from this, I will (4) lay out the opposing thesis that roles are constitutive for the development of individuality, which will prepare the way for (5) a discussion of the various aspects of role behavior. This discussion of the ambiguity of roles will (6) provide us with criteria that enable us to distinguish between alienating and nonalienating roles or between alienated and unalienated role behavior.

(1) THE ROLE PLAYER

Everyone is familiar with this type. There is the ambitious junior editor, who has his hair cut, buys himself a suit that fits just a little too well, and begins to imitate his boss's mannerisms. He takes part in important cultural events with wit and charm and he has an opinion on every contemporary issue. There is the financial adviser whose most prominent feature is the designer glasses he wears and who seeks to impress his customers with phrases like *flexibility* and *personal responsibility*. Or the rookie network newscaster with an air of optimism and vitality that fits perfectly with his network's image. He speaks, almost fluently, in clichés. In these cases we see the comic side of role behavior. For the junior editor the boss's mannerisms are simply "one size too large." The newscaster's professional cheerfulness is too unconnected from particulars for us to let ourselves be infected by it. In the financial adviser's expressions we hear nothing but the zeitgeist speaking. In their conformity and uniformity these dynamic young professionals resemble one another a bit too much, even when they act as though they were especially unconventional: the junior editor's deftness looks like a mask; the newscaster's informality feels artificial. In situations where role behavior is called for we all sometimes feel as if we were standing "beside ourselves," as if, in having "our strings pulled by unknown powers," we had lost ourselves.[2]

Naturally these are caricatures. But even here the question arises: to what extent are the persons sketched not themselves? Or put differently, from an internal perspective, why are we sometimes tempted to say that we are not really ourselves in a particular role or that we do not feel "at home" but are instead alienated from ourselves in situations where role behavior is called for?

The interpretative scheme bound up with the concept of self-alienation can easily suggest that we can distinguish between a real and a false—between an *authentic* and an *inauthentic*—self. Even if, as Dahrendorf expressed it in a 1958 monograph that introduced sociological role theory to Germany, the player of a role appears to us as a "pale, incomplete, strange, artificial man,"[3] the distinction between real and false, artificial and genuine, partial and whole, one's own and alien—in short, between what is oneself and what is not—still requires explication.

(2) DEMARCATING THE PHENOMENON AND DEFINING ITS CHARACTERISTICS

Once again, before turning to these questions, I will attempt to grasp the phenomenon more precisely by contrasting it with others. Two points are crucial in the cases I have just described: the alienated or alienating character of the behavior (as in the earlier example of the academic) is not due to coercion—to the forced character of the behavior in question—nor is it simply pretense or deception.

First, although the behavior described here is obviously related to a kind of heteronomy, when we have the sense that the people depicted in these cases are inauthentic, we do not think of them as externally coerced. What is disconcerting, rather, is precisely the extent to which they identify with what they are doing. The more their postures become second nature to them—the more they "become what they are" and believe what they say—the more alienated or inauthentic they become in our eyes. The network newscaster's cheerfulness is not the forced happiness of a hostage under pressure. To what extent, though, is someone forced when she identifies completely with a certain expectation or has made a demand entirely her own? Is a compulsion that has been internalized in this way still a compulsion? It is certainly not one in the usual sense.

Second, the kind of behavior at issue here is not pretense or deception. Someone who deceives is not inauthentic but fraudulent and mendacious. He withholds from us what he really thinks and feels. In the cases here, in contrast, what is one's own and what is alien are mixed together in a complicated way: the junior editor does not merely feign interest in the latest publications. He makes himself into a person who really has such an interest. And yet he differs from someone who is involved in something out of real interest, someone who is captivated and excited by *it*.

In both features we see that role behavior is a phenomenon that always also (or even primarily) concerns the relation someone has to herself in what she does. Thus the behaviors described here are not problematic merely with respect to the role players' relations to their surroundings. In a case of straightforward deception the deceiver remains in the end "intact"—she knows what she really wants and maneuvers to achieve a certain effect. In a case of coercion, one is compelled by an external power such that—to a certain extent—one's inner desires remain untouched. In phenomena of inauthenticity, in contrast, the subject is affected in its relation to itself. Someone who lies is not herself merely on the outside, whereas someone who is alienated is not herself also on the inside, and in a way that is not easy to understand. In a certain sense, then, the role player becomes just as alien to herself as to others, although again "alien" here does not mean unfamiliar—obviously she is aware of herself in her behavior—but rather a certain kind of impenetrability or inaccessibility to oneself.

In both coercion and deception the boundary between what is one's own and what is alien is preserved; in the cases that interest me, in contrast, there seems to be a complicated entanglement of the two where what is "one's own" itself becomes questionable or deficient. But, then, what kind of *appropriation* of behavior patterns is at issue in roles such that one can experience it as a *dispossession* of oneself? And if, in accordance with the literal sense of authenticity,[4] we perceive that behavior to be not *genuine*, what criteria of genuineness are we presupposing?

Before I go on to discuss the concept of a role in more detail, I must highlight two methodological problems that have already arisen in these first clarificatory steps. First, once again the negative evaluation of role behavior appears to rely on a normative standard. While discussing *drifting* and the idea of a process having a dynamic of its own in chapter 1, I appealed to values like self-determination and the capacity for action, which I claimed could be derived from our conception of ourselves as responsible persons. The present case, however, is more complicated. It is not yet clear what standard the suspicion of inauthenticity rests on or how it could be justified without falling back on the concepts of human nature or of the human essence that criteria such as genuineness and spontaneity appear to rely on. Solving this problem is one of my central aims in what follows.

Second (and related to this), there arises the problem of the interpretive sovereignty of individuals. Up to now I have left open the question concerning the perspective from which the cases here can be diagnosed as instances of self-alienation, and for this reason I have intentionally gone back and forth between external and internal perspectives, between third- and first-person perceptions of the problem. Clearly both cases exist: those in which others appear inauthentic to us and those in which we perceive ourselves to be so. This, however, does not relieve us of the problem of interpretive sovereignty. Can we describe someone as inauthentic or alienated who fails to notice this herself? Here, too, as already in the first question, the problem becomes especially urgent when we precisely do *not* want to understand alienation critique as grounded in a conception of the human essence. For the moment, however, I would like to postpone a consideration of this problem. As a first step, I ask what it could mean, in thinking about inauthenticity or self-alienation through roles in general, to speak of something like a "doubling" of the self into a superficial and a "deep," or into a true and a false, self. This is no less problematic as a *self*-interpretation than it is when spoken from an external perspective. Answering the question of interpretive sovereignty, then, will depend on how this model of interpretation can be understood.

(3) ROLES AND ALIENATION

What is a role, when this concept is taken from the theater and applied to the world of social relations? For sociological role theory all social interaction is role-playing in which socialized individuals encounter one another as bearers of roles,[5] which they perform within a framework of socially prescribed scripts or role expectations. "Social roles . . . are bundles of expectations directed at the incumbents of positions in a given society."[6] When viewed in this manner, a role marks the way in which the individual—as editor, financial adviser, and newscaster, but also as moviegoer, patient, subway rider, father, or owner of an attack dog—comes into contact with society. Every individual is typically the bearer of multiple overlapping roles, private as well as public. Like an actor in a play, one plays one's *part* in society and through this becomes part of it: "the idea that relates the individual meaningfully to society is the idea of the individual as a bearer of socially predetermined . . . modes of behavior."[7] Thus within sociological role theory the concept of a role is, in the first place, normatively neutral, providing a functional explanation for how society is possible.

If we think more carefully about the theater metaphor, we can distinguish various aspects of roles relevant to the suspicion that theories of alienation harbor regarding roles. We play roles *for others* and before them; roles are played according to a prewritten *script*; a role is, as a *part*, only a piece of the entire process; and roles are *artificial*—they are not identical with the person who plays them. Given a critical spin and applied to the social world, these features of roles give rise to an entire spectrum of critiques of social "appearance" and deception that we are already familiar with from Rousseau;[8] in addition, critiques of the division of labor and specialization can also take the form of a critique of role behavior.

THE CRITIQUE OF ROLES AND THE MODERN IDEAL OF AUTHENTICITY

The critique of the role-playing "homo sociologicus" as a "pale, incomplete, strange, artificial man"[9] gives expression to a general suspicion of roles as alienating that reflects the widespread intuition that there is a gap between a person's authentic self and her social roles. If "behind all roles, personas, and masks the actor [in a play] remains a real being . . . in no way affected by the parts he plays,"[10] this would also have to apply, according to Dahrendorf, to the "authentic self" behind its roles in social life.[11] Just as the actor is distinct from the role he plays, we, too, when taking on and embodying social roles (so it is claimed), remain *ourselves* behind these roles. On this view, the dynamic professionals in my initial examples would be inauthentic because their roles crowd out their true selves; they would be alienated from themselves to the extent that they experience themselves only through their roles. According to these intuitions, the *true self* is above all one thing: it is, original and untouched, something that exists *apart from its roles*. And for this reason it is something that is formed and limited—or alienated—by these roles.

These intuitions are not only widespread; they have also been immensely influential, having helped to shape the modern ideal of authenticity long before role theory in the narrower sense was developed. In this sense, for example, John Gagnon describes the development of the ideal of the modern "cosmic self" in terms of a self existing behind all roles: instead of "being composed of a limited and coherent bundle of socially given roles that would change slowly over the course of their lives and being judged primarily by the competence of their public performances, [they] began to experience the relationships which they had with others, what we would call 'the roles that they were required to play,' as increasingly detached from or alien to whom they truly were or what they really wanted to be."[12] The modern idea of authenticity, according to this description, develops as a critique of roles—or, more precisely, as a critique of roles as alienating.[13]

SWITCHING ROLES AND THE LIMITS OF THE ROLE METAPHOR

Now the implications of the role metaphor give rise to a problem.[14] In the theater the actor's role is something that can be cast off once the performance is over. After their tangled interactions, Hamlet and Laertes are both dead, but the actors playing them can go out together for a beer once their work is finished. In this case there is undeniably a distance between the role and the individual who stands on the other side of it.

In the case of social roles, however, the idea that they can be cast off so simply is misleading. To be sure, even in the social realm there are situations in which one must give a circumscribed and clearly defined "performance"— giving a brilliant lecture, making a good impression at a party—and then lean back, relieved, when it is over. Even the claim that, dressed in social roles, one *is not* what one *is* (in Sartre's unnecessarily paradoxical formulation) can be made sense of to some extent by thinking about the experience of switching roles.[15] The professor behaves differently in her seminar than she does at night with her friends in the bar. This becomes immediately clear when in the evening she runs into the student to whom she gave an oral exam that morning. The doctor, seen by her patients at a demonstration, feels she has been somehow caught. And the sales clerk, now almost devoid of solicitous cheerfulness, is not particularly enthused about running into her customer on the street after closing hours. Moving among different private and public roles, one not only fulfills different expectations but also associates these with different modes of behavior. And one is occasionally surprised oneself at how much—even down to the level of mannerisms—one changes. It is for this reason that we sometimes fail to recognize someone when we see her performing an unfamiliar role for the first time.

The fact that in the context of various roles we have different behavioral repertoires at our disposal does not, however, mean that somewhere behind these roles there is a true, substantial self that is unaffected by its roles, just as in the case of the actor there is a person behind the role. The question as to whether the professor is more herself in the seminar or in the bar, whether the doctor is more herself in the hospital or at the demonstration, is not easy to answer. And it is just as questionable whether the private realm, one's home, is the only place one can be oneself merely because there one can walk around with holes in one's stockings.[16]

In the case of social roles, as role theory conceives of them, the entire world is a stage on which *we all* are always *playing theater*, even outside narrowly circumscribed scenarios. The social world, even if conceived of via the meta-phors of stage, role, and performance, knows no *offstage*. The fact that roles still have their effects even where we take something to be our untouched innermost self leads Erving Goffman to conceive of the self as a "dramatic ef-fect."[17] And the fact "that the very structure of our self can be understood from the perspective of a performance" leads him to the now well-known image of the self as a hook or temporary hanger on which our various roles hang.[18]

But what would individuals be outside their roles? We could, of course, run into the junior editor, financial adviser, or newscaster on the street in a jogging outfit after work. And, presumably (one would hope!), they behave differently while shopping in the neighborhood or at home in front of the TV from how they behave at work. What, though, justifies our assumption that they are here (and not there) "themselves" and free from roles? The financial adviser who buys a loaf of bread once again acts within a role, this time that of the customer. And is he not also following a familiar pattern when he relaxes in front of the TV after work? It is not easy to grasp the place outside, the self apart from its social roles.[19] Where is the "true self" that exists behind the masks of roles to be found? What does it mean for individuals to develop "as a whole," and what does it mean to behave not artificially but immediately or spontaneously in social situations? It is precisely the idea of the authenticity and wholeness of persons prior to their being deformed through roles that is problematic.

Does it follow, though, from this thoroughgoing suspicion of roles that roles *do not* deform, that there is no standpoint from which we could judge the role behavior I have described as problematic? Does it follow that, since we always already exist in roles, we are necessarily identical with, or exhaus-tively constituted by, them?

QUESTIONING THE SELF-ROLE DICHOTOMY

Here the following dilemma arises: on the one hand, we do not know where to locate the self apart from its roles. On the other hand, if we are not to exclude the possibility of criticizing social roles—if we are to resist the idea that roles and the effects of socialization exhaustively constitute us—we must challenge the very dichotomy the role metaphor embroils us in.

According to the thesis I will now argue for, the dichotomy between self and roles is questionable and must be overcome. And for this reason the in-terpretive choice it imposes on us—between, on the one hand, a model of authenticity that appeals to a self behind all roles and, on the other hand, various theories that deny the distinction between self and roles and total- ize the latter—is a false alternative. While the distinction between mask and true self, genuineness and pretense, reality and appearance, becomes dubious when transferred from the theater to social reality, the choice between rescu- ing the true self from its roles, on the one hand, and an excessively positive valuation of role behavior grounded in a critique of the ideal of authenticity, on the other, is also a false alternative. My thesis, then, is that both these posi- tions remain trapped in the distinction between self and roles and in the false dichotomy that accompanies it. The task, for a theory of alienation, is precisely to dissolve this dichotomy in order to develop an alternative to appealing to a true self behind all roles. My claim, which might seem contradictory at first glance, is as follows: the fact that there is no authentic or untouched subject prior to its being socially formed through roles does not mean that we cannot become alienated from ourselves within them.

The objections against the critique of roles as alienating that derive from Helmuth Plessner's social theory of human nature and Georg Simmel's social philosophy can provide us with an understanding of the relation between self and roles different from the one suggested by classical theories of alienation.[20] The account of the constitutive function of roles for the formation of the self will provide us with a background that allows us to elaborate the potential for alienation inherent in various aspects of roles precisely without appealing to the idea that the real self is distorted by its roles; my account, instead, inquires into the conditions under which, *in* roles, one can determine and define one- self as something specific and articulate oneself as someone in particular.

(4) THE CONSTITUTIVE, INELUCTABLE NATURE OF ROLES (PLESSNER AND SIMMEL)

The positions of both authors can be reduced to the following common de- nominator: roles are less alienating than constitutive for the development of persons and personality. They are constitutive in the sense that they are di- rectly bound up with a person's development and, so, "productive." At first glance this position might seem to come down on one side of the two alterna- tives—an unconditional affirmation of roles—but after giving a brief account of the position, I will make use of it to move beyond the two alternatives.

Once the "productivity thesis" has been articulated,[21] it will be possible to distinguish between alienating and non-alienating aspects of role behavior.

THE HUMAN BEING AS *DOPPELGÄNGER*

Roles are productive. In and through them we first become ourselves. This is the essence of Helmuth Plessner's conception of the positive significance of roles (which he developed as a direct response to critiques of them as alienating). "The human being is always himself only in 'doubling' in relation to a role figure he can experience. Also, all that he sees as comprising his authenticity is but the role he plays before himself and others.[22] Roles on this view are not only necessary in order to make social interaction possible, whether this be a "being together" of individuals or a benign "passing each other by;" interaction mediated by roles is also constitutive of an individual's relation to herself. When Plessner speaks of a "doubling in relation to a role figure," he means that one depends on roles not only to become a "figure" of experience *for others* but also in order to become such a figure *for oneself*.

Plessner's thesis that the human being is a *Doppelgänger* is grounded in a comprehensive theory of human nature that, beginning from the fundamental concept of "eccentric positionality," is critical of every idea of immediacy or spontaneity.[23] According to Plessner:

> The distance that the role creates in family life, as well as in one's profession, work, or public offices, is the human being's characteristic detour to his fellow human being; it is the means of his immediacy. Whoever wants to see in this an instance of self-alienation misunderstands the human essence and foists on it a possibility of existence such as animals have on the level of life or angels have on the spiritual level. . . . Only the human being appears as a *Doppelgänger*, on the outside in the figure of his role and on the inside, privately, as himself.[24]

Although at first glance the talk of a *Doppelgänger* raises the suspicion that Plessner, too, is trapped in a model of doubling that relies on an opposition between authenticity and role behavior—between the inner and the outer— this suspicion turns out to be unwarranted: the *Doppelgänger* character of human beings is *illusory* because there are not two real entities there; our character as a "double" is a *construct*. There is not an internal division here to be overcome; rather, doubling is constitutive of the human self. "The human being cannot abolish his status as a *Doppelgänger* without negating his humanity. He cannot complain of this doubling and play it off against the ideal of an original oneness, for I can be one only with something, with someone, even if it is only myself. The human being gets a hold of himself in others. He encounters these others on a detour via roles, exactly as the others encounter him."[25]

If the other "gets a hold of himself" in the other, and if these two can encounter each other only through roles, then a self that is prior to or outside roles is a fiction. When Plessner says that "I can be one only with something, with someone, even if it is only myself,"[26] he is referring to a constitutive internal division that precedes all possible unity—it points to the fact that one's relation *to oneself* must also be conceived of as a certain kind of relation, namely, one mediated by a relation to the outside or to others. Thus I am not "someone" already at the outset; I can become someone only in relation to others and hence only via the roles in which we reciprocally encounter one another: "The human being gets a hold of himself in others." Behind all roles, then, there *is* nothing or, in any case, there is no "authentic being" there. No matter where we look, behind roles we find nothing we can grab hold of except for more roles that one "plays before oneself and others." We could call this an onion conception of the self: there are various layers but no inner core.

THE SCHOOL IN WHICH THE SUBJECT IS FORMED

These issues can be articulated in a similar way using Georg Simmel's account of the relation between social roles and individual existence. Roles, Simmel explains, are the "ideal form" "in which our existence has to clothe itself," and the ensemble of our roles is the "school in which the subject is formed." Two assumptions underlie this view: first, very generally, the subject, the identity of a person, is not simply given or *there* but is first developed or *formed*; second, taking on a role is an element of this formative process. When Simmel speaks of roles as an ideal form, part of what he means is that without them our existence would be unintelligible, too indeterminate, impossible to grasp. An identity becomes determinate only in taking on a determinate form—precisely this ideal form. If a role is understood as the *form* as opposed to the *content* of existence, this does not mean that the form is external to the content but rather that it is constitutive of it: there is no content without form.

Thus Simmel, too, embraces a conception of the relation between inner and outer that is completely different from the idea of authenticity as a role-transcending inwardness: the individual becomes constituted in her involvement with the outer (with others, the social form); the individual must externalize herself, give herself an ideal form in order to exist at all. What Simmel calls into question here is the contrast between inner essence and outer world and along with it a certain romantic conception of inwardness.[27] Here, too — in the view that taking on roles is a formative process — the idea of the productivity of roles comes to the fore; if something is formed, something that was previously unformed acquires a shape or "figure."

AN UNSOCIALIZED REMAINDER

But are we, then, socially formed through and through, nothing other than, as Simmel puts it, a "mere intersection of threads that society has spun before and alongside the individual"?[28] The question concerning the "unsocialized remainder" of personality, posed by Simmel elsewhere,[29] and the problem of "over-socialization" that occupies so large a place in the debate over role theory and the pragmatist theory of socialization,[30] can, for my purposes here, be set aside. Two points, however, should be noted:

First, on the basis of the theses I have discussed so far it is not necessary to deny the possibility of a bodily or instinctual foundation of the self described as socially constituted. What these theses deny, rather, is that without any relation to the social (for instance, via roles) the self can be shaped into a determinate form that would allow us to speak of a concrete identity or individuality. For the point of interest here it is not important (for the time being) what pregiven material makes up the starting point of the formative process that consists in the taking over of roles. Even if one can argue that this formation is always a *re*formation, that such structuring is always a *re*structuring, it is still the case that what is formed remains, without this formation, shapeless and indeterminate — unformed — and lacking in meaning. It is precisely this, however, that the idea of a true self existing behind all roles must claim: not only that there is something there but also that this something that claims to have primacy over the "falseness" of roles is already something determinate such that, metaphorically speaking, one would have only to remove the mask to find a finished form beneath it.

A second point must be clarified in order to avoid misunderstanding. Starting out from the productivity of roles and the self's formation in socially determined roles does *not* mean assuming an absolute *conformity* between an individual and her roles. Rather, this thesis assumes merely that the individual develops into what she is only by engaging with these roles. For, of course, someone who cannot identify with certain given social roles and conventions or who finds herself in tension with them is still a self or person. What is crucial is that even in this tension we remain related to our roles—even in this tension we do not find ourselves behind or outside our social roles. We must avoid at all costs assuming a preestablished harmony between individual and society; the tension between individual and society can be understood without relying on the idea of a too facile reconciliation, that is, without needing to presuppose a presocial self. (I return to this problem in chapter 10 in the context of the question concerning the potentials and resources of obstinacy or having a mind of one's own.) One can claim, then—in line with the ambivalence that Simmel expresses in various ways—that the individual *exists* through society but can also be threatened by it. And the unsocialized remainder, to the extent that it stands for the dimension of uniqueness or individuality, is, as I will argue, precisely not unsocialized but the result of specific constellations that various layers of socialization form with one another.

(5) ASPECTS OF ROLES AND THEIR AMBIVALENCE

We are now in a position to take up again the question posed earlier: if the idea of an inner or presocial self cannot be a source of normative standards, where are we to find the criteria in light of which roles can be criticized as alienating? My reflections here rest on two assumptions: the first holds that a certain duality or *ambiguity* is constitutive of roles. To the same extent to which social roles are constitutive and productive (and therefore enabling), they can also hinder, constrain, and alienate. They are, as it were, enabling and constraining at once. We should not, however, consider this constraint to be a necessary consequence of roles per se but to represent instead a way roles fall short of what they can be, precisely when the possibilities of expression and action are constrained *in them* (rather than by them). The second assumption takes seriously the idea that appropriating and adopting roles is a *formative process*. Then, however, various qualities of this formative process must be distinguished: it can be multilayered or one-dimensional; it can come to a standstill or it can "flow."

Both assumptions lead to the thesis that, while we are not alienated from ourselves *by* roles in general, we are sometimes alienated *in* roles. The crucial implication of this for the question of the true self is then that the true self is not masked by alienated role behavior but is hindered in its development, or formation, where true selfhood is something that can be formed and manifested only in unalienated or authentic relations to (and in) roles. (This claim also converges with my general thesis, namely, that the self's "truth" and "falsity," its authenticity and inauthenticity, are to be understood not as substantial properties but as ways of actively relating to something.)

Against the backdrop of this thesis and the distinctions just elaborated, I now return to the question of roles' alienating potential. I will proceed by attempting to specify the relevant problems with the help of the various aspects of roles already distinguished. Under the keywords (a) *outward-directedness*, (b) *standardization*, (c) *fragmentation*, and (d) *artificiality* (as contrasted, respectively, with *inward-directedness, uniqueness, totality*, and *genuineness* as forms of unalienated existence), I will articulate for each aspect of role behavior where its dual character—its productivity and its potential to be alienating—lies. This will enable us to elaborate criteria for diagnosing alienation within roles.

(A) "AN ALIEN HUMAN BEING"—THE OUTWARD-DIRECTED CHARACTER OF ROLE-PLAYING

First, there is the outward-directed character of role-playing: in roles we present ourselves before others and for them. Roles are public, even when performed in private. They are—from this perspective—alien, or "not one's own," since they are conveyed to the individual from the outside in the form of behavioral expectations. This critique is grounded in an opposition between the inner and the outer of the sort that Rousseau appeals to when (in reference to the theater) he decries the illusory self-relations of outward-directed individuals, for whom things are "ill at ease on the inside."[31]

This is a plausible explanation for the problem of the dynamic young man described earlier: when the up-and-coming editor has an opinion on every contemporary issue, he is reacting to the expectations conveyed from the outside to someone "in his position." He orients his opinions to "what people say" and is always tempted to display what he knows and to make it appear more significant than it is. The newscaster's cheerfulness, too, comes across as masklike precisely because it is a presentation directed outward. This by itself, however, does not yet fully capture the problem.

If, as the thesis set out previously claims, the subject must be formed, and if this happens only by engaging with social roles, then one can experience oneself as a self only in reacting to the demands and influences of others. There is, then—I return to this point in chapter 9—no pure inner self or, put differently, the so-called inner self differentiates itself through contact with what is outside or with others. The constitution of the self, then, is a process that depends on social interaction; it is not a stable object or substance that could only be "falsified" through the influence of others.[32] Understood in this way, only disturbances of this process, or of this relation between self and others, can be alienating, not the relation per se. It must then be possible to distinguish between relations to others that alienate and those that enable— that is, between forms of social interaction in which the individual becomes alienated from herself and those in which she first "comes to herself" or (also) between reifying and nonreifying modes of social interaction.

Sartre's analysis of the gaze and his phenomenology of intersubjectivity, as developed in the famous keyhole scene from *Being and Nothingness*, can help to clarify the problem of reciprocal reification (as well as the equally primordial nature of reification and enabling). The gaze of the other—in Sartre's example it is an other who catches us peeping curiously through a keyhole—makes us into a thing, an object. She makes us into something fixed, objectifies us as (in this case) someone who is curious, a keyhole peeper. If, in Sartre's terminology, the subject's "being-for-itself" is characterized by transcendence (because, as "projecting" itself, it is directed toward an open horizon of possibility), then we are reified—made objectlike—when we are made into something that is fixed by, or reduced to, what we factically are. The gaze of the other, according to this interpretation, represents the "solidification and alienation of my own possibilities"[33]—or, more dramatically, their "death."[34] But even for Sartre, who within the framework of a theory of intersubjectivity that remains negative through and through (because grounded in the view that reciprocal interaction *necessarily* fails),[35] there is a constitutive ambiguity here: it is also the gaze of the other that first makes me into a subject. Only in perceiving myself as the object of the other's gaze—hence here, too, only "via a detour through the other"—do I become conscious of myself. In the context of Sartre's ontology this means first detaching myself—as a subject—from my original immersion in the situation; (before being seen at the keyhole my condition is one in which "my consciousness sticks to my acts; it *is* my acts").[36] Yet, at the same time, it is the gaze of the other that first opens for me a field of possibilities for action. More concretely, only in seeing myself, mediated by the gaze of the other, as someone who jealously peeps through the keyhole (and who does so not because I am simply driven by jealousy) can I understand myself as someone for whom other options are possible. Translated into the conceptual framework of reification: the gaze of the other is as much reifying as dereifying or enabling. While, on the one hand, it makes me unfree by fixing me in my practical projects and identifying me with them (I am now the keyhole peeper, the jealous one), it enables me, on the other hand, to first come to an understanding of myself as someone who does one thing or another—and who could therefore also do something else. But, in that case, limiting the realm of possibility and opening it up are intertwined in such a way that they are difficult to disentangle. (The fact that Sartre impressively describes the phenomenology of this ambiguity but then, within the framework of his theory of intersubjectivity, tends to totalize the aspect of reification leads him, paradoxically, to fall back into precisely the ideal of authenticity he is trying to overcome.)[37]

This brings us back to the question I posed concerning the enabling and constraining forms of role-mediated social interaction, since in both role behavior and role ascription it is also their reifying features that appear to be problematic: the student who is clearly startled by his professor's presence in the bar fixes her in a reifying manner to her role as a seminar instructor—a harmless case. Men fix women to feminine roles and vice versa—less harmless. In such cases specific social roles and specific patterns of behavior are hypostatized and made into a person's "being." Here a part (a single role) is taken to be the whole (the person), and the specific patterns of behavior tied to it are reified into qualities that become inseparably tied to the person. A person's *doing* is made into a *being*. Understood in Sartrean terms, this implies in turn that when such mechanisms of reification have their source in others (through their ascription of roles), they fix me in a particular state, robbing me of my freedom to be something different from what I am for them.

But it is not only the case that here too—as the thesis introduced earlier implies—there is both enabling and constraint. The fact that someone is *made into something fixed* does not mean that her true self has been fixed as something behind the roles ascribed to her; it means merely that a field of possibility is taken away from her, the possibility of (also) determining herself differently—the possibility to be (also) something different.

With this a further feature of nonreifying role interactions (and their outward directedness) comes into view: a field of possibility for the appropriation of roles includes reciprocal negotiation. Even when one is dependent on others with respect to the definition of a role, how one understands that role and reacts to the expectations bound up with it is always a process of negotiation and interpretation. Thus successful role interactions are those in which acts of fixing the other with a "gaze from outside" come about and are broken through *at the same time*—a communicative form of interaction in the broadest sense in which individuals always also negotiate (verbally or nonverbally, harmoniously or conflictually) what they reciprocally make each other into. I emphasize that this is only in the broadest sense communicative not only because it involves more than merely verbal negotiation: we respond to gazes with gazes and body language, and resistance can be signaled through gestures. It is also the case that we are not limited to harmonious forms of negotiation in which one makes oneself into what one is in a spirit of mutual understanding: agonistic conflicts can also be nonreifying in this sense as long as they in fact occur as conflicts. Applied to our initial question, this means that the fact that others make me into what I am is not *in itself* alienating; nor is it the case that this is nonalienating only when, in "successful" relations of intersubjectivity, I can "come to myself in the other." Interactive relations are alienating or reifying in which no relation between subjects (however full of tension) comes about and, instead, acts of fixing the other turn into pure, one-sided subjugation that, rather than opening up fields of possibility, closes them down.

(B) "A PALE MAN"—STANDARDIZATION AND CONFORMISM

The next dimension along which roles are often criticized as alienating has to do with standardization and conformism. Roles are given in advance; their script is already written. Viewed in this way, they are a fixed form that individuals can only "fill in." The role expectations and repertoire of behaviors that characterize the junior editor or financial adviser exist prior to and in a certain respect independently of them. Roles imply standards for appropriate and inappropriate behavior, an entire set of expectations regarding competency and performance that must be met if one is to fulfill a role. This limits the possibilities for shaping one's own behavior and the space within which an individual can respond spontaneously. Thus from the perspective of alienation critique we are "caught" in roles and shaped by them; our own freedom, as well as the possibilities of expressing ourselves as individuals, are constrained. Standardization, then, stands in contrast to the aspiration for individuality and uniqueness.

Now the standardization or conventionality of roles is actually a constitutive condition of there being (social) roles at all. Roles are sets of rules. As with all social institutions, one cannot invent them oneself: like social institutions, roles are in a certain respect independent of and prior to the individual, even though they are at the same time constituted through the actions of individuals and—ultimately—can be kept alive only through them.

In order for something to function as a role there must be preformed patterns and behavioral expectations that make the role something individuals can recognize and manage as such. Becoming a newscaster or an editor, but also becoming a father or a revolutionary, always means taking over general norms and behavioral repertoires. This means that the conventionality of shared norms and practices is constitutive for the possibility of deviating from them. One can, for example, change and redefine the role of a parent; one can criticize, expand, or even dissolve the traditional form. What emerges, though, will always be a version of the parental role—more precisely, its redefinition—and it will, in one way or another, continue to stand in relation to the earlier forms and to the social practices bound up with them.

If roles are the ideal form in which we exist, then they cannot be individualized from the outset. If we require them in order to determine ourselves, to become something and someone, to form ourselves into subjects, then we also depend precisely on their conventionality. It is the form that first enables us to express who we are. Like language, whose rule-governed structure creates the basis for us to express ourselves within it, the conventionality of roles does not for the most part distort our individual possibilities of expression; rather, it puts at our disposal the conditions that enable us to define and express ourselves as something at all. It is the choosing and reshaping of roles that gives us the opportunity for individual self-presentation and self-development. The search for authenticity *behind* such forms would be, then, a meaningless undertaking—the search for authenticity *in* them would be a problem that constantly reposes itself.[38] If one accepts that following rules requires not only constant reinterpretation but a type of appropriation that cannot be understood as mere repetition, then individuality, originality, and authenticity are achievable only as a specific kind of *appropriation* of preexisting role scripts.[39]

With respect to standardization, too, roles can be seen to have a dual character that both enables and constrains individuality at the same time. Here again the problem of alienation emerges as the result of a tension between the preexistence of roles and their appropriation by individuals. It is necessary to distinguish here between the convention as a shared starting point and a conventionalism that makes individual appropriation impossible and thereby impoverishes or rigidifies the shared language, robbing it of its expressive possibilities. Just as a cliché reduces the possibilities for experience and expression, overly conventionalized roles block possibilities of individual self-expression and of individuals' identification with them. The figures sketched at the beginning of this chapter are not, then, inauthentic (or alienated) because they behave in accordance with certain roles but rather because of *how* they do so—because they act within rigidified forms of expression they are unable to appropriate as their own and whose possibilities of reshaping remain constrained.

If the possibility of authenticity does not depend on there being a self *behind* roles but on their being productively *appropriated*, then the framing of our problem can be deepened by using the conceptual resources of role theory itself: they enable us to conceive of the appropriation of roles as an internal requirement of the functional conditions of the roles themselves.[40] All roles must be translated and implemented by the individuals who carry them out. Roles are not simply given; they are *realized* only in being interpreted and implemented in a specific way. Everyone who learns to take on a role faces, on the one hand, a preexisting *script* and, on the other, the task of realizing it in her own way. In precisely the same way that individuals depend on roles in order to "come to themselves," roles depend for their continued social existence on subjects who appropriate them in specific ways. Thus every act of taking on a role is also a *modification* of this role. No description of a role—no *script*—could be so complete that it needs no interpretation. To be sure, our junior editor finds before him what he is supposed to do, and he adjusts himself to these expectations. But what precisely is expected? And who expects it? If in the "culture industry" one is expected to be up on recent developments, does the new editor's boss expect him to know the classical genres, or is it a familiarity with other cultural milieus that he is looking for? If one wants to demonstrate one's authority in relation to one's coworkers, what degree of familiarity or camaraderie should (or may) one display in doing so? What mixture of ambition and informal ease belongs to the profile of a successful newscaster, and how much down-to-earthness, on the one hand, and how much visionary energy, on the other, must the financial adviser radiate in order to be trusted? It is not merely that each case requires a complicated balance such that detailed "stage directions" are difficult to provide. Since these cases also involve processes of interaction that must adapt themselves to the situation and that require the integration of very different expectations—the secretary expects something other from the newly hired editor than the boss, the authors something other than his colleagues—most role descriptions cannot be more than mere sketches. What is required here is the adaption of general role expectations to a specific interpretation of a particular and concrete present situation. In order to achieve this—in order to elaborate the sketch and to find a path between various demands that are never unambiguous and sometimes, in cases of conflict, even contradictory—something beyond this is required: there must be an agency that can do more than merely react to given demands, an agency that is in a position—within the framework of these demands—to act independently.

Hans-Peter Dreitzel calls this component the subject-function, which denotes the "range of behavior that is more strongly determined by personality in comparison with role expectations that are fixed in content."[41] "Distance from roles," then, is a condition for successfully taking on roles and for their functional capacity: "In a role-based identity the person must understand herself in terms of a social role without, however, being absorbed into it without remainder."[42] If a distanced "standing back" is a condition for successfully identifying with a role, then it is the success of this relation that is of crucial importance. Alienation in roles means then—entirely in line with my reconstruction—the halting, disturbance, or flattening out of this relation, understood as a relation of tension and appropriation. Expressed in terms of these concepts, then, self-alienation is the loss of distance from one's roles. Dreitzel formulates this point as follows: "Alienation from oneself means a lessening of one's distance from roles and as a result of this a suppression of the necessary subject-functions in role playing through an excessive pressure of behavioral norm, which manifests itself in the fine-meshed and overly precise character of role expectations."[43] The junior editor is inauthentic or alienated from himself insofar as he becomes rigid in his role and acts, or is compelled to act, in an overly conventional or ritualized manner. He comes off as stranger than his boss (among other reasons) because the latter, more experienced and relaxed, has learned to allow himself room for deviating from his role and has found "his own style," in contrast to someone who must adapt to a new role and who reacts to this by overadapting.

But, even if distance and room for deviation are called for here, this does not imply a distinction between a "pure" self and the roles it plays. The subject function or the "part played by personality" in this relation of appropriation marks an individual's independence or obstinacy (or a having a mind of her own) in relation to her roles,[44] without making reference to a presocial core of the subject or to an individuality behind its manifestations. "It is not possible to isolate from these nomic functions something purely individual or, as it were, a pre-social component" of the subject.[45] What is described here, then, is a relation of tension between a person who is always already socialized and her social roles. Thus the contrast between standardization and the individual's uniqueness, which finds expression in the classical critique of roles as alienating, is a false opposition: what is important is not to express oneself in one's uniqueness but to develop oneself by engaging—possibly in distinctive ways—with social roles.

(C) "AN INCOMPLETE MAN"—FRAGMENTATION AND ONE-SIDEDNESS

The next respect in which roles can be understood as alienating concerns fragmentation and one-sidedness, or the absence of "wholeness" that Dahrendorf decries when he depicts the player of roles as an "incomplete man." Roles, as the *parts* individual plays in the fabric of social cooperation, are always a constraint as well: they always involve only a certain portion of the qualities and potentials we have at our disposal. This means not only that our own capacities are developed one-sidedly but also that in roles our possibilities for interacting with others are constrained. In social relations mediated by roles we take note only of pieces of one another: the editor does not need to concern himself with whether he likes the author "as a person" as long as he finds him interesting as an author. Of course, this means reducing the complexity of individuals: being fixed in a role not only excludes other possible competencies; it also fixes us to certain aspects of our personality.

The thesis that individuals are formed in and through roles also has implications for the problem of fragmentation or one-sidedness. That we are first formed into subjects through roles also means that, in taking on roles, we are formed into individuals with *determinate* and therefore also *limited* capacities and competencies. The process of being formed *into something* means precisely that we do not remain abstract human beings in general; rather, we become persons who—in the context of our activities—have specific possibilities of expression and behavioral repertoires at our disposal and who develop specific capacities. One then becomes someone who succeeds at being a father or a revolutionary, who as an academic holds this or that position, who as a journalist cultivates this or that style and in her dealings with others embodies this or that posture. However, to determine ourselves in this way is necessarily to limit ourselves. We cannot do everything and be everything at once. I am this (father, journalist, revolutionary) but not that, even if I can unite many different qualities and competencies in myself. One *is* someone at all only in doing something specific and hence in *not* doing something else. That roles never constitute a whole human being is unavoidable then. But even Marx's famous ideal of the unalienated whole human being—at once fisher, hunter, and critical critic—refers, properly understood, to someone who masters and is able to perform a wide variety of activities, someone who unites in her daily life a larger than normal number of roles and functions. The idea of a whole human being as an unlimited human being in general who stands behind her properties as hunter, fisher, and critic is a chimera and a false abstraction. She would be pure potentiality but not a real human being. (By the same token, the demand that we apprehend others as whole human beings rather than only in their limited roles is also nonsensical, at least in this formulation.)

But, once again, if the idea of wholeness is problematic, this does not mean that role behavior does not sometimes lead to one-sidedness, shallowness, and limitation and that no criteria for criticizing these phenomena can be found. More appropriate than the criterion of wholeness, which suggests that we already know what capacities and properties make up a whole personality, are criteria that—in line with my account here—focus on *how* things are executed, on the qualities of a person's process of development rather than on a fixed set of substantial properties. I would like to revise these criteria using concepts such as openness to experience, flexibility, and the ability to integrate experiences, by which I mean the following: the crucial question is not how many aspects of a successful life or how many features of an all-round developed personality someone realizes. The question is rather whether what she does leads her into a dead end or whether it offers her further possibilities for integrating and continuing her experiences—whether it limits her possibilities or opens up options for her.

Distinguishing among different qualities of *experience*, as John Dewey does in his reflections on education, can help to indicate in what direction we should proceed. If, as Dewey claims, the program of "new education" is to make experiences accessible to pupils, it is not the case that all experiences are equally productive. "Productive" describes essentially those experiences that make the "growth of further experience" possible, in contrast to those that inhibit that growth.

For some experiences are miseducative. Any experience is miseducative that has the effect of arresting or distorting the *growth of further experience*. An experience may be such as to engender callousness; it may produce lack of sensitivity and of responsiveness. Then the possibilities of having richer experience in the future are restricted. Again, a given experience may increase a person's automatic skill in a particular direction and yet tend to land him in a groove or rut; the effect again is to narrow the field of further experience.[46]

Without presupposing conceptions of wholeness or of the complete person, Dewey develops a conception of growth that is open to experience, the criterion of which is the ability to integrate new experiences ("the idea of continuity"): "The question is whether growth in this direction promotes or retards growth in general. Does this form of growth create conditions for further growth, or does it set up conditions that shut off the person who has grown in this particular direction from the occasions, stimuli, and opportunities for continuing growth in new directions? What is the effect of growth in a special direction upon the attitudes and habits which alone open up avenues for development in other lines?"[47]

These reflections can be applied to our set of problems: even if there is no core of a fully developed and (in this sense) unalienated personality, it is still possible to distinguish among qualitatively different ways of pursuing interests and having experiences (within the necessarily limited sphere of one's activity). From this perspective, alienation is present when such processes of experience are hindered or come to a standstill. What is problematic is when such processes lead to forms of specialization and one-sidedness that make it structurally impossible to broaden, transform, or redefine one's interests. Roles are dangerous when they fix someone so that there is no longer room for her to move among different roles. What is problematic with the editor, newscaster, and financial adviser is not that they develop only some of their capacities, nor that they are only editor, newscaster, or financial adviser and confront others in the first instance only as such. The problem arises only when it can be shown that their way of developing capacities and their adoption of these roles decreases rather than promotes the development of further capacities and possibilities for experience.[48]

(D) "AN ARTIFICIAL MAN"

Role behavior comes under the suspicion of being artificial (or fake), insofar as it is "performed," mechanical, and seems to be separable from the actor. One *learns* a role, and not only in the theater. What results is trained behavior.

Role behavior—*playing* a role—presupposes a doubling of the self that creates distance within the self. "I am someone else": I am not identical with the role I play. Being truly human, in contrast—so the idea goes—is not something we can achieve by playing. It begins, rather, precisely where our behavior is in some sense immediate and not subject to being questioned. In fact, cannot our unease at the network newscaster's cheerfulness be traced back to the fact that we see it as contrived and that we think of genuine cheerfulness, in contrast, as something spontaneous?

What, though, can be retained from this accusation of artificiality if we hold fast to the idea that individuals are first *formed* through roles? The first point is banal: if the subject, whenever it has specific qualities, is always shaped and formed, it is clearly not "natural." The idea of genuineness is therefore problematic. And if, as Plessner emphasizes, there can be no immediate relations, either to oneself or to others, this undermines the idea that uninhibited spontaneity constitutes our true, uncontrived self. (One sees this not least in "cultures of spontaneity," which arise again and again in reaction to fixed social forms; in them spontaneity itself is cultivated into such a form.)

There is, however, a second point: is not the critique of artificiality and the playing of roles—as the analysis of reification would seem to imply—reifying and essentialist? Very briefly (and returning to what was said in the introduction), someone is not an editor or a newscaster in the same sense that he has dark hair or is six feet tall. The former are not qualities one has but things one does—things that, insofar as one does them, could be done differently or not at all. The role-*playing* nature of what one does points not to a difference between essence and appearance but to a constitutive distance that follows from the fact that there is always a realm of possibility with respect to what one could be. This distance, then, rests not on *being* in essence something different from what one *professes* to be but on the fact that one always *could be* something different from what in this role or function one happens to be now. For, obviously, the editor *is* not an editor, the newscaster not a newscaster, and the revolutionary not a revolutionary. It does not belong to their essential qualities, to their nature, to be one thing or another. The artificiality of roles in its most positive sense refers to the fact that one is not fixed in one's roles, that there is no "substance" to be found behind one's roles. This is also the point of Sartre's analysis of bad faith, according to which a person behaves inauthentically precisely when she denies that her own existence is something to be "played" and that it is always lived within the realm of possibility. In the case of the waiter who plays at being a waiter (another famous example from Sartre's *Being and Nothingness*), it is precisely the concealing of the role-*playing* nature of his behavior that is taken to be untruthful and reifying. Conversely, what is called, in the language of role theory, distance from roles is a presupposition of being able to act authentically in a role. Only someone who knows she is playing a role and does not pretend to be identical with it, and who, at the same time, knows that she cannot avoid playing roles, counts as "truthful" in Sartre's sense. In his provocative inversion: "True human existence is always played." It is precisely making roles natural, not their artificiality, that is problematic from this perspective. The artificiality of roles should not be opposed to genuineness but to a way of using, structuring, and playing this role so as to open up a sphere for action. Reifying or alienating roles, then, are those that no longer allow the contrived character of roles to appear and that mask their nature as something that must be played.

(6) SELF-ALIENATION IN ROLES

From the perspective proposed here, social roles are to be understood as simultaneously limiting and enabling. To the extent to which roles can limit individual development, they also make this development possible. To the extent to which they compromise an individual's wholeness, they also first make it possible for her to acquire real existence. To the extent to which the influence of others brings the individual outside herself, she also first "comes to herself" through them. In these considerations we can find some indication of how to answer the question raised previously concerning whether we can still speak of alienation in roles if we abandon the idea of a self or an essence behind all roles. The criteria with the help of which one can criticize roles as alienating are to be found precisely in roles' potential as enabling or productive: the alienating or nonalienating character of a role is measured according to the extent to which it is capable of forming a subject (or of helping it to become a reality) that is, at the same time, not "already there." As we have seen, the problem is not *that* we play roles but *how* we play them. Thus, when roles bring about alienation, it is because of deficiencies in the roles themselves and deficiencies in the way they are appropriated.

APPROPRIATION AND DEFICIENCIES OF APPROPRIATION

With some people one has the impression that they are recognizable in every situation regardless of the role they are playing at that moment; they seem to remain themselves in every social role. At the same time, there are others—the young professionals described earlier—with whom one has the feeling that they completely disappear behind their roles. The difference here lies in the specific ways they take on their roles, and on the basis of this thought various characteristics of successful or unsuccessful appropriation can be enumerated.

Successful role appropriation can be measured, for example, by the degree of interest a person has in what she does in a role—by the degree to which she *involves* herself in a role's demands. This coheres with the observation that problematic role behavior, for example in a seminar, can disappear at precisely the moment when "things get serious," when a serious discussion begins in which the participants are engaged, regardless of the social positions or roles from which they argue. Just as one can forget oneself, so to speak, while engaged in a concentrated activity, the same thing happens in the interactions among the seminar participants without the role relationships themselves disappearing.

Successful role appropriation can be measured, then, by the degree to which someone *identifies* with a certain situation or role. In this spirit Stanley I. Benn discusses the relation between roles and alienation by asking whether an individual "finds herself" in her role or understands (or can understand) her fulfillment of the role as a part of her personality:

> So one may judge whether a role enters into the self by the degree of satisfaction or dismay occasioned by success or failure in it. The completely alienated worker or the disaffected conscript soldier takes no pride in his achievements in the role or accepts with equanimity the criticisms of his superiors because the role means nothing to him. . . . But when a role is truly a part of the self, what the role makes of it affects his consciousness of his identity; having the role is a necessary part of being the person that he is, and his performance counts for him as a stage in self-creation.[49]

Involvement, interest, and identification stand in contrast, then, to the attitude one could call *instrumentalism*: a disengagement that is not an expression of indifference or distance to the role's demands—our eager young careerists, for example, clearly seem more like cases of overengagement or overidentification. What is crucial here is a specific deficiency in the kind of interest that results when one engages in behavior with a merely instrumental attitude. An instrumental interest in something is an interest in which what one does or what one is interested in is merely a means to an end. Someone who attends a concert in order to prove that she is part of the cultured elite, someone who goes to a party in order to be seen, someone who argues intensely for an opinion because she cannot be left out of the discussion, someone who is exuberant because it is part of her image—all have instrumental relationships to what they do. The rigidity that goes along with such a posture signals a lack of identification, whereas someone who identifies or engages with her role more spontaneously usually exhibits a wider range of behavior in playing her role: she retains distinctive character traits or idiosyncrasies that are not (and need not be) repressed but can instead be worked into the role. And she can permit herself deviations from the standard expectations. Someone who can actually identify with her roles, then, exhibits—precisely in performing her roles—a dimension of obstinacy (or having a mind of one's own).

OBSTINACY AND THE MULTIDIMENSIONALITY OF ROLES

Finally, a new problem emerges that leads us back to the question raised earlier concerning the normative standards at work when we describe alienation as a problem. If one requires a distance from roles in order to relate to roles, the suspicion arises that there must already be an agency—existing outside roles—that enters into relations with its roles. But who distances herself here from whom? If we identify a dimension of obstinacy in the successful appropriation of roles, is there not then a previously existing character, a presocial agency that stands over and against the roles? Where does the potential for real identification come from? What is the source of the surplus that makes possible the "subject-function" that Dreitzel speaks of? These questions can be answered with the help of two points:

First, role constellations—at least in modernity, precisely where they first become a problem—typically involve multiple roles: one is always engaged in several roles at once.

Second, every life history is marked by a succession of previously adopted roles. Roles accumulate, therefore, and enter into various constellations in different individuals. And, viewed as a formative process, every instance of being shaped by a role constitutes a situation from within which the next role demand is encountered. Role constellations are multidimensional in both respects, which means that the role demands that apply to a person must be integrated both vertically and horizontally. It is, then, precisely this multilay-eredness—the fact that humans are shaped in the course of their lives by a constellation of roles specific to each case—that one can identify as the source of character, uniqueness, and obstinacy.

One must imagine the subject that stands in the "intersection of social circles" (Simmel),[50] then, as a subject that also contains the dimension of its own life history and that, as something shaped, formed, and developed, can also take up a distanced (and sometimes resistant) relation to current demands. The individual who is confronted with a role is not a blank slate but is always already shaped in specific ways. Goffman's metaphor, according to which the self is only a hook on which roles hang—like pieces of cloth-ing—does not go far enough, because he does not take into account (to keep within the metaphor) that the hook is transformed by the different pieces of clothing that hang (and have hung) on it.[51]

THE TRUE AND FALSE SELF

To what extent, then, has my analysis overcome the dichotomy previously discussed? The distinction between the subject and its roles that many critics of roles take for granted can no longer be understood as a distinction between two entities (a mask and a true self) but only as a distinction between two kinds of activity, successful and unsuccessful appropriation. In fact, alienation in roles looks more dramatic if we do not start off from the idea that there is a true self behind its roles. If we first take on a specific shape, even for our-selves, within roles, then alienating roles not only force us to conceal or mask ourselves, they inhibit us already in the construction of our identity. If it is not only before others that we express ourselves in roles, then in alienating roles we actually lose *ourselves*. This is true, however, not in the sense that we already exist as someone different, as someone who, in these roles, we precisely are not, but rather in the sense that we cannot develop into someone in the roles in question. One must not therefore imagine the loss of self or the loss of authenticity (through roles) as a process of being divided into two selves. From the claim that underneath the roles there "is" nothing at all it follows that, when roles limit us in an alienating way, there is nothing left over behind these roles—or, at least, no self with determinate features. Formulated differently, there exists no true self as a counterpart to the false self as long as the true self is something that can be formed only by successfully identifying with roles. What results from alienation in roles, then, is less a distortion of, or a coming away from, the true self than an inner void.

Someone who has to fear losing herself in a role, then, does not have very much to lose. Expressed less polemically, and philosophically more productively, the problem here is that no determinate self has developed.[52] As Adorno notes in *Minima Moralia*: "The outward-directed human being has normally not lost his individuality; in the outward-directed society he never attained it." The true self does not lie dormant under its roles; rather, pathological forms of role behavior impede the development of the true self—a self that is true in the sense of having the capacity to relate to itself and the world in an active and appropriating way.

This also means that the position that overaffirms or totalizes roles—the view that concludes from the lack of a true self behind roles that it is futile to try to find elements of alienation—is false. Authenticity and alienation *in* roles are both modes of performing them.

With respect to the standards and criteria for successful or unsuccessful forms of appropriation: although there is no Archimedean point from the perspective of which we can distinguish authentic from inauthentic selves, it is also not the case that we are therefore forced to appeal to something that is accessible only to introspection. The criteria that define alienation are to be sought in externally manifested performances and actions that show themselves to be problematic.

CODA: SIMMEL'S ACTOR AND AUTHENTICITY IN ROLES

Georg Simmel's essay "The Philosophy of the Actor," in reflecting on what an actor must achieve in taking on a role, offers some interesting suggestions as to how to understand the interpenetration of persons and roles.[53] Here, too, the question arises as to how a role's objective content—the demands of its pre-existing, given "matter"—relates to the actor's creative individuality in interpreting a role. In this essay Simmel is interested in understanding how what is individual and what is universal are mediated so as to yield the "particular law" to which a role is subject:

There is not simply, on the one hand, an objective task, fixed by the author, and, on the other hand, a real subjectivity of the actor, such that the task is merely for the latter to be fit into the former; rather, above these two elements there arises a third: the demand the role makes on this actor and

perhaps on no other—the particular law that comes for this actor's personality from this role.[54] With this a false objectivity is overcome that makes
the actor into the marionette of his role, and implies that all actors should
play the same role in the same way. At the same time, a false subjectivity is
overcome, according to which the actor only has to play himself as nature
made him, so to speak, and the role is merely the accidental guise in which
his individuality is presented. Rather, the actor has before him an ideal of
how his individuality is to form this role such that what results is a maximum
of total artistic value.[55]

Simmel's main idea here is that, when a role is taken on successfully,
the actor's subjective disposition, individual character, and personality, on the
one hand, and the objectively given role, on the other, interpenetrate one
another. This, however, does not relativize the objective requirements or turn
them into something subjective. An artistically perfect form of interpenetration of actor and role is, in turn, subject to an objective constraint or, better,
to a subjective-objective constraint since there is an objectively correct—an
"obligatory"—way in which a particular artist has to fulfill the universal demands of a specific role. It is necessary *for her* to play it in the specific way she
plays it. On the other hand, this obligation is completely "custom-fitted" to her
specific personality; it is valid only for her and for the particular combination
of her and the role. For this reason it makes sense to speak of a particular law
rather than a universal law that requires every actor to play the role in a certain
way. The actor, then, plays "herself" in playing a role. At the same time, this
does not mean that the role is *immediately* given for her or that her playing it
emerges out of "her nature." If an actor playing Hamlet expresses himself in
his performance, this does not mean that he needs only to present himself on
stage as he "is," nor that prior to the performance, before he has given shape
to his role, he is already Hamlet. To say that his personality expresses itself
in his playing of the role does not mean that he simply has, without his own
participation, a "Hamlet nature" and therefore needs only to reproduce what
he already is without forming and structuring the role. What occurs, instead,
is a form-giving interpenetration of the individual's character with the material and its objective demands. The ideal actor (or the one who is ideal for a
specific role) does not express *herself*, she expresses *herself in her role*.

If then his vital impulses, the coloring of his spontaneously acting temperament, push off themselves in the direction of this form, if the ideal figure,

which in the realm of his personality preforms Hamlet with those "invisi-
ble lines," is reproduced from his preexisting reality without resistance, as it
were—then "he plays himself" in the perfect Hamlet. To be sure, this Hamlet
is perfect only for him, not for his given reality but for the ideally demanded
form that develops out of this reality and is one with it only through a hap-
penstance of nature.[56]

7

"SHE BUT NOT HERSELF"—SELF-ALIENATION AS INTERNAL DIVISION

Our life as we lead it is just our life, except that some elements in it seem like intruders, interpolators. Some thoughts we have, emotions we feel, some of our beliefs, desires, and actions are experienced as not really ours. It is as if we lost control, as if we were taken over, possessed by a force which is not us.

—JOSEPH RAZ, "WHEN WE ARE OURSELVES"

IN THIS CHAPTER I DEAL with cases in which one experiences one's own desires and impulses as alien, cases in which one sees oneself as dominated by desires that one has, but as if from an alien power, or cases in which one's own behavior leads one to feel like a stranger to oneself. These are situations in which one wants to say "that can't be me," but in which, at the same time, one is oddly incapable of rejecting the behavior one experiences as alien or of dismissing the desires one feels so distant from. In this sense being alienated from oneself means not being able to identify with oneself or with what one wants and does, which seems to be not really "part of our story" and not really to belong to our own life. How are we to understand that? And, conversely, when are desires really *our own* and when are we really *ourselves*? My claim is that in these forms of self-alienation there is a certain way in which one is not accessible to oneself in one's own desires and that this phenomenon can be explained without appealing to an authentic "core self."

I will again proceed by first (1) elaborating the phenomenon with the help of an example in order next to (2) bring out the characteristics that make *self-alienation* a plausible interpretation of the described situation. From this arise two sets of questions. The first has to do with the internal structure that characterizes a division of this type within a person's own will, the second with the standard in relation to which certain of our desires are able to claim authority and others not. I address both sets of questions in sections (3) and (4) in conjunction with an extended discussion of Harry Frankfurt's account of the person. I conclude (5) that his model is incapable of resolving the problem of how our desires can acquire authority if what we are interested in is overcoming processes of internal division in the name of emancipation. Finally, (6) the view of self-alienation as practical inaccessibility to oneself will yield some clues as to how the dilemma elaborated here can be resolved.

(1) THE GIGGLING FEMINIST

H., a self-professed, reflective feminist of strong convictions, catches herself over and over again communicating with her lover like a silly, giggling ado-lescent girl. She rejects such forms of feminine coquetry as unemancipated, as the mannerisms of a "little girl." She has long understood that the idea that women must present themselves as cute, petite, and harmless in order to be attractive is the projection of a world dominated by men. Yet, as she discov-ers to her irritation, she constantly falls back into these patterns of behavior against her will. She experiences her own behavior, so starkly in contrast to her convictions, her self-conception, and her life plan, as contradictory and as not really part of herself. It triggers in her a feeling of disconcertedness when she sees herself behave in such a manner: "That can't be me." Formulated somewhat dramatically, it is as if in her giggling something were speaking through her that is not herself.

(2) DEMARCATING THE PHENOMENON AND DEFINING ITS CHARACTERISTICS

One can describe the discrepancy that makes the situation depicted here an experience of self-alienation as follows: H. cannot *identify* with her impulse to giggle and with the desires she suspects lie behind it. The talk of feeling alien in relation to herself indicates that more is going on than (or something different from) a mere rejection of certain behaviors. She desires and does things that do not "fit" or belong to her, things that at the same time she has no influence over. She is *internally divided* insofar as she seems to be split into two parts that do not stand in a coherent or meaningful relation to each other. Similarly to the academic in chapter 1, she feels herself to be a "help-less . . . bystander to the forces that move [her]."[1] And yet what is at issue here is nevertheless (to return to the Heidegger quotation from part 1) "a power that is she herself." How precisely, though, can we explain that a person can do and desire things that at the same time do not belong to her? Who is alien to whom here? When, and having which desires, would she be *herself*?

In what follows I elaborate the features that make the conflict I describe a problem of self-alienation.

1. The Significance of Desires. The behaviors of her own that she rejects are not merely insubstantial inconsistencies that occur at the periphery of her personality and have no vital importance for her. The part of herself that she experiences as alien stands at the center of her personality and is of great significance to it.[2] Her behavior, then, is no mere quirk, not merely a vestige of previously learned behavior that is inconsequential for her. (She is not someone whose feminism resides merely at the surface of her personality and who would almost be relieved to be able to discard its strong demands; she is, rather, a woman whose identity is deeply informed by her feminist convictions, who owes much to them, and who in many other respects successfully leads an emancipated life.) One can imagine that in reflecting on these issues H. discovers that her pattern of giggling is intertwined with deep-seated desires and thoughts, for example, with the fact that her idea of romantic relationships corresponds far less to the picture of a symmetric relationship between equals than she could admit. Her giggling, she discovers, is an expression of the need she feels to be protected, as little as that fits with her otherwise self-confident manner. (It would be excessive to regard behaviors that are really involuntary and trivial—without explicable meaning[3]—as symptoms of an internal division.)

2. The Incompatibility of Desires. To speak of an internal division further presupposes that the opposed sets of desires are mutually exclusive or at least that pursuing one of them stands in significant tension with pursuing the other. H.'s desires are incompatible insofar as they—at least for her—suggest relationships and forms of life that are mutually incompatible: whereas, on the one hand, she wants to be an independent woman, she also, on the other hand, longs for a love relationship in which she is dependent but protected. This is a case, then, in which the inconsistency between those desires becomes an explicit problem, at least in the protagonist's own self-conception. (Otherwise there would be no reason for a stronger reaction to her own behavior than

mild bemusement.) The two attitudes sketched earlier are understood by our protagonist as an opposition between an emancipated and an unemancipated way of life. As such they are mutually exclusive. To borrow a distinction of Charles Taylor's: they contradict each other *qualitatively* and are therefore incompatible in a different and stronger sense than that they merely cannot be realized simultaneously.[4] In contrast to this, for example, the desire she occasionally has to play competitive sports conflicts with the rest of her life only because of time constraints. This desire, even if it were to remain unfulfillable, is not an alien element in her economy of desires, and—as long as it is not reinterpreted and integrated into the framework of more fundamental life decisions—she will not have the impression of being alienated from herself regardless of whether the desire is fulfilled or not.

3. The Inauthenticity of These Desires. That the existence of certain desires is interpreted as alienating implies, further, a very specific attitude to those desires and a corresponding understanding of their nature. When we regard our own desires and behavior as alien to us, we understand them as desires that we do not *truly* (authentically) have. When H. experiences her desire for protection or subordination to a man as an alien part of herself, she distances herself from it not merely in the sense that she rejects it; she understands the desires she interprets as alien as being *not really* her *own*; they are not her authentic desires. The assertion "they don't belong to me" is more than just a confused way of saying "I don't want that." What is implied, rather, is that they are *not genuine*. These desires, one could say, masquerade as her desires. This calls into question—places under suspicion or expresses a reservation about—the authority of the desires she in fact has. Talk of self-alienation—this is the important point—presupposes the possibility of criticizing desires, which takes the form of doubting their authenticity.

This feature also distinguishes the conflict in which our protagonist finds herself from inner ambivalence.[5] Someone is ambivalent when she stands between two of her own desires; in this case both sides represent desires—even if qualitatively incompatible in the sense explained earlier—that are equally her own and can therefore each claim an *equal right* to authority. So understood, a conflict of ambivalence is a *tragic* conflict.[6] (In this sense, for example, one can stand ambivalently between two lovers or be ambivalent about deciding for a life with or without a child.) In contrast to this, the potential for conflict in *inauthentic* or *alien* desires, or in desires one understands as such, resides in the fact that one rejects a desire and therefore cannot identify with it but still cannot be rid of it. H. would not say of herself that she stands between the desire for emancipation and the desire not to be emancipated or that she has both desires simultaneously. She rejects her desires not to be emancipated. Whereas a conflict of ambivalence is due merely to the fact that one cannot realize the two desires simultaneously, an inauthentic desire is one that one *truly* does not even have.[7] In the one case we must simply decide; in the other we must find out what we *really* want. This presupposes not merely that one of the two desires is more important but that one of them corresponds more to oneself. The question then is how we can make sense of these presuppositions—how one can distinguish real from unreal, authentic from inauthentic desires if both are desires one in fact has. Is it so clear whether her giggling or her normally self-confident manner better represents H.'s authentic desires? When is she really herself: when she no longer giggles or when she no longer distances herself from her giggling?

4. Self-conceptions. Understood in this way, conflicts of this type concern what is often called a person's self-conception or identity. What is at issue for the young woman who is in internal conflict over her girlish behavior is clearly who she *is* and how she *conceives of* herself. It is not for her merely a question of whether she should decide in favor of one form of life or another (and about the consequences this would have in each case) but rather of what her actions would make of her and of how she could understand herself in them. The role of interpretation and self-interpretation is crucial here: H.'s behavior is not contradictory as such. It is contradictory insofar as it contradicts her feminist self-conception. Without entering into such reflexive relations oneself—not merely *doing* this or that but *conceiving of* oneself in this or that way while doing it—the entire phenomenon of self-alienation would be inexplicable. One can understand one's behavior or one's desires as an alien element of oneself only because one has an implicit or explicit conception of what belongs or should belong to one, because one can integrate certain things into one's self-conception and not others.

5. Freedom and Emancipation. If self-alienation in the present case means being driven by desires that one in some sense does not really have and thus becoming someone one really is not, then one is not really free when controlled by such desires. As Raymond Geuss writes: "Someone is 'free' in the full sense only if he does what he really wants to do, that is, only if he acts out of a genuine, authentic, or real desire. The authenticity of the desires that motivate action is an essential component of freedom."[8] Unmasking inauthentic desires has in this respect an emancipatory significance, if processes of emancipation involve more than casting off foreign domination and oppression and

also involve emancipation in relation to the alien power "that we ourselves are."[9] Such processes of emancipation typically include a complex process in which someone wants to become different from what she is and at the same time interprets this as corresponding better to who she is—as being "freed into being herself," as the promising formula would have it.

Now in order to examine the relation between real desires, the self, and self-conceptions, as well as to articulate what justification there can be for speaking of self-alienation here, two sets of questions must be analyzed in relation to the example sketched above:

First, how can we understand the claim that alienating, inauthentic desires are those that are alien to the person and that nevertheless mysteriously compel her in certain ways? How exactly are we to understand the fact that one has such desires, but does not really (authentically) have them, that one supposedly—and paradoxically—at once has and does not have them?

Second, what kind of criteria can there be for establishing which of two conflicting desires is one's own in this strong sense? What authorizes desires? What makes them our own or alien? Bound up with this is the question of under what conditions a self-image or self-conception is appropriate or fitting.

I will discuss these questions by critically examining the views of Harry Frankfurt, whose theory of the person, as we will see, is relevant in various respects to reconstructing a theory of alienation.

(3) THE ALIEN CHARACTER OF ONE'S OWN DESIRES

The first problem—how one's own desires can be alien to oneself and how we should understand the distancing from desires that is bound up with this— can be investigated with the help of the model of the will developed by Harry Frankfurt in his paper "Freedom of the Will and the Concept of a Person."[10]

According to Frankfurt, the defining characteristic of persons resides in a specific structural feature of their wills, namely, that they can relate evaluatively to their own desires. Frankfurt elaborates this claim with the help of a hierarchical model: persons relate to their "first order desires" by means of "second order volitions." A second order volition is a desire to have or not to have a first order desire. So, for example, one can have a second order volition not to give in to one's first order desire for a cigarette. What makes someone a person is not merely having desires but being able to take a position with respect to them and to distance oneself from them.

Besides wanting and choosing and being moved *to do* this or that, men may also want to have (or not to have) certain desires and motives. They are capable of wanting to be different, in their preferences and purposes, from what they are.[11]

This conception of the person has several important implications for our problem:

First, not every desire that one has is *one's own* merely because one has it. It is a positive relation to one's desires—which Frankfurt later calls identification—that makes them one's own in a meaningful sense. Just as one can identify with one's desires in order to make them one's own, one can also be alien with respect to them (be alienated from them) insofar as one does not identify with them.

For Frankfurt the paradigm case of this kind of alienation is the unwilling addict. Someone who is an unwilling addict is dominated by a first order desire (to take drugs) that contradicts her own second order volition (not to take drugs or, more precisely, not to give in to her first order desire for drugs). This is a case, then, in which first and second order desires diverge. In a way that is structurally similar to our feminist, the unwilling addict is internally divided—at odds with herself—because she is driven by desires she does not *really* have, which is to say, by desires she does not have at the level of her second order volitions. She is, as it were, unable to turn her second order volition into effective action. Exactly like our feminist, she experiences her powerlessness in the face of the continued presence of an unwanted desire as alienating. In this sense, her continuing desire to take drugs is one she "does not really have" because she does not affirm it on the second order level. This enables us to explain nonparadoxically how desires can be at once alien and one's own: an alien desire is one that I in fact have—on the level of first order desires—but with which I cannot identify—on the level of second order volitions. Calling a person's desires *alien* does not mean that she does not *have* them; it means, rather, that she has not *made them her own*. Here, too, the situation is not one of merely conflicting desires (as discussed above in conflicts of ambivalence) but rather a rejection of a desire that one experiences as an alien element. Allying oneself with the second order volition, one has, so to speak, taken sides against the lower level desire. And the specifically alien character of these desires is not that one is not *aware of* them—the unwilling addict is aware of her desire for drugs all too well—but rather that one does not make them one's own. Understood in this way, a condition of self-alienation is one in which a person has failed in some way to bring her first and second order desires into agreement.[12]

Second, the account of the person that emerges from Frankfurt's discussion is of great interest for the problem of alienation. For Frankfurt the decisive criterion for the ascription of personhood is the capacity to develop second order volitions. What distinguishes us from other living beings is not the capacity for rationality (or language or other human characteristics) but the structure of our will. If being able to distance oneself from one's own desires—being able to take a critical or affirmative stance to them—is the distinctive characteristic of persons, it follows that the possibility of a divergence between what one factually *is* and one's *project* (for oneself) is constitutive of personhood. Put differently, a person is not determined by the "raw material" of her desires but rather by how she gives form to them (and along with them herself). Authentic desires, then, are not natural or given but rather higher-level, shaped desires; being oneself or being in agreement with oneself is not a natural or immediate condition but a higher-level process, the result of which Hegel refers to as the "purification of the drives."[13]

This becomes clear in the contrast between an unwilling addict and a "wanton." A wanton is an addict who will-lessly gives in to her addiction and allows herself to be determined exclusively by her first order desires without taking a position to them in the form of a second order volition. What distinguishes the wanton from the unwilling addict is not the result—both in the end succumb to their desire for drugs—but rather the fact that the former does not reflexively relate to her desires. For a wanton, who lacks the capacity to take a reflexive position to her desires—and, so, to evaluate her own desires— every desire that moves her is immediately *hers*. She does not distance herself from her desires and hence knows no internal division. For Frankfurt it is for precisely this reason that a wanton does not really have her own desires and is not really a person. She lacks the capacity to distance herself (for example, from her desires)—and therefore lacks the feature that for Frankfurt constitutes the core structure of personhood.[14] If the wanton, therefore, is *one with herself*, it is at the price of the essential feature of personhood. Conversely, it follows that real "being one" with one's desires is achieved only on the higher level of reflective will formation—precisely when first order and second order desires agree. The wanton, who does not give form to the raw material of her desires, is not, as one might think, herself to a particularly strong degree; she is not authentic in the sense of being immediate or spontaneous. Rather, she is not capable of real authenticity because she lacks personhood, a higher-level structure that first makes it possible for something to be authentic or inauthentic. One might say that because she does not have a relation to herself she also cannot be in agreement with herself. For that reason she is not alienated from herself, but *has lost* her self.

What follows from Frankfurt's account of the will for our example and our two problems? The model of second order volitions allows us to give a nonparadoxical answer to the first question as to how something can simultaneously be an alien desire and one's own—as to how H. can simultaneously have and not have her desires, can both desire and not desire something. Her second order volition to be emancipated is directed against her first order desire to behave coquettishly, like "a little girl."

How, though, does this help us to solve the second problem regarding the authorization and disowning of desires? The position that emerges from Frankfurt's account of the person with respect to the authority of desires at first appears to be simple: *real willing* is not found in lower-level, immediate desires; what one really wills, according to Frankfurt, is what higher-level, reflexive volitions aim at. In the case of H. this means that what is decisive for her as a person is not the giggling that she cannot hold back but rather the desires that lead to emancipated behavior. This answers the question of what makes one's desires one's own or of what *authorizes* them: the higher-level volition is the authority that makes a desire one's own; it has the power to define what is one's own and what is alien and what belongs to a person or does not. And not being alienated means bringing one's desires into agreement with this higher-level volition. This follows simply from the formal structure of the will as Frankfurt defines it.

(4) THE AUTHORIZATION OF DESIRES

It is not so simple, however, to solve the second problem raised by our example. For it is possible also to question—and it is even probable that H. sometimes asks herself this, too—whether the second order volition for emancipation that we have taken to be authoritative in fact corresponds to H., whether it is "in keeping" with who she is. Could it not be that the uncontrollable impulse against which she defends herself expresses something that she does not have at her command but that is nevertheless undeniably a part of her personality?

We see here that the question of the authenticity of desires—the question of what really belongs and corresponds to us—cannot be answered with the formal, hierarchical structure that Frankfurt's model offers us. An unsympathetic misogynist, for example, might claim that when H. distances herself from her giggling and her fantasy of protection this shows that her feminism is a masquerade. In truth, according to the claim, it is precisely when she wants to rely on a man's instinct to protect that she is "fully a woman" and when she giggles she is really herself. How, then, are we to decide in which position our young feminist is really herself and what corresponds to, or is more appropriate for, her? How are we to decide whether the tension between self-image and reality that reveals itself in H's conflict is due to an illusory self-image or simply to the difficulties that have to be overcome in the course of emancipation? What makes desires or impulses authentic? What authorizes them as really *mine*?

The difficulty before us is as follows: if one were to ask H. why she does not consider her desire for protection to be a real desire of hers, the answer "because I don't want to have it" would be just as inadequate as the assumption that this desire is her own simply because it is there. A "barren assurance" (Hegel) is not enough.[15] Everyone knows that one is not simply and immediately what one would like to be and that one does not merely decide to follow whatever desires one has. The fact that H. prefers to be emancipated is—without further elaboration—not decisive. It would be just as mistaken to think that she is herself precisely in the uncontrollable giggling that spontaneously breaks out in her despite the constraints her feminist self-image imposes on her. For if, to follow Frankfurt, it is constitutive of being a person that we can want to be different from what we are (precisely because we can desire that our desires be different from what they are), then authentic desires are always evaluated and formed. This means that the question of their authenticity is a question about the *appropriateness* of this evaluation. It is a question of which of our second order volitions are appropriate or on what basis we identify with some of our desires and distance ourselves from others. But this means it is a question of their *justification*. When H. distances herself from her disposition to behave coquettishly, she makes a certain claim of authority—and according to the considerations just discussed, she must do this. But what legitimizes this claim? How can she be sure that her second order volition is her real, authentic desire, the one that is "her own"? The question here is the following: what truly authorizes a second order volition? What makes it one's own?

Frankfurt's model does not allow us to answer this question. In order to come closer to an answer, it is necessary to examine more precisely the nature of the process of identification that underlies will formation, as Frankfurt has done in (among other places) his essay "Identification and Externality."[16] I will argue that even his reflections here (and in other essays) cannot solve the problem; yet examining the reasons for this failure will bring further dimensions of our problem into view.

IDENTIFYING WITH ONE'S OWN DESIRES

What exactly does it mean that we can *identify* with one desire but not with another? On what basis are desires alien or our own? What makes them belong to me or not? And to what do we appeal when we distance ourselves from expressions of emotion? Identifying with something means regarding it as belonging to oneself, as a part of oneself. Conversely, desires, feelings, impulses, and passions with which one cannot identify can be seen as *external*. Frankfurt addresses these issues in discussing a case of a violent outburst of temper. When one apologizes for such an outburst—"I don't know how that could have happened; somehow in this moment I wasn't myself"—one means to show that what was expressed in the outburst does not correspond to what one really feels, but one does this without denying that in that moment one was in fact under the sway of a feeling of rage.

One could understand this distancing such that—as in the case of the feminist—we do not identify with these impulses inasmuch as they cannot be integrated into our self-image: "we regard them as being in some manner incoherent with our preferred conception of ourselves, which we suppose captures what we are more truly than mere undistilled description."[17] It is obvious that this does not solve our problem. As we saw before, the fact that a certain behavior "does not fit" with us, that it does not agree with our preferred self-image, is not sufficient to explain its being external or alien. For, in the end, one's self-ideal can be just as alien or inappropriate as the impulse that does not fit with it.[18] Cannot persistent impulses that run counter to one's self-image even serve to uncover illusory aspects of it?

Even if one is not to be identified with all that spontaneously bursts out of oneself, one also cannot reasonably claim simply to be identical with what one *would like* to be. In any case, simply appealing to what one would like to be, which is nothing more than a declaration of intention, cannot do any justificatory work. The question whether an impulse or a desire is alien or one's own (is internal or external) cannot be determined solely by the person's attitude toward it. As Frankfurt himself says: "It is fundamentally misguided to suggest that a passion's externality is entailed by the person's disapproval of it, or that its internality is entailed by his approval."[19] If this were so, then instead of saying "That's not me" it would be more appropriate and less confusing to say "I don't want to be like that." This, however, would leave the phenomenon we are attempting to explain untouched. If calling something alien has any explanatory value, and the process of identification is to have a higher authority than that of mere wishing, we cannot simply make a desire, disposition, or feeling into something alien by declaring it to be such, just as a certain ideal image of ourselves cannot become *our authentic* identity by declaring it to be so.[20]

This is a question of interpretive sovereignty, of the conditions under which it can be said of a certain interpretation that it really captures who we *are*. The problem, which Frankfurt himself recognizes, is that the authority and status of even second order volitions can be called into question; they can themselves be alien or external: "Attitudes towards passions are as susceptible to externality as are passions themselves. This precludes explication of the concepts of internality and externality by appealing merely to the notion of orders of attitudes."[21] What we need, then, is a criterion for the internality or externality of desires that goes beyond merely subjective attitudes, a description of what it means to identify with something, a criterion according to which identification means more and is grounded in something other than merely a positive view or attitude. If identification is to *authorize*, it must involve something beyond a mere subjective wishing, something more compelling or decisive. And it is not easy to see where this is supposed to come from if what is at issue is the status of one's own desires, not an objective account of what one *ought* to desire or an appeal to what content "real desires" can have. (What is at issue in the case of H. is not whether it is right to be a feminist or not but whether she really is or wants to be one, whether she *corresponds to* or *fails to be herself* in what she does; it is not a question, then, of being in agreement with what is objectively good or right but of being in agreement with herself.) The problem of finding a criterion presents itself with such urgency because we also lack any essentialist criteria for being in agreement with oneself; that is, we cannot claim knowledge of a human essence that would make such a judgment possible.

BETWEEN DECISIONISM AND THE CORE MODEL

It is instructive to see why Frankfurt cannot solve this problem within the framework of his model. Frankfurt remains undecided between two opposing models of explanation, which, translated into Heideggerian terminology, one could characterize as *resoluteness* and *thrownness*. The first emphasizes the active elements of the identification process (making decisions), whereas the second emphasizes the passive (fateful) elements. Both models, however, run into difficulties: the first cannot justify the authority of desires; the second falls back into an essentialism that makes it impossible to capture aspirations for self-transformation and emancipation as they appear in our protagonist's initial feelings of alienation.

(a) Resoluteness. Sometimes (in the essay we have discussed) Frankfurt characterizes the process of identification in which one relates to one's own desires and passions as a kind of decision with a fundamentally active character: "it appears to be by making a particular kind of decision that the relation of the person to his passions is established."[22] However, Frankfurt has a difficult time characterizing the specific nature of this kind of decision such that it has the binding force and necessity it is supposed to have: "In any event, the nature of decision is very obscure."[23] There are good reasons for this difficulty. As explained above, the authorization of desires cannot be a merely voluntaristic process. The decision in question must be determined by something that — in a way that is indeed difficult to grasp — comes from a "deeper," "weightier," or better founded stance. A further point is also crucial for my way of posing the question: the resoluteness model cannot really explain the possibility of self-alienation as it appears in our case. If identification is conceived of decisionistically — if we make our desires our own by means of a simple decision — it is possible to fall into a condition of irresoluteness that threatens our identity. This dissolution of identity, however, is not equivalent to self-alienation. According to this model, every decision (as long as it is sufficiently firm) results in an "agreement with self" that cannot be further questioned or evaluated. The question "What do I really want?" is then no longer meaningful. It can refer only to the intensity or resoluteness with which one wills. The question "Am I really resolute?" cannot be meaningfully posed or, at best, only rhetorically. The problem of a desire's authority in the sense of its legitimacy has no place here. Applied to H., who questions her identification with her second order volition for emancipation: in the decisionist version of Frankfurt's position the problem cannot be posed such that there could be a correct answer to the question of what she should identify with. From this perspective the only problem is that she asks this question at all, that she is not sufficiently resolute in leaning toward one of her desires. She cannot fail to be herself in deciding for one side or the other; her identity is threatened merely by the fact that she is undecided.

What, then, authorizes the authenticator? According to this model, the authenticator authorizes itself. A desire is authorized by the fact that one has decided for it. It is this decisiveness that stops the threat of a regress of higher-level desires. This is where we hit bedrock and "the spade is turned." For the purpose of answering our question, however, the spade hits bedrock too soon. The authority of desires, as it arises for the problem of self-alienation, can be neither questioned nor justified on this model.

(b) Thrownness. The second version of Frankfurt's account, which I associate with the term *thrownness*, explains the problem of identification differently. Even if identification with one's own desires still has an essentially active character here, Frankfurt emphasizes the passive dimension—the intractability (*Unverfügbarkeit*) of one's deepest commitments and identifications—in speaking of "ideals" and "volitional necessities." The account of the person that Frankfurt develops over time in his writings attempts to do justice to the intuition that persons are characterized by a dimension of intractability. Persons are beings who relate to their desires by shaping them; their will "carves a path" for itself through the desires and needs that confront them on the level of their first order desires. At the same time, however—and Frankfurt emphasizes this more and more as his work develops— this dimension of the will should not be misunderstood voluntaristically. The possibility of relating evaluatively to one's own desires does not mean that a person's will is completely unbound or uncommitted: a person cannot will just anything; she is not free to redesign her will from scratch.

Frankfurt is concerned here with the will's limits, with the limits of what one is free to will. He even goes so far as to claim that it is precisely these limits that make up the character of a person: "The boundaries of his will define his shape as a person."[24] Conversely, someone who could will everything would have no identity as a person: "Since nothing is necessary to him, there is nothing that he can be said essentially to be."[25] Frankfurt gets to the heart of this topic with his concept of volitional necessities: there are things we cannot help but will and, on the other hand, things we cannot will. This in turn depends on what we are really committed to, what we really "care about," what is unalterably important to us: "Our essential natures, as individuals, are constituted, accordingly, by what we cannot help caring about. The necessities of love, and their relative order or intensity, define our volitional boundaries. They mark our volitional limits, and thus they delineate our shapes as persons."[26] Someone who was capable of everything, who had no volitional limits, would, according to Frankfurt, have no identity. By the same token, following one's volitional limits means being in agreement with oneself.

Once again Frankfurt elaborates his point with a striking example: the case of a woman who has decided to give her child up for adoption but who realizes in the decisive moment that she simply *cannot*.[27] It is significant that Frankfurt does not interpret this decision in what would seem to be the most natural way, as a victory of first order desires over second order volitions—as a triumph, for instance, of spontaneous emotion over reason. For if the woman cannot make the second order volition to give the child up "her own" even though she has it, then the force that prevents her from doing so in the decisive moment operates on a level that, according to Frankfurt's hierarchical model of desires, is higher than that of her second order desires.[28] Volitional necessities, then—sometimes Frankfurt speaks of ideals, but this can lead to misleading associations—are the authority that decides which second order volitions a person can embrace. Thus, one cannot follow just any second order volition, not because pure, unevaluated desires conflict with it, but because one *cannot* follow some second order volitions when considered from the higher authority of one's volitional necessities.

The crucial point here is the following: according to Frankfurt's account, the limits set by volitional necessities, although they place constraints on what we can do, do not constitute *compulsion* in the conventional sense. If, as has already been said earlier, these limits make up our identity, then they represent something like our deepest fundamental commitments, and these are ineluctable because they are what constitute us as a person. For Frankfurt, someone who questions or denies her volitional necessities betrays her identity. According to this view, the mother who wants to give up her child is threatened with the loss of her identity—and from this threat comes the necessity she cannot escape, the force she yields to when she finally decides to keep her child instead. This necessity, however—and this is Frankfurt's main point—is not compulsion since conforming to it means remaining in or coming into *agreement with oneself*.

In order to understand this account more precisely and to be able to evaluate its implications for the problem of the authorization of desires, I would like to summarize briefly the implications of Frankfurt's claims for the problem of alienation we have just examined:

1. On the one hand, self-alienation can be understood, with Frankfurt, as being "delivered over to" our own desires and longings. (We could call this

"first order" alienation.) These desires can take on an overwhelming power that presents itself as a "force alien to ourselves." This is not due to their irresistible character alone: "It is because we do not *identify* ourselves with them and do not want them to move us."[29]

2. These feelings and passions are the raw material that we relate to evaluatively or with respect to which we form our will.

Whether a person identifies himself with these passions, or whether they occur as alien forces that remain outside the boundaries of his volitional identity, depends upon what he himself wants his will to be.[30]

Hence the volitional attitudes on this level, in contrast to unformed *first-order desires*, can be shaped and structured and are wholly at our command: they are "entirely up to" us. A crucial implication of this account is the distinction between *power* and *authority*. Passions, according to this account, have *volitional power* but no *volitional authority*. Frankfurt elaborates: "In fact, the passions do not really make any *claims* on us at all. . . . Their effectiveness in moving us is entirely a matter of sheer brute force."[31]

3. What we do not freely have at our command, in contrast, is our *volitional nature*, the deep structure of our will itself. On the level of volitional necessities we are determined; here it is not "entirely up to us" how we determine our will; our volitional nature determines us. Yet our volitional necessities determine us in a different sense from that in which passions or first-order desires do: they compel us, one could say, not as *alien* powers but rather *to be ourselves*. They are not a brute force because they are not an external power but rather the power of what we really want or really *are*. "It is an element of his established volitional nature and hence of his identity as a person."[32] For this reason Frankfurt can claim in his adoption example that the mother experiences the limitation of her will—her "not being able to"—as a kind of liberation. Self-alienation, then, means acting against one's volitional nature. Hence the mother who wants to give up her child has formed a second order volition that conflicts with her volitional nature. If she acted in accordance with this second order volition, she would alienate herself—a "second order" alienation. This means that it would run counter to what constitutes her as a person; it would undermine the *conditions of her identity*. Self-alienation on this level consists, then, in not being in agreement with one's own person, with what constitutes oneself as a person.

The assumption of a volitional nature appears, then, to solve the problem of finding a criterion for authentic desires and their authorization that I have raised in conjunction with the theme of self-alienation. The standard for the appropriateness or inappropriateness of identifying with a desire is our volitional nature; our desires—our *real* desires—are authorized in relation to it. In what follows, however, I will explain why this, too, fails to solve the problem raised in our initial example.

CRITIQUE OF THE MODEL OF THROWNNESS

The talk of attempting to find out *who one is* already raises a suspicion, namely, that this concept takes us back, though in an interesting and methodologically sophisticated way, to an essentialist core model of the self of the type I criticized in the introduction (even if it is not vulnerable to some of the criticisms I raised there). In part 3, chapter 9 I will take a more detailed look at the account of the person or the conception of the self at issue here. For the moment I am interested only in the practical implications that follow from this solution and its model of the person.

Volitional necessities, as Frankfurt describes them, are not only what ineluctably makes up the identity of a person; they are also not subject to questioning or critique—they cannot and need not be justified. They are factical and contingent. According to Frankfurt's conception, asking the mother who cannot give up her child "Why can't you do it?" is no longer a meaningful question. She could answer only by saying "Because that's how it is." This is not due only to the emotional strength of her commitment; it is due to the structure of personhood as Frankfurt conceives of it. The intractable commitments in question are *conditions* of the possibility of her own identity; they are what first make her into a person, into someone who can develop further desires for this or that. If giving up the child undermines the mother's identity, it is no longer possible to ask meaningfully whether keeping the child would destroy her plans for the future. There would then be no basis for such plans. This has an important implication for our inquiry: there is no place from which it is possible to question or criticize the influences and formative processes that have constituted this identity. A volitional nature, though volitional, is in the end *nature* and therefore not something one has at one's command.

One could indeed suspect—contrary to Frankfurt's interpretation—that the mother in question (one assumes a situation in which her life with the child would be very difficult) is not in a position to let her second order volition determine her action because she is too deeply stuck within traditional ideas of maternal love. These ideas, one could say, prevent her from making a self-determined decision that accords with her plans for the future and her life plan more generally. There would, then, be two possibilities: a) a calling into question of oneself (of the person one has become); and b) a tension between identity and self-determination, which is precisely what Frankfurt excludes with his idea of being "liberated into oneself."

If Frankfurt's account excludes such questioning and critique, however, then *self-transformation* is no longer a possibility: every radical self-transformation manifested in an abrogation of one's volitional necessities would represent a loss of self. If we ask, from Frankfurt's perspective, how desires can become authentic, the answer can only be through a process of comparing and adjusting one's desires to one's volitional necessities. Asking oneself what one really wants means, then, becoming clear about one's volitional nature, which is accepted as "untractable"—as given and not subject to questioning or alteration. This has implications for the possibility of emancipation as well as for the emancipatory nature of the question concerning the authenticity of desires that interests me here.

It should now be clearer why Frankfurt's model is unsatisfactory as a solution to the problem of authorization: Frankfurt underestimates the role of reflection, justification, and evaluation that accompanies the process of identifying with one's own desires (or that at least must potentially be able to accompany it) if these desires are to be able to become one's own in a robust sense. In this respect his two apparently opposed models meet in a common point: what the idea of volitional necessities shares with the decisionistic model is that neither has room for a process of reflection and evaluation that could guide our taking a position in relation to our own desires. Either we make decisions about what we identify with "just because"—as an ultimately unjustified and unquestionable choice—or there is nothing at all for us to decide, and all we have to do is carry out what our identity as defined by our volitional necessities requires of us. In both cases—when Frankfurt understands the process of evaluating our own desires decisionistically and when he completely brackets out the element of decision—we do not really decide *ourselves*. The unintended implication of such a conception is that our desires remain in a certain respect "raw facts" (Charles Taylor), even in the case of higher level desires. Insofar as both ultimately take place without reflection, there is no question of "forming" one's own desires.[33] This, however, undermines Frankfurt's own intentions: if the process of interpreting and evaluating desires is bracketed out, it is difficult to distinguish the situation of the mother who *cannot* give up her child out of volitional necessity from that of the addict who *cannot* resist taking drugs, even though, as we have seen, it is precisely this difference that Frankfurt's account aims to explain. Although we find in Frankfurt the suggestion that (unreflected or first order) passions have volitional *power* but no volitional *authority*—that they exercise power over us but possess no authority—he has failed to make clear how precisely the authority of such claims can be justified (if the talk of authority is to have normative significance). To summarize my objection: although for Frankfurt desires become one's own only when one *appropriates* them as such, this process of appropriation or identification can be properly understood only if we are able to distinguish between appropriate and inappropriate identifications, that is, between successful and failed processes of appropriation. In the following section I will again take up the problem of identifying with one's own desires with a view toward its relevance for understanding how processes of emancipation are possible.

(5) BEING ONESELF AND EMANCIPATION

The emancipatory character of questioning the authenticity of desires (or of suspecting them to be inauthentic) is due to the fact that, in inquiring into the appropriateness of given desires and attitudes, one presupposes the possibility of criticizing them and thereby of calling oneself, as one is and has become, into question: one can want to become other than one is. Critically examining our desires and dispositions—the doubt "Does this impulse, this desire *really belong to me?*"—can make it possible to make our life more decisively our own and to "move more freely" within it. Applied to Frankfurt's adoption example, the question of whether the mother who cannot give up her child has allowed herself to be trapped in patterns of socialization that make her unfree is part of such critical examination. H.'s case, too, has this general structure. Whereas Frankfurt would be concerned only with determining which of her two sets of desires corresponded to her volitional nature—is she "fully a woman" or a feminist?—for H. herself the problem poses itself differently: she aspires, in cases of doubt, to question critically even her volitional nature. For Frankfurt she would be alienated from herself if, acting contrary to her volitional nature, she attempted to be something other than what she "is"— independent, perhaps—while still longing to be protected, whereas H. would consider herself to be alienated precisely if she "blindly" followed this nature.

And whereas for Frankfurt she would be *authentically* herself only if she were free of tension and without ambivalence, the alternative view would hold that the struggle against her deepest attachments and formative influences cannot take place without such tensions. According to the one position, such an attempt at emancipation is a condition of not being alienated; according to the other, it is a threat to the unity of the self.

THE DILEMMA OF EMANCIPATION

Now it may be that in certain situations one would do well to recognize that a particular way of life simply does not correspond to who one is; and, of course, it could in principle be the case that the standards H. sets for herself are too demanding. On the other hand, would we not be suspicious if H. were suddenly to reveal to us that the whole story of emancipation was nonsense and was never right for her—that, having recently fallen in love, she was happy to have finally embraced a feminine role? If someone like H., who, because she "could not do otherwise," ended up in a form of life in which she were protected by her husband while assuming a subordinate position in relation to him, would she not be just as problematic (and a candidate for alienation) as someone who was in constant tension with her aspirations?

We can see the problem that the demand for emancipation is faced with: where is the criterion to come from that enables us to decide which of these two sides is more appropriate to who she is, or which part of herself is really her?

An unevaluated, merely factual "agreement with oneself" can obviously not be the criterion we are looking for. Are not the most preposterous conversions routinely accompanied by a claim to have finally found oneself? And does not resignation also lead to a kind of agreement with oneself? If H. were to adopt a traditionally feminine way of life, one would have to wonder whether doing so was an act of resignation in which she *gave up* rather than *found* herself. By the same token, however, if she were to succeed in overcoming her opposing impulses, one could ask whether she was committing herself to too rigid a self-ideal, one that required her to deny too many parts of herself—possibly resulting in a personality that was completely rigid in its self-control. Formulated somewhat paradoxically, the suspicion is that both might be cases in which being in agreement with oneself is achieved at the price of a loss of self and where her self-conception as a whole would be false, manipulated, inappropriate, or illusory.

It is common enough that we question ourselves and others in this way, and not doing so would be costly. But what can such a doubt about one's own identity—an "objection" to oneself—be based on if we lack a secure standpoint that could reveal one's *true self*, even on the model of a volitional nature? How, then, is emancipation, as an "emancipation from alien powers" that we are ourselves, to be conceived? Here the dilemma of emancipation becomes clear: every attempt to pose such questions and to justify this kind of doubt is like trying to pull the carpet out from under oneself.

The proposal I want to make to solve this dilemma can be formulated as follows: emancipation and the self-critique bound up with it must be understood as a *free-floating enterprise*—an undertaking that cannot be grounded in advance but only in the course of the process itself, a process in which one cannot appeal to something that one already is and in which one can at the same time "come to oneself." This means that emancipation must be conceived of as "rebuilding on the high sea"[34]—where a critique of alienation is the driving force and means of such a rebuilding. (And here, too, as suggested in part 1, what is important is the *how* and not the *what* of this process.)

In what follows I attempt to describe the processes of self-alienation and emancipation when understood in this sense. In so doing, I will approach the problem gradually, "from the outside," that is, from the negative conditions of authentic will formation (as proposed by John Christman and Raymond Geuss). (Although in the end we will see that even these conditions rely on a positive vision of what it is to be oneself.) In the next step I will then elaborate my proposal (in line with the idea of emancipation sketched previously) that authentic "being oneself" is to be understood as a mode of being freely accessible to oneself.

MANIPULATION AND CONSTRAINT

Under what conditions must the process of will formation have taken place if it is to count as my own will? Two such conditions are:

First, the formation of my desires must not have been due to *manipulation*. We do not recognize desires as our own if we have reason to believe that they came about through manipulation. Desires can be authentically my own only if I was free in their formation and if they came about without the manipulation of others. H., for example, might conjecture—or we could conjecture about her—that her behavior is a product of manipulative conditioning, a consequence of her gender-specific socialization. Thus, to follow a suggestion of John Christman,[35] we must take into account the history of the development of a trait or the genesis of a desire—and thereby rule out manipulation—in order to judge the authenticity of desires.

Second, as Raymond Geuss emphasizes in his reflections on the problem of true interests, will formation must take place under conditions in which the *alternatives* at my disposal are alternatives I can really want to choose among. Following Geuss's account of the "optimal conditions" of choice,[36] we can say that what I really want cannot be the result of a choice between alternatives that are inappropriately constrained. Something will count, then, as an authentic desire only if it emerges from a choice among acceptable alternatives. Applied to H.'s case, the alternative between protection and emancipation that H. sees herself faced with would, if this description is correct, be unacceptable. Neither of the two possibilities—emancipation without protection and protection without emancipation—can rationally be what she really wants. If it should turn out, then, that in a patriarchically organized society women were systematically confronted with the choice between such alternatives, then in important domains—at least for women—the conditions for forming authentic desires would be lacking.

The exclusion of manipulation and the idea of optimal conditions or acceptable alternatives are clearly two basic conditions that must be satisfied. But they help to clarify only the preconditions of authentic will formation. And the difficulties with these suggestions are obvious. Given that one is always influenced by one's environment—is always in some way socialized—when is the boundary of manipulation crossed? And given that alternatives are always constrained, what constitutes sufficient and acceptable alternatives?

What exactly constitutes unacceptable manipulation if one assumes that the formation of desires and dispositions is always shaped by outside influences and that socialization necessarily involves being influenced by others? Apart from the drastic but hardly plausible cases of brainwashing that are frequently discussed, the manipulation condition does not go far enough as long as we cannot distinguish between manipulative and nonmanipulative influences. It pushes back the question of what is *one's* own and what is *alien* without answering it. In our debate, for example, both sides could argue that H. is dominated by alien influences and manipulation: the antifeminist would point to indoctrination by feminist "ideology"; the feminist, in contrast, would trace back the conceptions of love and family that she cannot shake loose to a deep-seated conditioning by a patriarchal environment and its gender-specific socialization, elements she must liberate herself from in order to become herself. While it is correct that the genesis of desires should be taken into account in judging their authenticity, the absence of alien influences is by itself inadequate as the sole criterion of what counts as a successful genesis. Here we run into a problem we already encountered in discussing the appropriation of roles: to what extent are formative influences *alien* if *one is constituted* by precisely such influences? Just as in the case of roles it made no sense to presuppose a pure self lying underneath or behind its roles, it makes no sense, in the case of will formation, to assume that there are pure desires that exist prior to all social influence. As for the case of appropriating roles, criteria must be developed that enable us to distinguish between what is one's own and what is alien other than by appealing to something "unspoiled" or uninfluenced by others.

If, on the other hand, as Raymond Geuss formulates it, "agents' 'real' interests are the interests they would have formed in 'optimal' (i.e., beneficent) conditions,"[37] and if these optimally favorable circumstances are spelled out (as Geuss does in his discussion of true interests) in terms of "perfect knowledge and freedom,"[38] then this idea, if it is to refer to more than the absence of external obstacles, also calls for an elaboration of the conditions under which perfect knowledge is available and can be acted on in perfect freedom. Here, too, substantial assumptions come into play that are more difficult to articulate the more subtle the constraints that must be taken into account. (This is easy in the case of the considerations that Geuss first introduces—hunger and extreme deprivation—but it is more difficult when what is at issue are possibilities for development, as is the case in my emancipation example.)

(6) BEING ONESELF AS SELF-ACCESSIBILITY

What we need is a positive description of what it means not to be determined in what one wills by alien powers. I will sketch out a proposal for providing such a description, which, on the one hand, does not rely on an independent criterion—an Archimedean point that defines the true self—and, on the other hand, goes beyond a merely factual "agreement with oneself." This proposal aims to broaden—or, better, to refine—the idea of a coherent self-conception into one of a self-conception that is both *coherent* and *appropriate or fitting*. Appropriateness in turn is to be determined by the criterion of *self-accessibility* (as revealed in one's practical engagement) and of *having oneself at one's command*: one is oneself when one is accessible to oneself and can "move freely" in what one does: so understood, being oneself is not a state but a process; it is not something one *is* but a way of taking part in what one *does*. In accordance with this, the attempt to identify alien desires and to replace these alien "intruders" with desires that are one's own (as defined by the idea of emancipation I have discussed) is a free-floating, self-balancing developmental process.

EVALUATED COHERENCE AND APPROPRIATE SELF-CONCEPTIONS

This again leads us back to our example: the source of the dilemma was the difficulty of finding a criterion for determining which of H.'s desires and behaviors correspond to who she is, which of her desires are her *own* and which "intrude" into her personality as *alien* elements.

Given the significance of self-conceptions for the problems we are considering, an obvious possibility for defining what is alien would be to appeal to a self-conception's *internal coherence*. This relocates, as it were, the question at issue: it is no longer a question of whether what I want and do really *fits me* but whether the various things I want and do—the things I identify with and that matter to me—*fit together with one another*. Instead of looking for a criterion within ourselves that would enable us to determine what really belongs to us, we are now asking whether a person is consistent or coherent in her expressions and activities, whether she is able to bring the diverse parts of her personality into relation with one another and to integrate them. On this criterion, whether a desire, a passion, or an impulse "fits" us cannot be decided by examining an individual desire but only by looking at how our diverse desires "hang together."

Self-conceptions become important here for various reasons. I understand a self-conception, provisionally, as something that establishes connections among our attitudes and desires and gives them a certain order. These connections are essentially *interpretive*. Neither individual desires nor the connections among them are independent of interpretation or objectively given: whether Gisela Elsner's predilection for luxury consumer goods fits with her socialist views, or H.'s giggling with her feminism, is a question of interpretation and self-interpretation. It is not traits and desires themselves that must fit together but a person's interpretations of them. What is important is whether I can integrate what I want into the conception I have of myself as a person. Appropriating or identifying with one's desires essentially means weaving them into a coherent interpretation. Being internally coherent, then, consists in having, developing, and pursuing desires and plans that can be integrated into a *coherent self-conception.*

Now it is easy to see that the idea of coherence alone is not sufficient to answer our question: delusions can also be internally coherent! We must therefore be concerned not only with the internal coherence of our self-interpretations but also with their appropriateness. What, though, makes a self-conception *appropriate or fitting?* In order to pursue this question, it is first necessary to further elaborate the idea of a self-conception.

Having a self-conception or *conceiving of oneself as something* involves taking a stance toward oneself and one's life—understanding or interpreting oneself in a certain way—that is distinctive of the type of being we are and is constitutively bound up with the way we lead our lives as persons. (It is for this reason that Charles Taylor speaks of the human being as a self-interpreting animal.)[39]

Self-conceptions involve two elements. First, we not only do and want particular things; we also relate to the fact that we do and want them and in doing so we *understand* ourselves *as* someone who does and wants those things. Second, having a self-conception means establishing *connections* among these individual elements. Taken together, this means that a self-conception is based on more than merely an inventory of objectively given traits and actions; it is an internal principle of organization, an attempt to make our desires and actions "hang together" and thereby give them *meaning.* Loosely formulated, developing a self-conception means "making sense of" oneself. In chapter 9 I will return to the difficult questions bound up with this, such as how we are to picture this process and how much coherence a successful relation to oneself requires. Here I only want briefly to anticipate a misunderstanding: self-conceptions should not be taken to refer exclusively to sophisticated, higher-order interpretations of the sort a person has of herself when, for example, she understands herself as a "feminist" or "leftist." Self-conceptions need not always be fully explicit; they can sometimes inform what we do without being expressly articulated. And they are not always fully coherent from the start; for our purposes it is enough to say that they are oriented toward coherence.

It is also important that a self-conception has a dual character: it is at once an *interpretation* and a *project*—a self-interpretation as well as a projecting of oneself. In my self-conception I understand myself as the person I am and at the same time I project—or fashion—myself as the person I want to be. Neither involves merely an objective inventory of facts.

As an *interpretation* of what constitutes us, the self-conception we develop starts with a given material, the facts of our life history. On the basis of this we attempt to understand who we are and what constitutes us. At the same time, this material is chosen, interpreted, and structured. There is no "naked truth" here; the various aspects of our lives are meaningful only if we make them so. It might, for example, be true of someone, objectively considered, that he comes from a "good family," has enjoyed the best of educations, is a connoisseur of art and wine, and has had asthma since early childhood. But this does not mean that all these traits automatically belong to his self-conception. He could take his asthma as the basis for an intense identification with Marcel Proust and understand his chronic suffering and the distance from the world it involves as an essential aspect of his personality or he could, surprised each time he has a new attack of shortness of breath, barely perceive it as an annoyance and repress its implications. Even his solid bourgeois background need not become the object of a positive or negative identification (pride or shame); coming from a particular kind of family can also be more or less significant for one's self-conception.

As a *project*, on the other hand, a self-conception defines who one would like to be or what one thinks one ought to be. If I understand myself as a feminist or as someone who looks after her friends, I not only interpret who I *am*; I also ask myself who I *want to be* and I orient my future actions and desires toward conduct that fits this conception. There also belongs to this an implicit value orientation—that I find it correct to orient myself in this direction. In this respect a self-conception is closely related to a self- or ego-ideal that expresses "what is important for me in life, what kind of human being I would like to be, what I would like to strive to be."[40] It seems clear that both components, interpretation and project, are interrelated. Thus my project for myself will more or less shape my self-interpretation; conversely, my project for myself can be the result of a particular self-interpretation: I become a feminist because I interpret certain of my life experiences in a particular way; I interpret them in that way because I am a feminist. And, of course, both interpretation and project shape what one is. As Jonathan Glover notes: "the way we think of ourselves helps to shape what we are like."[41] This tension, between interpreting and projecting what one is, is essential to the idea of a self-conception. One might call this the reconstructive-constructive or the hermeneutic-creative character of self-conceptions.[42]

Now the following implications of this account are of interest for our question concerning the distinction between appropriate and inappropriate self-conceptions: what constitutes someone as a person does not lie before or behind her self-conception but is interwoven with it. Identity is not an objective fact beyond interpretation. This accentuates our problem. If everything is interpretation, and if interpretation always creates its object, how can we distinguish correct from false interpretations? How is it possible to distinguish self-conceptions that correspond to who we are from those that do not? When does someone understand herself correctly or incorrectly? How can a self-conception, as I have just described it, be false, illusory, distorted, or inappropriate?

My proposal for answering these questions rests on the following assumption: self-conceptions neither merely reflect objective facts, nor are they mere inventions. Self-conceptions have foundations to which they can do justice in varying degrees. It could be, for example, that someone understands himself incorrectly if he denies the role that asthma has had since early childhood for his relation to himself and to the world, or that he understands himself incorrectly if, under the influence of a particular subculture, he denies his connection to bourgeois values and forms of life. Our suspicion that such a person understands himself incorrectly and that his self-image is illusory does not rest only on the fact that we know he actually had a particular sickness or family background; it is typically also based on what we take to be signs that his background is of greater significance than he thinks it is. We notice, for example, that some of his behavior contradicts his self-conception or, more generally, that it is difficult for him to act in accordance with the image he has made of himself.

Here there are parallels to the general problem of interpretation: an interpretation—including that of a text or a work of art—is powerful when, among other things, it can bring together a large number of significant details and establish connections among them. It is the more compelling the less it is forced to exclude facts that do not sit well with it. Naturally, these are not hard and fast criteria; in the end, the question whether certain aspects of an interpretation run counter to it is also a question of interpretation. And this is an unending process: when there is doubt, an interpretation is valid so long as it is not replaced by a more compelling one.

My thesis, then, is as follows: in the theoretical realm (or when we observe things) an interpretation that does not fit means that we do not interpret things appropriately, we do not *understand* them. If this is carried over to the domain of practical relations to self and self-conceptions, an interpretation that does not fit means that something "stands in their way," that the practical relations to self and world that correspond to them or by which they are guided are marked by *functional disturbances* that are expressed in various forms of distortions and inhibitions of action. Whether one's self-conception and the way of leading one's life that follows from it fail to fit with who one is depends on whether there are practical inhibitions and contradictions in what one does and in how one understands oneself in doing it.

Whereas an inappropriate interpretation of a picture or a text means that we are unable to *understand* it sufficiently,[43] having an inadequate self-conception means that it does not "work" or *function*: we cannot live with it or act within it. In both cases there are, as mentioned above, only "soft" criteria. Yet these criteria are so frequently applied and appear so self-evident that it is difficult for us to imagine our relations to world and self without these (mostly implicit) practices of judging and understanding.

What follows from this for my initial question concerning the authenticity of desires is that authentic desires are those that can be fit into an appropriate conception of oneself, where appropriateness is determined by whether that conception "works" or functions.[44]

SELF-ACCESSIBILITY AND THE INHIBITION OF ACTIONS

What does it mean, though, that a self-conception does not "function"? I would like to elaborate this idea as follows: the crucial point is whether my self-image, my self-conception, and the desires and projects bound up with it result in my being or remaining *accessible* to myself in them and in being able to act freely on the basis of them. At issue, then, is a kind of inner mobility and self-accessibility.

If H., for example, adapts herself to the traditional role of a woman, is she not forced to do so at the price of closing off essential parts of her personality, not only parts of her history and her social surroundings but also some of her fundamental desires and longings? But a closing off of this kind means that a part "of herself" (as we can now say without being too sensational) is not accessible, that she is forced to avoid certain things and is unable to integrate them, that there will be taboos and "no-go areas" in leading her life that she cannot integrate into her self-conception. There will then typically be strategies of avoidance and rigidification—a familiar phenomenon.

That functional disturbances are to be conceived of as disturbances of accessibility to oneself and to the world is still a very vague and unexplained claim. I propose to elaborate it (tentatively and incompletely) by listing some symptoms of such disturbances:

※ *Rigidity* in relation to oneself can, for example, be identified as one such functional disturbance. Here one is not accessible to oneself insofar as one rigidly holds to previously made decisions and is thereby unable to integrate opposing impulses. As Martin Löw-Beer has shown,[45] a certain lack of contact with oneself can also be seen in the moralistic traits that characterize rigid personalities. The way in which rigid personalities hold on to things that have outlived themselves or to things they are unable to live out gives rise to an objectifying attitude toward themselves that can be described as a lack of vitality and an inability to take part in their own lives. Löw-Beer articulates this point in his striking example of a man who believes that he must love a woman because she meets certain criteria he considers important. It is not only that these criteria are too impersonal; the stance he takes to himself when demanding this of himself is an objectifying one, not one appropriate to leading a life. Similarly, it could also turn out (contrary to the interpretation I set out previously) that it is rigidity that hinders H. from giving in to her "feminine" impulses.

※ Very generally one can consider *rigidity*—rigidly holding on to previously established norms and self-images without being able to adapt them to new situations—to be a disturbance of self-accessibility, insofar as it means closing oneself off from new experiences and conflicting emotions. In line with this suggestion, Richard Sennett characterizes a "purified identity" as a pathology. The search for too much coherence that does not allow itself to be troubled by anything that conflicts with it is, then, just as problematic as too much discontinuity: "the enterprise involved is an attempt to build an image or identity that coheres, is unified, and filters out threats in social experience."[46] An adequate self-conception must be open to different outcomes and experiences; an inadequate self-conception is not.

※ While inaccessibility to oneself means being closed off to experiences, it is also characterized by an inaccessibility to reasons. A person who is not accessible to herself cannot translate rational insights about herself or her life into action. The asthmatic, for example, who denies his sickness because he cannot integrate it into his self-image does not succeed in acting on the entirely available intellectual insight that he needs medical care. A self-conception in which one was accessible to oneself, in contrast, would not block insights of this type.

※ Similar to this is the phenomenon of not having access to one's emotions or of having inappropriate emotional reactions. Part of self-accessibility is reacting in emotionally appropriate ways—for example, mourning in the case of illness and loss[47]—and being able to relate to these reactions. An appropriate self-conception is able to integrate such reactions; an inappropriate one suppresses them. Illusory self-images, for example, are often those that suppress experiences of illness or failure. Phenomena of self-deception also belong to this set of problems. Presumably someone who is constantly self-deceived will be inaccessible to herself, since she must protect herself from evidence that might help correct her self-deception.

Hence self-accessibility in general can be characterized as a complex cognitive and emotional state that includes being sufficiently familiar with oneself to be able to perceive one's own needs, to interpret them, and to draw practical consequences from them. Our true self, then, is not merely one that is acquired in the absence of compulsion; it is, formulated positively, a self-relation in which we can move freely and in which we are accessible to ourselves.

In relation to the topics discussed in this chapter, self-alienation means not being able to move freely in one's life, being inaccessible to oneself in what one wants and does. It includes a form of internal division and estrangement from one's own desires that consists in a limitation of one's power to have oneself at one's command in all that power's complex manifestations. Conversely, overcoming self-alienation occurs through a gradual recovery of self-accessibility, without this requiring the Archimedean point of the true self that defines one's real needs. Thus the form of the question H. must pose to herself is not "What do I really want?" but rather "What am I actually doing in what I already do, and *how* does that happen?" It would then be an unforced, transparent relation to her desires and behavior and an openness in dealing with them that allowed us to determine her unalienated or "true" desires.

THE NORMATIVE STATUS OF ALIENATION CRITIQUE

I conclude with a question that also emerged in each of our earlier chapters: why is self-alienation problematic? What normative standard justifies regarding a condition of internal division with respect to one's own desires, as I have described it here, as problematic? In the case of internal division the immanent character of such a standard is obvious: can I will that my will not be my own or the desires I pursue not be mine? Here, with the help of Tugendhat's terminology, introduced previously, one can speak of a hindrance in the well-functioning of volition itself. From what standpoint, though, can we identify a well-functioning will or hindrances to the same?

If individuals are not immediately given to themselves, they are also, to a certain extent, capable of being deceived about themselves; they can understand themselves falsely. As external observers, for example, we can draw their attention to contradictions between the desires they express and particular behaviors that run counter to those desires. As a first step, one can claim that in uncovering such contradictions the subject has no privileged access to itself and that for this reason one can criticize individuals from the outside in a way that remains immanent.[48] As with a psychoanalyst's interpretations, interpretation from the outside and self-interpretation must agree if an interpretation is to claim validity. Even such agreement, however, is no final guarantee against shared deceptions. Here, too, there is no Archimedean point, although this does not imply that interpretation and reflection are simply arbitrary and subject to no constraints.

COMPLEXITY AND COHERENCE

In concluding I would like to discuss one more objection: is my model's idea of having oneself at one's command, as developed in relation to the problem of internal division, also too robust, and does the view I have sketched invoke too harmonious a conception of coherence? Do not alien desires and parts of ourselves—the existence of different, not always compatible, parts of ourselves that we do not have at our command—belong just as much to our "own life" as those constitutive, intractable aspects of ourselves outside our command (cf. chapter 5)? Are not inconsistencies and contradictions part of the complexity of persons, without which we would not be ourselves and which we therefore cannot (and ought not to want to) banish from our lives? I will return to these questions in connection with the postmodern critique of the subject in part 3. For now I will note only briefly: first, whether certain experiences and parts of ourselves are part of our lives depends on how we can integrate these initially alien elements at a deeper level. In order to count as our experiences (however disconcerting), there must be someone who can have these experiences. Perhaps this capacity for integration must even be all the stronger the more one comes into contact with experiences of "otherness." What is required, then, is not coherence in the sense of harmony or a seamlessly unified meaning of life but a capacity, underlying one's discontinuities, for relating to what one feels and does.

Second, self-accessibility and the functional capacity of one's own will are open criteria the nonfulfillment of which manifests itself in practical conflicts or, more precisely, functional deficits. Self-accessibility, then, is a question of degrees, and it can manifest itself and be attained only in dealing with such conflicts. The problem arises because, and to the extent that, H.'s internal division hinders her in doing what she really wants, in being able to move freely in her life. What an unalienated life requires, then, is not that all ambivalences, disunities, or disharmonies in a person be completely sorted out; it requires instead the capacity to be able to react to such problems—or inhibitions of functioning—when they appear. In cases of doubt that can also mean—contrary to the accusation that the unalienated self is too harmonious—first making them into conflicts.

Third, self-accessibility, or having oneself at one's command, as our distinguishing it from rigidity has shown, does not mean having "everything under control" or keeping to a strict model of who one is at any cost. Perhaps one should characterize the capacity in question in a more favorable way: it is about being familiar and able to deal with oneself.

8

"AS IF THROUGH A WALL OF GLASS": INDIFFERENCE AND SELF-ALIENATION

I, say I. Unbelieving.

—SAMUEL BECKETT, THE UNNAMABLE

THIS CHAPTER IS ABOUT INDIFFERENCE as a kind of self-alienation and loss of self—hence about phenomena of alienation in which one perceives the entire world as alien and indifferent, in which one loses one's relation to the world and "withdraws one's feelers" from it. To what extent, though, is indifference alienation, if the capacity to distance oneself from certain involvements in the world can also be understood as freedom? At issue here is the relation between self and world as well as the thesis that it is not possible to understand *self-realization* outside a successful relation to the world. Again, I organize my discussion around (1) an example that I then (2) interpret with an eye to the concept of self-alienation. In doing so I (3) distinguish two aspects of alienation: detachment from one's practical involvement in the world and the loss of identification. Then, with the help of ideas from Harry Frankfurt and Hegel, I (4) elaborate the problem of indifference—the ambivalence between freedom and loss of self—in order, finally, (5) to be able to determine the relation between freedom, indifference, and alienation.

(1) THE INDIFFERENT MAN

The character of Perlmann in Pascal Mercier's novel *Perlmann's Silence* illustrates a case of self-alienation as indifference. Perlmann is a once ambitious and still generally respected professor of linguistics, who—in Mercier's description—has "lost his faith in the importance of academic work" and who ever since looks "upon academic work as if through a wall of glass."[1] The previously ambitious academic now reacts with indifference to critiques of his work. As if under "a local anesthetic,"[2] he experiences the positions he once defended as though they were no longer his; his identification with them has dissolved. This condition of complete indifference, not only to his discipline but also to the entire way of life bound up with it, at first sets in for him almost unnoticed and without apparent reason. It is not, for instance, because his interest in linguistics has been replaced by other beliefs or passions. Nor is the distance that becomes increasingly noticeable during the three-week conference he has organized due to a critical view he has of the factory-like nature of contemporary academia. Perlmann is not a rebel. The opposite seems rather to be the case: once he has distanced himself, everything that was meaningful to him before appears as mere busywork. The world as a whole has submerged—without apparent cause—into the haze of indifference and become unreal. The projects he previously participated in with interest have suddenly receded into a distant region. It is not only, though, that the world becomes alien to him; in this condition he also becomes alien to himself. One has the impression that with the fading of the world Perlmann himself becomes diffuse and unreal; having become a "man without opinions," his own identity becomes strangely ephemeral.

(2) DEMARCATING THE PHENOMENON AND DEFINING ITS CHARACTERISTICS

Several features of this example suggest that Perlmann's situation can be understood as a case of self-alienation.[3]

1. The course of events described is not merely the manifestation of a process of *self-transformation* and the displacement of interests that accompanies it. There is at first nothing else that occupies the center of Perlmann's attention in place of his work. What occurs is more radical: his interest in the world in general dissolves. In the one case, metaphorically speaking, the spotlight of interest moves from one place to another, whereas here the spotlight fades altogether. In contrast to a change of orientations, no new points of reference come on the scene to replace the old ones; no new interests and projects replace the earlier ones. As difficult as it might be in the case of a radical

transformation to balance out the discontinuity between an earlier and a later self, this problem differs from a condition of radical indifference in that in the former one is still *entangled* in, or tied into, the world, whereas in the case of indifference one seems to be completely disconnected from it. Thus the problem to be understood in what follows is not discontinuity but *radical detachment* (and the problem of meaninglessness that accompanies it).[4]

2. Why, though, is Perlmann's indifference alienation? The metaphor of being under local anesthesia makes it clear that Perlmann must have previously understood his work and position as part of himself: he *identified* with it. Part of the process described here is that things he previously understood as integral parts of himself suddenly appear to him external and distant. (One could characterize this process in psychoanalytic terms as a withdrawal of libidinal cathexis.) We can recognize here the feature of processes of alienation discussed previously: that we can be alienated only from things we were previously connected to. Of course, one can always separate oneself from earlier interests and projects. They do not necessarily remain a (now "anesthetized") part of myself simply because I once had them. What must be explained (in accordance with the structural characteristics of alienation set out in chapter 3) is to what extent in this case, too, detachment still represents a *relation*.

3. Why is this a case of *self*-alienation and not one of alienation from the world? Is it not the (external) world that has become alien to Perlmann? If he cuts himself off from an external world he has become indifferent to and withdraws *into himself*, why should he become alienated from himself in doing so? Discussing Perlmann's crisis as a case of self-alienation, and hence as a problem he has not merely with the *world* but with *himself*, rests on a weighty assumption: his indifference in relation to the world has consequences for his relation to himself. If what he has done, what was important to him, and what he identified with have become alien and inaccessible to him, then, so my interpretation, he becomes alien *to himself* to the extent to which the *external* world becomes alien to him (and to which for that reason he can no longer relate). The condition of indifference affects a person's relation to herself along with her relation to the world. This leads to a conjecture that I will explore further in what follows: insofar as our projects and interests connect us to the world, our relation to them is what first allows us to determine ourselves *as something*. The fact that we, in a certain respect, first become "real" through these relations implies a concept of *self-realization* whose distinctive feature is that it conceives of self-realization not in terms of an individual's inner growth or "coming to oneself" but as a certain kind of relation to, engagement with,

or involvement in the world. According to this view, one can secure an identity for oneself only via a "detour through the world"; one can *realize* oneself only by engaging with the world. (I take up this topic again in chapter 10 in my discussion of romantic inwardness.) In that case, self-alienation must be understandable as alienation from the world and, conversely, alienation from the world (from meaningful others and from the other in general) must manifest itself as self-alienation.

(3) INTERPRETATIONS: THE LOSS OF RELATIONS AND IDENTIFICATION

In the following sections I will discuss two interpretations of alienation: as a loss of relations (a loss of involvement in the world) and a loss of identification (a loss of affective attachments to the world). Although these two aspects of alienation are closely related, they illuminate different aspects of the problem.

INDIFFERENCE AS A RADICAL LOSS OF RELATIONS

How precisely are we to understand radically alienating detachment as a phenomenon of alienation? How are we to imagine the termination of involvement in the world we have been describing? Obviously not as a detachment from this or that particular thing: in a strange way Perlmann does not seem to be alienated from anything specific, but rather from the world in general. This peculiar condition of complete disengagement manifests itself, for example, in his astonishment at the fact that he can no longer seem to manage to have "views," even though it is part of his profession to take positions on theoretical issues. "What had it been like when he still had opinions? Where had they come from? And why had the source dried up? *Can you decide to believe something? Or do opinions just happen to you?*"[5] Someone who asks such questions has not grown uncertain merely about one position or another; he has lost the foundation that enables him to develop positions at all. In a certain sense he now asks his questions "from nowhere." He has "catapulted himself" out of the processes and relations he was once part of. Even Perlmann's astonishment points to a process of alienation. Is it not generally the case that one simply *has* opinions? This is not to say that we do not form, refine, and revise opinions—that we do not sometimes develop our positions as a result of prolonged learning processes. Yet it is usually not the case that we begin from a condition in which we have no opinions in order then to enter a space where we have them. Forming opinions is a process of transformation, something that is "carried out" and in the course of which new opinions develop out of existing ones, new information is added to old, and a new constellation of opinions is formed. Thus already the question *where* opinions *come from*—formulated this abstractly—points to a problem. It is difficult to see how someone who asks this question could ever come to have opinions. We can also formulate the problem more generally: what Mercier here calls opinions are the fundamental orientations and stances by means of which one finds one's way in the world and creates order for oneself out of it. We acquire these orientations, however, only in "finding our way," only by actually doing it. If we ask ourselves what we *ought* to do, we are already in the middle of doing something; if we are uncertain what opinion we should have about something, we already have an opinion, however diffuse, and we are asking about its correctness.

THE VIEW FROM NOWHERE

The phenomenon of losing one's points of reference can be understood, following Thomas Nagel, as taking the perspective of the "view from nowhere," a view that transcends one's own involvements in the world and allows one to look at life and the world from the outside.[6] In this sense, losing the points of reference within the world from which one acts and suspending the actions in which one is normally absorbed means no longer regarding as important what used to be important (and what presents itself as important only when one is involved in one's life rather than observing it from the outside). One could claim that the "question of meaning" becomes a problem in precisely the moment when such a loss of relation to the world arises since from a nonsituated, external perspective one's own life must appear objectively meaningless. It is for precisely this reason that, as Nagel acknowledges, the view from nowhere harbors a risk of alienation.[7] Nagel, however, believes this alienation to be unavoidable. On the one hand, things can appear important and meaningful only "from the inside;" on the other hand, he claims, we cannot evade the possibility of taking a standpoint "from the outside." We are in a position, then, to take both perspectives, the subjective and the objective, without, however, being able to reconcile them.

According to Nagel, it is this irreconcilable tension that inevitably produces in our lives what one could call the *absurd*. Thus, for him, alienation, or at least its possibility, is constitutive of how humans relate to themselves and to the world. This implies that alienation can no longer be formulated or evaluated as a *problem*, but only as part of the human condition. (This view, in fact, reflects an entire tradition that found expression above all in existentialist literary texts of the 1950s; it is not accidental that Nagel makes reference to the now mostly forgotten buzzword of the time: the absurd.)

It is also possible, however, to give a different assessment of the phenomenon, the starting point of which is suggested by Nagel's own account. From the perspective of the broadly pragmatist thesis noted earlier—that our practical involvement and dealings with things in the world are the primary ways (both temporally and constitutively) in which we relate to self and world (and which precede the possibility of distancing and detachment)—the loss of relations and the radical detachment from the world described here can be understood as a kind of *failure of apprehension*. If, given this thesis, one accepts that we *cannot* meaningfully abstract from the practical relations that constitute the world for us, then what we have here is the loss of relation to something that we are at the same time *always already* related to—a relation of relationlessness. Of most importance for my argument here is that what Nagel conceives of as a *dissolution* of a relation turns out to be (from a Heideggerian or broadly pragmatist perspective) a *failure to apprehend* a relation that as such is foundational. Nagel fittingly describes the problem of the meaning of life that inevitably arises from the perspective of the absurd as "a form of skepticism at the level of motivation."[8] From the pragmatist perspective, however, these questions of meaning could turn out to be pseudoquestions, in the same sense in which pragmatists accuse epistemological skepticism of raising pseudoquestions.[9] Nagel himself cites such an objection raised by Bernard Williams: "Perhaps, as Williams claims, the view *sub specie aeternitatis* is a very poor view of human life, and we should start and end in the middle of things."[10]

INDIFFERENCE AS A LOSS OF IDENTIFICATION

I come now to the second interpretation (or second aspect) of the experience of alienation that is characterized by indifference: the loss of identification as the loss of affective attachments to oneself and the world. In order to justify the diagnosis of this phenomenon as alienation, our task here, too, is to understand how this kind of dissolution of relations remains nevertheless a relation.

I argued that relations to self and world are constitutively bound up with one another in such a way that alienation from the world necessarily leads to self-alienation. This thesis has two implications that must be further explicated. First, the self determines itself "from within the world." It constitutes itself by identifying with projects and through an affective as well as a cognitive "investment" of things in the world; it constitutes itself through its interest in these things and its involvement with them. What we need to understand in all this is what identification means here. Second, this presupposes a claim about the boundary between inner and outer, or between myself and the world, that can be articulated with the help of William James' *Psychology*.

I will briefly clarify these two implications now so that, in the fourth section of this chapter, I can explain why becoming distant from and indifferent to the world is a problem for the individual (since she obviously *can* distance herself from any such identifications) and hence why, to return to the opening example, Perlmann's situation is to be understood as a loss of self and self-alienation and not as an (in his indifference) heightened independence and freedom in relation to the world.

IDENTIFICATION

The claim that what constitutes us is inseparably bound up with our identification with projects in the world points to a kind of interweaving of self and world that in the previous chapter we called identification.

What, though, does it mean to identify *with something*? In order to explain this I will start with the question of what it means in general to *identify something*. I can identify *something as something* (or someone as someone). I do this when I identify the sparkling thing on the floor as my earring that has fallen there or the man who is standing over there as the person who stole my handbag yesterday. I can also identify a strange tingling in my stomach as nervousness or as hunger. Identifying something as something means, then, establishing a correspondence. In order to do so I make a kind of comparison: I note that the man standing there has the same haircut and the same facial features as the one I saw yesterday in the subway just before he ran off with my handbag; I compare the earring lying there with the one that I possessed until just now. I remember that I always feel this rumbling in my stomach when

I am hungry and that it stops when I eat something. I identify something as something, then, by discerning correspondences such as these.

But what does it mean to say that *I* identify with something or someone? What does the process of the comparison look like when someone identifies with her soccer club or her child? Clearly, what goes on in these cases cannot be a direct comparison or one that establishes a real correspondence. I cannot be identical with my soccer club nor with my child in the sense in which the two earrings prove to be identical or the same thing. Talk of identifying with something or someone can have only a figurative meaning. More precisely, I identify with the well-being or fate of someone or something. When someone identifies with her child, she identifies with the child's well-being; when someone identifies with a soccer club, she identifies with its successes or defeats. I want my club to win; I desire happiness for my child. The identity here is not between me and the soccer club or between me and my child but rather between my child's desires and my own or between the club's (or club members') hopes and my own. When the club wins, I feel that I have won. When my child is successful, I am proud. I am "identified" with the club or with my child's well-being insofar as my own well-being and the satisfaction of my desires are bound up with my child's well-being and the fulfillment of the club's hopes.

What distinguishes, though, wishing something (or someone) success from identifying with something? What does the talk of identifying mean beyond wishing that things go well? When one identifies with something, one makes it a part of one's identity or self-conception. In the one case I am satisfied with the success of something or I am pleased if someone is doing well, while in the other I tie my fate to that of the other person or thing in such a way that its fate is constitutive for my identity. In the one case I remain—despite all my goodwill—separated from the person or thing I wish well; in the other there seems to be a kind of introjection or "taking in" of something into myself. This is why we sometimes suspect an unhealthy lack of distance when we say that someone is completely identified with something.

It is difficult, however, to explain how we are to imagine this "taking in." Perhaps we can only recognize it by its effect, one that William James pointed out and that Harry Frankfurt, too, repeatedly emphasizes: one recognizes that one is *identified* with something when one feels vulnerable with respect to it. I experience the soccer club's defeat as my own. When my child is doing poorly, I do poorly. Identifying with something, then, means more than just a greater amount of goodwill, even if it may not always be possible to define clearly the boundaries between the two phenomena. The crucial (structural) point, however, seems to be the following: in the one case there is someone who wants something and relates to something, but who also remains separate from the object of her concern. In the other case we understand the identity in each instance as constituted through this relation; it is unimaginable outside this relation and is defined by it. For this reason the identity of someone who identifies with something is "entangled" with it.

This model—this basic pattern of identification—has two implications that will concern us. First, becoming engaged on the side of something that I identify with in this sense is not an act of altruism since my own fate is interwoven with that of the thing (or person). Second, if I identify with something, that thing has more than instrumental significance for me. The sponsor who wishes the soccer club success so that her investment pays off has (at least in this respect) not identified with it. The club's success is for her a means to the end of economic success. Their fates are interwoven with each other in a certain sense, but not in the way that identification implies. (This can be seen in the fact that the sponsor will drop the club if it continues to lose, whereas the fan who really identifies with the club remains true to it in good times and bad.)

"A FLUCTUATING MATERIAL" (WILLIAM JAMES)

With this in mind we can further articulate the thesis of the entanglement of self and world. If one accepts—as the claim that alienation from the world is self-alienation seems to presuppose—that the self constitutes itself in its identificatory relations to projects, persons, and objects in the world, then the separation between inner and outer and between self and world is called into question.

William James's pragmatist conception of the self attempts to do justice to precisely these points. James distinguishes the empirical self ("Me") from the "pure ego." What is of interest here is not this distinction itself but the account he gives of the Me. James ascribes various dimensions to the Me: a material dimension (which includes the body) as well as social and spiritual dimensions. The distinctive characteristic of the Me—James understands it as the "self in its widest sense"—is a certain form of identificatory relation: "It is clear that between what a man calls me and what he simply calls mine the line is difficult to draw. We feel and act about certain things that are ours very much as we feel and act about ourselves. Our fame, our children, the work of our hands, may be as dear to us as our bodies are, and arouse the same feelings and the same acts of reprisal if attacked. And our bodies themselves, are they simply ours or are they us?"[11] What James calls the self, then, is not a fixed entity with a clear dividing line between inner and outer. Things belong to me more or less (or constitute the Me more or less) according to how strong this identificatory relation is.

We see, then, that we are dealing with a fluctuating material,[12] the same object being sometimes treated as a part of me, at other times as simply mine, and, then again, as if I had nothing to do with it at all. In its widest possible sense, however, a man's Self is the sum total of all that he can call his, not only his body and his psychic powers but his clothes and his house, his wife and his children, his ancestors and friends, his reputation and works, his lands and horses and yacht and bank account. All these things give him the same emotions. If they wax and prosper, he feels triumphant; if they dwindle and die away, he feels cast down.[13]

What is my own—what belongs to me (myself)—is not, then, somewhere inside; it constitutes itself in relating to the external world. As mentioned earlier, the world includes social relations and relations of recognition, in addition to the world of things and the property one can acquire within it; that is, it includes, in addition to the yacht, nonmaterial goods such as honor as well. Thus, if identification means understanding something as "part of myself," I am everything I can identify with. I am not myself prior to or beyond these identifications but *in* them.

What does this imply for Perlmann's indifference and for the relation between self and world it involves? Perlmann can be described as someone who can no longer identify with anything; his indifference means a loss of identification. In the novel this process of losing his identifications is vividly described: when his views are called into question—as a rival does at the conference—he no longer feels dejected and attacked as he did when he was still ambitiously pursuing his career and he no longer experiences that feeling of triumph when he wins an argument. It no longer feels to him as though it were *his* triumph, as though it belonged to him, even though he brought it about himself. The fact that everything has become indifferent to him produces the impression that it was not *he* who wrote the text or *he* who won the argument. (This is expressed, too, by the metaphor of local anesthesia.) But if the Me, as James suggests, is pieced together out of precisely such affective investments in the external world and such identifications in the world, then the question arises as to what exactly *he*, Perlmann, really *is* under such circumstances if so little of what constituted who he is still remains. If, according to James, the self is a "fluctuating material" that can expand or shrink and be wider or narrower, then the self is as large or wide as the circle of its identificatory relations. Perlmann's self, then, has "shrunk" in his phase of indifference; he experiences what James calls a "shrinkage of our personality, a partial conversion of ourselves to nothingness."[14] Against this backdrop one can claim that the indifference to the world into which Perlmann falls threatens *himself* as well and that his indifference to the world goes hand in hand with an indifference to himself. If nothing is important to someone any longer, then he is also no longer important to himself. Precisely this phenomenon can be understood as a process of self-alienation that is mediated by alienation from the world.

But why is a shrunken self of this kind an alienated self? Why, in order to realize oneself, must one actively take part in the world? The background assumption here is the following: it appears to be part of leading a life as a person that one pursues projects in one's life or has aspirations for one's life such that one is not indifferent to everything. This assumption, as one can see, implies a conception of self-realization as an active appropriation of the world, as I presented it in the introduction in connection with Hegel and Marx. One can sharpen this basic point by saying that the self must *realize* itself *in the world* in order to become real. But why is that so?

(4) THE AMBIVALENCE OF INDIFFERENCE— FREEDOM OR LOSS OF SELF?

Even if someone who is indifferent can be diagnosed as having a "shrunken self," what justifies thinking of this as a problematic process of self-alienation and loss of self? To be sure, "withdrawing one's feelers from the world" and "clipping" one's ties to others (and to everything that is "other" more generally) is not without consequences. To what extent, though, does such a withdrawal mean that an individual is alienated from herself or even threatened with regard to what constitutes her identity? How small may a shrunken self become without it amounting to a loss of self, and how far can one withdraw into an inner citadel without thereby losing oneself?[15] This seems to presuppose certain assumptions about what belongs to a complete or at least to a sufficiently extended self—assumptions that are not so easy to make, precisely when one assumes that the self is malleable.

This leads to two general questions: first, why should one have to be interested in the world? What is wrong with indifference? And, second, what justifies the claim that if someone abandons her interest in the world she also loses interest in herself? Can one not take the world to be unimportant and still consider oneself important? In the end the answers to these two questions will be connected with the point that is crucial for the concept of alienation, namely, the extent to which indifference, too, is a (deficient) *relation*—and therefore understandable as alienation.

I want briefly to expand on the problems here. In this case, too, one is tempted to say that there is a fundamental ambivalence.[16] If being detached from the world (when evaluated negatively) appears to be an instance of alienation, one could also suspect that it harbors an *emancipatory potential*.[17]

Does not the possibility of withdrawing or distancing oneself from the world also contain a potential for independence? By withdrawing from the world and pulling back from one's identifications, the "area open to attack" in which one can be wounded becomes smaller. If, following James's line of thought, we no longer place value on our clothes, our children, and our projects, then losing them or seeing them do poorly can no longer grieve us. One could even envy our indifferent Perlmann as someone who is suddenly free from all cares and no longer bound by anything, someone who lives in a state of complete agreement with himself. Insofar as he no longer cares about his earlier views and becomes less and less concerned with his reputation, he can no longer be wounded and no longer needs recognition. It is like Hegel's characterization of the ancient Stoic: "He no longer counts as part of himself everything that belongs to desire and fear, and this puts him in the position of being an alien to himself."[18] The Stoic who withdraws from the world into himself is "identical with himself" inasmuch as he no longer directs himself (his will) toward what is "other" and inasmuch as he is not tied to the world by desire or fear. Someone who no longer wills and desires has nothing more to fear. This constitutes his sovereignty, the sovereignty of someone who is indifferent. On this view, complete indifference would be the height of freedom. Dependent on nothing and no one, defined as nothing and no one: indifference makes one free.

But, given what has been said previously, can I "be in agreement with myself" without being attached to things in the world? Can I be free without wanting something in and from the world? And to what extent is someone free to whom her life does not matter? As Martin Löw-Beer says, it is "doubtful that a person is autonomous if it does not matter to her how she lives."[19] But why is that so? What is ultimately at stake here are the conceptions of

personal identity, freedom, and self-realization bound up with the stances I
have sketched earlier.

In what follows I take up two very different approaches, both of which
consider the freedom of indifference to be deficient. In examining the phenomenon of boredom, Harry Frankfurt develops the claim that the withdrawal
of interest from the world leads to a loss of vitality or an emptying of life that
results in the destruction of personality, a dissolution of the person (or of what
constitutes a person as such). Hegel's discussion of the ancient Stoics is also of
interest in this context because it points out the deficiencies of a conception
of freedom based on indifference. Whereas Frankfurt offers an argument that
appeals to the implications of what it is to be a person and that is to a certain
extent grounded in a view of human nature, Hegel offers an immanent form
of argument directed at the self-contradictory and incomplete nature of freedom "in the citadel." I will present both arguments and then examine to what
extent they support my claim about the problematic nature of indifference
and its status as a form of alienation.

"LIVELINESS" AND AVOIDING BOREDOM

For Harry Frankfurt, it is "wholeheartedness" in identifying with specific desires that constitutes the self's unity and it is commitments and volitional
necessities that define its contours. For this reason the fact that we are *in general* interested in something—that something is important to us—is so fundamental. Indifference, the absence of such interests and of "care" in general
amounts to a dissolution of the self. This suggests that indifference—the loss
of identifications, becoming indifferent to the world—can be understood as a
threat to personhood. Accordingly, someone who is not interested in anything,
like someone who has no ties, has no identity. A person for whom nothing is
important leads "a life without meaningful activities."[20] Someone who constantly confronts life with indifference lives, as Frankfurt explains, a life in
boredom precisely because nothing in such a life can be significant. What
speaks against leading such a life? Frankfurt takes a very decisive position
here: "I believe that the avoidance of boredom is a very fundamental human
urge. It is not a matter of distaste for a rather unpleasant state of consciousness" (89). His argument is based on a certain view of human nature: a life of
boredom means in a certain respect not really being alive: "It is the essence
of boredom that it involves an attenuation of psychic liveliness" (89). The self,
according to this view, is not alive in a real sense, not alive as a person, if it
cannot actively relate to the world through identifications. Having interests

and investing the world with significance are necessary conditions of being a person at all. For this reason Frankfurt also argues that the self—in an existential, not a biological sense—can be understood only as an active, expansive self. It constitutes itself in relating to the world. We *are*, as persons, insofar as we relate to a world through identifications that enable us to experience it as meaningful, and personhood dissolves when this is lacking.

The justification Frankfurt gives for this diagnosis is interesting, as well as the implications it has for the connection between a person's relation to self and her relation to the world. His view, not so distant from Marxist and pragmatist positions, combines two theses: first, that we develop or "come to" ourselves as persons by relating to the world; second, a thesis concerning the development of our capacities to perceive and differentiate: if nothing is important or significant in the world, then the "organs" do not develop—one can think of the development of sensory organs—that are capable of perceiving the world in its diversity.

Being bored entails a reduction of attention; our responsiveness to conscious stimuli flattens out and shrinks; distinctions are not noticed and not made, so that the conscious field becomes increasingly homogeneous. The general functioning of the mind diminishes. Its tendency is to approach a complete cessation of significant differentiation within consciousness; and this homogenization is, at the limit, tantamount to the cessation of conscious experience altogether (89).

If nothing in the world interests us, we become stunted. If nothing makes a difference anymore, we lose our capacity to differentiate.

Thus the self as something definite and differentiated develops its capacities to perceive and differentiate only through contact with a differentiated world in which things are significant. If, on the contrary, nothing in the world is important and we are not tied to it by any interests, then our organs of perception do not develop. This leads to a loss of liveliness: we are dulled and remain undifferentiated. The "active self" ceases to exist. "A substantial increase in the extent to which we are bored undermines the very continuation of psychic activity. In other words, it threatens the extinction of the active self" (88). Thus, if (radical) boredom leads to a loss of self, avoiding boredom is an imperative of self-preservation: "What is manifest by our interest in avoiding boredom is therefore not simply a resistance to discomfort but a quite elemental urge for psychic survival. It is natural to construe this as a modification of the more familiar instinct for self-preservation. It is connected to 'self-preservation,' however, only in an unfamiliarly literal sense—in the sense of sustaining not the life of the organism but the persistence of the self" (89). Self-preservation here is not understood in a biological sense, since clearly the natural person continues to exist even if she retreats from the world without interests. But the person, as someone who leads an active life of her own and relates to it, dissolves.

In this sense our interest in the world and the process through which we imbue it with significance represent constitutive conditions of a person's acquiring a relation to self. We relate to ourselves and are important to ourselves to the degree to which the world is important to us. That follows conceptually from the fact that we determine ourselves—give ourselves specific properties—through the things that are important to us. Persons relate to themselves and are important to themselves in what they do.

Can something to whom its own conditions and activities do not matter in the slightest properly be regarded as a person at all? Perhaps nothing that is entirely indifferent to itself is really a person, regardless of how intelligent or emotional or in other respects similar to persons it may be (90).

And, insofar as (according to this account) taking oneself seriously—regarding oneself as important—can mean nothing more than taking oneself seriously in what one does and what one cares about, it is inseparably bound up with taking the world seriously. This is why indifference with respect to the world is tied to indifference with respect to oneself. A world that has become lifeless and insignificant goes hand in hand with a subject that has become lifeless and insignificant. This means that the question raised earlier regarding what is false or problematic about indifference can no longer be seriously posed: it is not only that someone cannot be autonomous who is indifferent to how she lives; someone who is indifferent to how she lives does not exist at all as a person.[21] Applied to the example of Perlmann this means that it would not be only his intellectual capacities—his intellectual capacity to differentiate—that would fade if he continued to find nothing important and could no longer form opinions in any areas of life. In general, one could witness the emotional and cognitive "wasting away" of one's own personality: alienation from the world would result in self-alienation.

"THE SPURNING OF EXISTENCE" (HEGEL'S CRITIQUE OF STOICISM)

Hegel's critique of ancient Stoicism (or of Stoicism as a way of conducting one's life) is helpful for shedding further light on the relation between freedom and indifference. Stoicism, of course, is not to be equated with indifference, and Perlmann is no Stoic. Nevertheless, there is a point of contact between the two that helps to illuminate the question I have posed. On Hegel's account, a Stoic is someone who seeks to attain "inner freedom" by becoming indifferent, by disengaging from the external world. In relation to the world, he cultivates, as Hegel puts it, "not a dull but a willed indifference."[22] What merely happens to Perlmann (becoming indifferent to the world) is for the Stoic a strategy: "He no longer counts as part of himself everything that belongs to desire and fear, and this puts him in the position of being an alien to himself" (290). Expressed in the same terms we have already used, the Stoic keeps the "area open to attack" in which the world can affect, disappoint, or enslave him as small as possible. If I do not want honor, no one can affect me by dishonoring me; if I reduce my needs to what is absolutely necessary, I do not lose my freedom when they are not met. In this sense Stoicism means a "spurning of existence" that appears to itself capable of withdrawing from social and natural sources of compulsion (294). It is crucial that this strategy is conceived of as a means for attaining freedom: the Stoic seeks to attain inner freedom through indifference to the external world. According to Hegel's description, the Stoic's will is "the will of the subject, who . . . firmly does not permit himself to be moved by anything other (desires, pain, and so forth), who wants only his freedom and is prepared to give up everything else—one who, if he experiences external pain or misfortune, separates this from the interiority of his consciousness" (288). In separating himself in this way he is free "in his thoughts" since he is no longer tied to the world, which could otherwise challenge his independence.

What is important for our inquiry is the argument Hegel employs to criticize an inner freedom attained in this way. His critique of a freedom gained by renouncing attachments as empty and abstract leads to an alternate model of freedom that is defined positively. When the freedom that results from the "spurning of existence" fails to give itself any specific properties, a contrasting picture of freedom emerges—a positive, actually realized freedom of the individual who is capable of giving herself specific properties in the world and of understanding and realizing herself in her relations to the world.

What then is problematic about the Stoic's inner freedom? There are several related problems to take note of. First, Stoic freedom, indeed the entire Stoic existence, is defensive. When Hegel discusses Stoicism in the form in which it was historically most influential—he focuses on late Roman rather than Hellenistic Stoicism—he draws our attention to the social and historical conditions of the Stoic's stance: "The power of the spurning of existence is great; the strength of this negative attitude is sublime. The Stoic principle is a negative moment in the idea of absolute consciousness; it is also a necessary appearance of the time. For if the reality of the world has been lost, as in the Roman world, and real spirit or life has disappeared in the abstract universal, then consciousness, whose real universality is destroyed, must retreat into its individuality and preserve itself in its thoughts" (294). Stoicism is described here as a reaction to the loss of "real universality" and the "reality of the world" that—with all the greatness that Hegel grants it—bears the scars of this loss, a deficiency that reveals itself in the resigned and private character of this reaction. "The noble Romans therefore have demonstrated only the negative, this indifference in regard to life and to everything external. They were able to be great only in a subjective or negative manner, in the manner of a private man" (296). The Stoics' conception of sovereignty—as a "flight from reality"[23]—is characterized, then, by powerlessness with respect to the external world, and it bears this as a kind of blemish. The question is then: is there freedom in the "freedom of the private man"? Or, formulated differently, is that really freedom or merely freedom in a deficient form?

Hegel's response is that the Stoics' "subjective or negative manner" points to a deficient form of freedom. Their freedom remains "abstract freedom" or "abstract independence" (294); the independence of Stoic consciousness exists "only in thoughts." "Abstract" here means something like "not having become real" or not determinate in its content. "But Stoic consciousness goes no farther than concepts; it does not succeed in knowing the content, or what the work is that it should perform" (289). We have here, then, a freedom that, in Hegel's terms, yields no "ethical [*sittliche*] reality," but exists only in the individual's subjectivity: "What matters is not that the condition of the world should be rational or just but only that the subject as such should assert his freedom in himself" (294).

This means, however, that it is questionable whether an individual can be free in a purely inner sense, whether the incapacity to materialize freedom socially or to give it "reality" must not have an effect on the individual's freedom (and the reality of her self). One could call this the "worldlessness" of this kind of freedom: the subject that is free merely inwardly does not give itself a world; it does not externalize itself and does not realize itself in the world. "The ethical reality is not expressed as an enduring, created work that repeatedly creates itself" (288). And Hegel's critique of this is that this freedom is merely an ideal and not a reality; it does not therefore provide the point of reference freedom needs in order to realize itself. This freedom remains "formal" and attains no "content" (290).

The underlying idea of freedom here can be understood by turning to Hegel's *Philosophy of Right*. Formulated schematically, the basic thought is that freedom must give itself reality, must *determine*, concretize, or realize itself as something, and this has two aspects. On the one hand, the merely negated world, as negated, remains external to the individual, hence alien and not subject to her influence. Actual, realized freedom, in contrast, consists not in abstracting from the world but in appropriating it. The important point here is that this appropriation is a transformation. The abstract, negative freedom of withdrawing from the world, in contrast, remains, in its withdrawal, bound to what it withdraws from (or negates); it can reject it but not transform it. Realized, positive freedom in Hegel's sense refers, then, to an appropriative transformation (or transformative appropriation) of the conditions under which it realizes itself.[24] Freedom means being able to make something— namely, the conditions under which one lives—one's own. And, conversely, an independence that preserves itself only by disregarding the actual world remains abstract. As Allen Wood puts this point:

> We do not achieve true self-sufficiency in relation to an other by escaping it or separating ourselves from it—as by Stoical aloofness from our external condition, or Kantian detachment from empirical motives. Such a strategy is self-defeating, like the strategy of the neurotic personality that avoids the trauma of failure by precluding from the outset any possibility of success. True independence in relation to an other is achieved rather by struggling with otherness, overcoming it, and making it our own.[25]

On the other hand, the person remains unreal because she lacks all specific properties. Becoming a person for Hegel means "putting one's will into something," and that also means giving oneself specific properties by willing something in the world. In such a relation to the world, the person first realizes herself as a person, and in that her freedom first becomes concrete.

Hegel can be understood here as developing a dialectic of freedom and determinacy. If I identify with nothing, then nothing limits me. I can then do anything. The problem, however, is that being able to do anything also means that I elude being "grasped" and that I have no determinate contours. I am not a specific person who wants and is able to do specific things; instead, my freedom remains empty and abstract. As long as I do not put my will into anything determinate, this freedom is not real but only an indeterminate possibility. Hence the individual who locates her freedom in not identifying with anything, in not determining herself as anything and not putting her will into

anything, falls prey to an erroneous idea of sovereignty and independence—
erroneous, because such a position is grounded in a one-sided and formal idea
of freedom or independence. (Thus Hegel and Frankfurt share the idea that a
person must commit herself to and identify with something in order to make
her freedom concrete.)

A will that remains indifferent to its concrete properties is therefore not
free in the full sense. It is indeed free to renounce identifications, but at the
price of the self's emptiness and impoverishment. On this basis one could
also argue against what Nietzsche would later call the "free spirit."[26] Freedom
of choice, then, is only the formal aspect of freedom. The freedom of indifference, of distancing and renouncing identifications, is incomplete, and it
becomes complete only when the will determines its content by choosing
something determinate or orienting itself positively toward something.

Of course, the negative or merely formal side of freedom has for Hegel
its own rightful claims (and not merely historically): the "right of indifference" consists in the requirement that in order to be able to determine oneself freely, as something, one must be able to abstract from that very quality.
Raymond Geuss has pointed out that in his positive conception of freedom
Hegel attempts to integrate both the act of reflection (which depends on the
dissolving of attachments) and that of identification. The individual who determines herself must—in agreement with Frankfurt's theory of identification
and wholeheartedness—determine herself as something. She must do this,
however, in a reflective act of free choice that presupposes the possibility of
distancing herself from what she is at present. Thus for Hegel—in any case
one can describe his attempt in this way—negative freedom is a constitutive
condition of positive freedom; negative freedom is sublated (*aufgehoben*) into
positive freedom. One can sharpen these thoughts even further by returning
to the views of Frankfurt discussed in chapter 7: for Hegel commitment is not
only (as for Frankfurt) a condition of freedom; it is also the case (in contrast
to Frankfurt) that freedom is a condition of having commitments. (This same
structure underlies the theme of the free appropriation of self and world that
I will contrast in part 3 with the processes of alienation diagnosed here.)

(5) INDIFFERENCE, SELF-REALIZATION, AND ALIENATION

My discussion of Frankfurt and Hegel has the following implications for
the question of how indifference can be understood as a phenomenon of
alienation:

One can conceive of indifference as alienating insofar as it can be understood as a deficient mode of asserting one's independence. It is deficient because in it real independence—which would consist in being able to relate to projects one has set for oneself in the world in an identificatory and appropriative manner—is not yet realized. If, as I propose, we can call this kind of relation *self-realization*, then indifference threatens individuals' possibilities for *realizing* themselves. The aspect of freedom that is part of indifference—dissolving one's entanglements in the world—points, in contrast, to the fact that one must realize *oneself* rather than some inescapable trait or commitment or some objective idea, that (therefore) individuals must make what they do in the world their own by freely appropriating it. This presupposes the possibility of distancing oneself. To the extent that indifference includes the experience that a world of established meanings can suddenly become meaningless—that one can distance oneself not only from social norms one has been subjected to but also from the entire network of meaningful relations in which one previously found one's orientation—it is also an emancipatory, even a "dereifying" experience. It is in seeing that the world can become meaningless and that I can distance myself from it that I first experience that it is I myself who gives the world this meaning and who is actively involved, not merely passively wrapped up, in it. In this respect indifference is not only an experience of powerlessness but also of power: the world is not significant in itself but only through me; things are not important of themselves; instead, I make them so by identifying with them. This realization becomes an instance of alienation when one fails to conclude from it that one must *give* the world meaning oneself—that is, when indifference turns into a sense that it is impossible to be involved in the world as a being that actively shapes it. In other words, the world becomes mine when I (actively) appropriate it for myself.

Hence indifference, the possibility of distancing, and also, at times, the fading of the world, as Perlmann experiences it, can be understood as the obverse side of identificatory relations to the world. On the other hand, if indifference is total, it becomes an experience of alienation. Taking up my account of alienation as a relation of relationlessness, one can then argue that the separateness from the world that an attitude of indifference produces, or from which it arises, is illusory; even in indifference there is still a relation to the world—a defensive relation that has been shown to be deficient.

PART THREE

ALIENATION AS A DISTURBED APPROPRIATION OF SELF AND WORLD

CONSIDERED FROM THE PERSPECTIVE OF the subject, alienation is a deficient relation to world and self that, according to my thesis, can be understood as a disturbed relation of appropriation: alienation is an impeded appropriation of world and self.

Whereas the first part of this book undertook to introduce the historical and systematic issues bound up with the concept of alienation, and the second attempted to elaborate my initial suggestions for reconstructing the concept of alienation, the aim of this third part is to bring these threads together once again by evaluating the results of my discussion of cases of alienation and systematizing them conceptually. Against the backdrop of the analyses we have so far compiled, I will articulate a conception of self-alienation as an impeded appropriation of self and world and situate it in relation to other positions. Before moving on to the three chapters of this last part I would like briefly to summarize what I have said thus far.

SELF-ALIENATION AS A DISTURBED APPROPRIATION
OF SELF AND WORLD

1. Taking up a formulation of Ernst Tugendhat's, self-alienation can be understood as a way of *not having oneself at one's command*. Being alienated from oneself means, in other words, being *inaccessible to oneself* in what one wants and does.[1]

2. Having oneself at one's command is not a merely theoretical but a practical form of relating to oneself: a *process* of *practical (self-)appropriation*. This idea refers to a broadly conceived capacity of being familiar with oneself and being able to deal with oneself that neither aims at nor can be reduced to complete self-transparency and that neither entails nor presupposes complete control or self-command. It is a productive process of practical (self-)appropriation, and it is the basis of a successful relation to self. Conversely, alienation can be defined as a disturbance of such a process of appropriation.

3. Self-appropriation is mediated by an *appropriation of the world*. Since the relation to self at issue here can be articulated only in terms of the relation one has to one's own desires, interests, and actions—which are directed toward the world—self-appropriation always occurs as an appropriation of the world. Hence self-alienation is also *alienation from the world*, and, conversely, alienation from the world is self-alienation. This is why indifference counts as an instance of alienation.

4. Thus the model of alienation presented here does not appeal to a self that is authentic and unspoiled in its inwardness, and overcoming alienation does not mean withdrawing into an unalienated inner self. My account of alienation leads to a conception of *self-realization* as a process of "giving oneself reality" in the world that transcends the distinctions between inner and outer and between an inner life and an outer world. Inner life, too, is an inner *world*.

5. The concept of self-appropriation and the account of self-alienation as self-accessibility has further implications for the relation between alienation and heteronomy. Being accessible to oneself is a prerequisite of, but not identical with, self-determination; by the same token, the ways of not having oneself at one's command that I have discussed up to now cannot be reduced to heteronomy. Not being able to identify with what one wants and does is both more than and different from *heteronomy*. Yet a life that one has not been able to appropriate is in a significant sense not one's own.

6. In contrast to a merely passive *identification*, the concept of appropriation emphasizes the productive and active character of an unalienated relation to self and world. Calling the process of appropriation *productive* should
be understood in the following way: the self that is capable of becoming alienated first emerges *in* this process. There is nothing that exists already as *something* outside the process itself. What is appropriated does not exist apart from
the process of appropriation.

7. Beginning with relations of appropriation has the methodological implication that what it is to be oneself in an unalienated way no longer depends
on the model of an (inner and substantial) "agreement with self" but finds
its normative criterion in the idea of a successful process of appropriation.
(Following Ernst Tugendhat, it is a matter of the *How*, not the *What*, of appropriation.) Hence the criteria for successful appropriation are located in
this process itself, in the functioning of this process *as* a process. In examining the various phenomena, I suggested that such a process is *disturbed* if it
fails to "work" (or function) in a certain respect. An inadequate capacity for
integration and problem solving, as well as a lack of openness and inclusivity
in the process of appropriation, are symptoms of such a functional deficiency.
On the basis of the cases we have examined, this can be generalized as follows: alienation means the halting of processes of experience, and someone
is alienated who cannot *relate to her pregiven conditions* or appropriate them.

8. A diagnosis of alienation hovers, then, between subjective and objective
perspectives. For, as is clear, the question of when a self-conception "works"
can be controversial, and the question of what the pregiven conditions are to
which one must relate always rests on interpretation (see chapter 7). At the
same time, the "qualified subjectivism" proposed in chapter 3 turns out to
depend on certain assumptions that have a material content. Insofar as the
validity of these assumptions must itself be supported by interpretation—as
in many psychoanalytic models—and hence be justified as presuppositions,
what we have here is not a vicious circle but one that constantly enriches
our understanding in a kind of reflective equilibrium. As we will see (above
all in examining postmodernism's opposing view), the given conditions that
must be appropriated are neither given independently of interpretation nor
completely contingent.

9. The openness of the process of appropriation and its experimental character imply that overcoming alienation need not be described as a "coming to
oneself" or as reconciliation but can be conceived of instead as an open-ended
and never-ending process.

STRUCTURE OF PART 3

The next three chapters further elaborate the relation between appropriation and alienation in the following way:

Chapter 9 systematizes the conception of the self that has been implicit in my analysis up to now into an "appropriative model" of the self and defends it against various objections. I will show that alienation critique can dispense with essentialist presuppositions without thereby becoming arbitrary. Chapter 10 further locates the set of problems surrounding the theme of alienation: against the backdrop of the negative foil of self-alienation, I will discuss the relations between freedom, self-determination, and self-realization and criticize the romantic conception of authenticity using a model of self-realization derived from Hegel and Marx. In conclusion I will take up the thesis of the sociality of the self that runs throughout my reflections: here I will argue that a successful relation to self also rests on a successful relation to the social world.

9

"LIKE A STRUCTURE OF COTTON CANDY": BEING ONESELF AS SELF-APPROPRIATION

Nana is an animal with an outside and an inside. If you remove the outside, you get what's inside. If you remove what's inside, you catch sight of her soul.

—KAJA SILVERMAN, *HARUN FAROCKI: SPEAKING OF GODARD*

Was he ready to claim that a self, a person in the psychological sense of the word, had no solid core and nothing whatsoever in terms of substance, but was a web of stories, constantly growing and subject to a constant process of relayering—a little like a structure of cotton candy at a carnival, except without material?

—PASCAL MERCIER, *PERLMANN'S SILENCE*

IN CONJUNCTION WITH THE PHENOMENA discussed in part 2, I described self-alienation as an inadequate *power* and a lack of *presence* in what one does, a failure to *identify* with one's own actions and desires and to take part in one's own life. Conversely, one is not alienated when one is *present* in one's actions, *steers* one's life instead of being driven by it, independently *appropriates* social roles, is able to *identify* with one's desires, and is *involved* in the world—in short, when one can appropriate one's life (as one's own) and is accessible to oneself in what one does.

How, though, are we to characterize the *self* that becomes alienated *from itself* as described here? What conception of the self underlies the analysis of cases of alienation carried out in part 2? What form does the problem of the self and its unity take when addressed from the perspective of the threat of a *loss* of self as it has been understood here? I understand talk of the "self" and of a person's "identity" in roughly the same sense they have in everyday language, as concepts that address what could be called the (psychic) *continuity* or the (psychic) *unity* of a person.[1] What I mean here is the more or less stable "agency" that we presuppose when we understand ourselves as acting persons or what we have in mind when we say "this is who I am."

The present chapter summarizes the implications of my analysis up to now with the aim of presenting an "appropriative" conception of the self and defending it against objections and rival positions. In contrast to essentialist views, this conception emphasizes the fluid and constructed character of self-relations in which we are not simply *given* to ourselves. Unlike the poststructuralist critique of the subject, however, it insists on the possibility of distinguishing between successful and unsuccessful ways of appropriating ourselves. Only in this way can one speak of self-alienation while avoiding the trap of essentialism.

The first section of this chapter, "The Self as a Process of Appropriation," develops an *appropriative conception of the self*, borrowing both from Hegelian and (broadly) existentialist positions. This conception will take shape in the course of examining and responding to objections from two directions. The first of these raises objections to my critique of essentialism or to the ostensible implications of an antiessentialist approach; it charges that antiessentialism denies both the unity of the self and its intractability (*Unverfügbarkeit*, or its being outside our command). These objections will be discussed in the second section, "Intractability and Inwardness," in conjunction with two positions that regard my model of identity as too weak: (1) accounts that more strongly emphasize the intractable elements of personal identity (those outside our command) and that endorse a more substantial model of the unity of persons than I do and (2) positions that insist on an idea of inwardness as the individual's internal refuge from the world. Finally, in the third section, "Self-Invention and the Multiplicity of the Self," I deal with objections from a second school of thought. Here I engage with the discussion inspired by poststructuralists and social constructivists, which accuses the appropriative model of the self that I develop here of residual essentialism and too strong a conception of the subject. In this section I discuss (1) the theme of self-*invention*, as it is contrasted in this discussion with self-*discovery*, and against these (in my view) false alternatives I argue for the idea of self-*appropriation*. Afterward (2) I examine the idea of the multiplicity and the hybrid character of identity, which contrasts with my conception's emphasis on the appropriating subject's *achievement* of unity. Finally, since these ideas have found an echo in contemporary cultural critique, I discuss (3) the soundness of such critiques by examining an empirical case, the construction of identities on the Internet.

1. THE SELF AS A PROCESS OF APPROPRIATION

In the introduction to part 2, I grouped under the name of the "core model" of the self those views that operate with the idea that one is "with oneself" (*bei sich*) or authentic when one is in agreement with an inner essence or with a kind of internal "original pattern" of oneself. According to these views, one realizes oneself by allowing this essence to be expressed and one can "find oneself" by turning back to that essence. Calling this a core model is apt because it presupposes (metaphorically speaking) an *inner core* that contains what one really is. This model has been criticized in two respects: first, for the reifying implications of its implicit essentialism and, second, because of the dichotomy between inner and outer inherent in the metaphor of a core and the accompanying idea that the true self is located somewhere "inside," independent of its expressions and manifestations. How can the descriptions of cases of alienation in the previous chapters avoid these objections? To what extent have we succeeded in diagnosing alienation *without* a core model?[2]

DOING, NOT BEING—ALIENATION CRITIQUE WITHOUT AN ESSENTIAL SELF

With respect to the academic in our first example the diagnosis is obvious. The core model would claim that he has missed his essence—his authentic self, his inner character—in going from being a bohemian city dweller to being a suburban father. He is, according to this conception, alienated from himself in the life he leads to the extent that there is a discrepancy between what he *does* and what he—authentically—*is*. My own interpretation takes a different approach. The problem is not that he does something that he *is* not but that he is *not present in* what he does. I described this as "letting oneself drift" and analyzed it as a "masking of practical questions" that leads to us not really doing what we do, insofar as we do not ourselves decide (or perhaps do not even understand as the possible object of decisions) what we could have decided on and shaped. On this model, self-alienation is an alienated *action*—not an agent's "falling away" from a self imagined as a substance underlying its actions, but a *mode* of this action. One is not alienated *from something* (one's authentic self) but rather *in* one's performance of actions and hence in what one does or *how* one does it.

My interpretation of the second example, too, explicitly contradicts the assumption that the self has an essential core. Since my analysis of this example emphasizes that alienation occurs not *through* but *in* roles, it also rejects the assumption of an authentic, unfalsified self that underlies its falsifying roles. If, in opposition to this view, we ask how one can *appropriate* one's roles, the answer is that alienated or unalienated (inauthentic or authentic) behavior describes a mode of acting or doing. Authenticity resides in certain ways of behaving in roles—that is, in certain ways of shaping what one does in roles and in "obstinately" giving them a meaning of one's own—rather than in an unspoiled pure or genuine self, understood as something that exists prior to and apart from roles. And if, as my interpretation insists, in cases of alienation through roles the "true" self cannot even come into being behind the "false" self, then the decisive standard is not what one *is* in distinction to one's roles but rather what one is not able to *do* in them.

The third example (the feminist) suggests in various ways that the problem of one's own desires being experienced as alien could be solved only by presupposing an essentialist self as an underlying standard. How, without referring to such a standard, is one able to decide in which of two conflicting complexes of desires and behaviors a person is really herself? Here, too, I have attempted to show that one can understand the conflict described without such a standard. If my diagnosis of an "inner division" can be contrasted with a condition of "agreement" with oneself, then this agreement is to be defined as an *internal* coherence between the characteristics, desires, feelings, and attitudes that constitute who one is and not as an agreement of one's various features with a center or core. Insofar as this coherence must also be characterized by an inner mobility and an openness of access to oneself, a *mode* of doing, or praxis, comes into play. According to this reconstruction, the criterion for distinguishing between one's own desires and those that are alienated or alienating lies in the functioning of this praxis.

Finally, in the fourth example (Perlmann's indifference) the diagnosis of alienation relies on dissolving the dichotomy between "core" and "outer shell." It is only because the self exists in identifying with its projects that indifference to one's projects can be described as alienating. This idea presupposes not a finished self that then seeks the projects that are suitable for it but rather a self that constitutes itself in identifying with its projects and that acquires specific properties only in relating to them. Again, the self (or "true" self) is not something that exists separately, apart from its activities. In this respect the self is relational; it constitutes itself in its relations to the world, and its authenticity in turn melts into a "doing" that consists in identifying with something or in appropriating the world.

If one is not an agent in what one does, is not present in one's life but is instead driven by it, does not identify with what one wants, and is not involved in what one does, this does not imply that one is somehow "really" someone else. And yet there is an identifiable discrepancy, an analyzable deficit or contradiction, in what one does.

OUTER, NOT INNER—THE EXTERNALIZATION OF THE SELF

These conclusions also agree with the implications of my discussion of what I called in the introduction (in reference to Jameson) the container model of the self.

The container model presupposes a self that demands to be expressed but that also is already "there" prior to this expression: "a self that cries for expression." According to this model, self-alienation is always characterized by a discrepancy between inner and outer or between the self as it lives in the container and the self as it appears outside it, where it is constrained, distorted, and made into something alien. The self would like to express itself, but as soon as it enters the external world it is threatened by distortion and deformation. The concern of the container self is how it can move undamaged from inside to outside, but my objection to this model is directed at the very dichotomy it presupposes. Without externalization—as my account implies—there is nothing there to be damaged. The self, as what makes up who we are, cannot be separated from its expression and externalization in the world. There is not first a self about which one could ask how it should express and realize itself; rather, what we call a self is formed *in* expressing and externalizing itself, and through this it, in Hegel's words, "gives itself reality."[3]

The academic's alienated situation, then, is precisely not to be described as the tragedy of someone whose true self is not adequately expressed in the life he lives, such that he is unable to "recognize himself in it." Perhaps he *is* not what he appears to be in his life, but he is also not something different *inside* that has simply not found its proper expression. In the case of the role player, too, the opposition between inner and outer is out of place. Whereas a model focused on inwardness would claim that a person's (external) roles alienate her from what she is inside, my analysis implies that even when role behavior is a false (distorted, rigid, lifeless, artificial, constrained) expression of oneself, the "correct" expression of oneself can only be a publicly accessible articulation of who one is. The problem of unwanted and concealed desires can also be explained without relying on the model of inner and outer. These desires do indeed express themselves, and we recognize them as candidates for authentic desires precisely because we cannot dispute their power, since they manifest themselves by blocking, distorting, and hindering a person's free accessibility to herself. Thus, if we ask what H. really wants, neither she nor we can decide that by looking into what is "inside" her, but only by asking what she actually (already) is doing in what she does and to what extent her actions show signs of being inhibited. As Jean-Luc Godard remarks: "How can one portray a person's inner life? By directing one's entire attention to her external life."[4]

The discussion of Perlmann's indifference also calls into question the division between inner and outer, between (inner) self and (outer) world, insofar as Perlmann's feeling of the unreality of the world and himself can be traced back to the fact that he has lost the possibility of externalization, which alone would allow him to become real.

"BEING ONESELF" AS APPROPRIATION OF SELF AND WORLD

The conclusions of my analysis up to now can be summarized as follows: if processes of self-alienation can be analyzed as ways in which actions are disrupted or constrained rather than as a falling away from or a distortion of a substantial essence, then one is not alienated *from* something but *in* the performance of an action. In this account an unalienated "agreement with self" is conceived of as an active process of externalization. Thus the self's "being" is dissolved into something practical (the performance of an action) that has no ontologically independent entity underlying it; in other words, the unity of the self has no metaphysical foundation. It is an ever renewing achievement of integration in which, in accordance with Kierkegaard's demand, one carries out the "task of becoming oneself through one's own deed" without the self being already given prior to and apart from this integrating activity. What is crucial for the conceptions of appropriation and externalization I have proposed is that, in contrast to more strongly essentialist, expressivist models, here it is not possible to make out any "doer behind the deed" (Nietzsche),[5] no self that exists *prior to* and *apart from* the deed. On the other hand, insofar as a self emerges *in* its deeds, it does so within a process where what exists beforehand is appropriated and simultaneously transformed—a "web of stories . . . subject to a constant process of relayering" in which the self constitutes itself by relating to itself and the world in an appropriative manner. Being oneself is the result of such a process of appropriation and externalization—and it first exists as such.

My account also implies a conception of expression different from that of the container model: what is expressed does not exist independently of its expression—hence (here, too) not prior to or apart from the act of expression. Whereas in the one case the expression is merely a reflection of what is already inside, in the other it first *produces* what is expressed. This entails a reinterpretation of the kind of expressivism that a theory of alienation presupposes (and with it the problematic Promethean aesthetics of production that I referred to in part 1 in my discussion of Marx). In what follows I will provide a sketch of this revised expressivism by engaging with the views of Charles Taylor. Instead of starting with a given, as the classical model does, I will propose a performative-constructivist interpretation of "the human being, who simultaneously produces himself and his world."

TAYLOR'S CONCEPT OF ARTICULATION

In his theory of articulation the Canadian social philosopher Charles Taylor productively explores the relation between what is previously given and what is constructed or made. Taking over themes from Romantic expressivist conceptions of human nature and from Hegel's conception of spirit,[6] Taylor understands becoming oneself—the process in which we constitute ourselves as what and who we are—as a continual process of articulation in which we clarify to ourselves what we desire and value and develop a corresponding self-understanding. The crucial feature of his account is that the act of articulating does not merely serve to make our desires and attitudes public; in an important sense, it first creates them: "To give a certain articulation is to shape our sense of what we desire or what we hold important in a certain way."[7] According to this model, we first become accessible not only to others but also to ourselves through articulation. Thus, it is not the case that we want, value, or care about something and then give expression to these valuations in a process of articulation; rather, the process of articulation itself has a creative dimension. If we need articulation in order to determine ourselves or to give our self-conception a certain shape, then articulations do not express something independently given; rather, they represent, as Taylor explains, "attempts to formulate what is initially inchoate, or confused, or badly formulated. But this kind of formulation or reformulation does not leave its object unchanged."[8] In this sense articulation does not simply find what it articulates; it does not simply *uncover* something that was given prior to and independently of being articulated. Rather, it simultaneously *creates* what it articulates. Thus the concept of articulation can be understood antiessentialistically. As Hartmut Rosa explains: "What is to be made 'clear' through expression or articulation not only cannot be known objectively from any perspective; it does not even exist independently of the expression or articulation. Every expression and articulation simultaneously changes what is articulated or expressed. The medium of expression and what is expressed merge in this way since expression is no longer to be understood as a previously existing something's becoming manifest but (at least partially) as its production."[9] And in Taylor we read: "Expression partakes of both finding and making."[10] The interesting point, then, is that in a certain respect articulation must accomplish *two things*: it *makes* or creates what is articulated, but it must simultaneously *correspond to* what it finds before itself as unarticulated (the material, as it were, that it deals with). And one could regard it as the very point of Taylor's approach to try to hold in balance the constructive and the interpretive-disclosive elements of successfully becoming oneself.[11]

ARTICULATION AND SELF-APPROPRIATION

Taylor's account is useful in several respects for my reflections on the relation between self-appropriation and self-alienation.

First, Taylor's approach provides suggestions that are helpful for solving the problem discussed regarding the criteria for successful relations to self. Although articulations are constructed, they are not arbitrary. Taylor holds on to the possibility of judging articulations to be successful and unsuccessful or correct and false: "There are more or less adequate, more or less truthful, more self-clairvoyant or self-deluding interpretations. Because of this double fact, because an articulation can be *wrong*, and yet it shapes what it is wrong about, we sometimes see erroneous articulations as involving a distortion of the reality concerned. We do not speak of error but frequently also of illusion or delusion."[12] This criterion, however—and this is crucial—focuses our attention on distortions *of* the expression and not distortions *by* the expression. And the talk of illusion or blindness indicates that what is at issue here are defective processes of articulation—an erroneous *How* of articulations—that (in the terminology I have proposed) can be traced back to disturbances of various aspects of the accessibility of self and of world.

Hence our self-interpretations, which operate within such articulations, are—as I discussed in detail in chapter 7—constitutive of what we are and of the experiences we can have with ourselves and the world: one has such experiences (only) within such interpretations. At the same time, however, these interpretations (as appropriations of ourselves) are not arbitrary; they cannot arbitrarily construct what we are. There is also here a kind of relation of fit. The attempt to make oneself into who one is and the attempt to understand oneself as who one is are two sides of a practical reflective equilibrium. It is possible, then, to arrive at what Holmer Steinfath demands as the implication of a consistently applied antiessentialist conception of expression: "a concept of identity that can do without the idea that subjects necessarily have at their disposal a solid core or 'frame' defined by their highest values and without needing to stylize identity formation into an act of self-mastering choice."[13]

Conceived along these lines, the interpretive appropriation of ourselves constitutes what it appropriates, just as it, at the same time, depends on something previously existing that it can be more or less true to. Formulated differently, if self-appropriation is a complex process with many preconditions (comparable in this respect to the psychoanalytic process of "working through"), this is precisely because appropriation (and having oneself at one's command) is not simply a relation of gaining power over something, but relies on relations of fit as well as on processes of transformation and of responding to the specific characteristics of the situation. We behave in an appropriative manner to what we find before us; we behave in an appropriative manner—in many respects—to our own given conditions. Thus appropriation refers not to a limitless power to determine ourselves and the world but to ways of dealing with situations that we must relate to and to which, in doing so, we can respond in more or less adequate ways.

Second, the model of articulation sketched here sheds light on a further problem. As I have understood them, both processes—appropriation and articulation—are subject to the suspicion that they still rely on an "essentialist remainder." If it is difficult to conceive of the process of appropriation without a "given material"—ultimately there must already be something there to be appropriated—then a process of articulation always deals with something that it seeks to express. If, as we have seen in connection with Taylor, articulation

164 ALIENATION AS A DISTURBED APPROPRIATION

is neither a *creatio ex nihilo* nor merely a reflection of something that already exists, then—if one radicalizes Taylor in an antiessentialist direction—what previously exists enters as material into a process that can be described as a "process without substance": nothing underlies this process in the (substantial) sense that it must constitute the process or remain identical to itself throughout it. At the same time, this is a process in which we are always already involved. It is therefore meaningless to look for a beginning of the process or to ask about the conditions prior to such a beginning. In the moment in which we articulate ourselves, the process of transformation has already begun. Insofar as it is at all accessible to us, the "previously existing something" is always already articulated, and insofar as it is to be articulated or determined as something identifiable, it is no longer separable from its articulation.

This can be carried over to the process of (self-)appropriation: self-appropriation is always at once a finding *and* an inventing, a constructing and a reconstructing—a process in which what is appropriated first acquires a shape through its appropriation (see the section titled "Appropriation" in chapter 4). Hence, understood in terms of the capacity of self-appropriation, the self is *simultaneously given and made*, and, similarly, the process of self-appropriation knows no "outside." In the moment in which we relate to ourselves we are always already appropriating what we are. In neither case does the fact that something always already enters into the processes described here lead us back to essentialism.

RECAPITULATION

The conception of the self that underlies my analysis of alienation can now be summarized in terms of the following ideas:

BEING AS DOING In my analysis the *being* of the self or person is dissolved into a *doing*, into the performance of an action. This means—in line with existentialist themes[14]—that the self is conceived of as a relation to self or as a "relating to one's own existence" that is always already a worldly existence and must be understood within the context of a totality of practical situations. The self is defined, then, as the "sum of one's actions" (Sartre).[15]

IDENTIFICATION We are what we do and what we identify with. The self, as I argued above with help from William James, is always a self "in the broadest sense." As John Christman notes in summarizing the recent analytic discussion of autonomy and personal identity, the true self is no longer an ontologically independent entity: "The true self is the set of characteristics with which the person genuinely identifies."[16]

RELATIONALITY The self is a *relation*. It does not arise self-sufficiently out of itself but is fundamentally relational.[17] As something that "establishes relations among relations," it constitutes itself in and through the relations it has to others and to "the other" more generally and it has no being outside these relations. Even when it individuates itself, it does so from within these relations.

FLUIDITY Identities as I have described them are fluid and always "selves in the making."[18] This fluidity derives from the fact that the self is not given but must first constitute and realize itself—from the fact, then, that it first forms itself in relating to and externalizing itself in the world, in the course of which it repeatedly transforms and retransforms itself. If we ask about the unity of the self, it cannot be located in "remaining self-identical" but must be sought in the particular ways in which it integrates itself. (I discuss the integration necessary for selfhood later in this chapter.)

RELATION TO THE WORLD The subject appropriates not only itself but also, and at the same time, the world. The self, as it has been understood here, is an acting and worldly self, one that always finds itself already acting in the world and cannot be separated from it. It can understand itself only from within the world and in its involvements with it.[19]

ARTICULATION AND EXTERNALIZATION Immersed in the world, the self does not exist in a closed-off inner space where it could be found in isolation from the external world. One can understand this conception (in analogy to Marx's externalization model of labor) as an "externalization model of the self." As Hegel says, "an individual cannot know what he is until he has made himself a reality through action."[20] Our self-relation, then, always depends on and is inseparable from our externalization or articulation of ourselves. This means that we cannot be separated from how we express ourselves in the world (in what we do and say) and from how we give ourselves specific qualities by acting in the world.

EXCURSUS: "SELVES IN THE MAKING" (CASSAVETES)

"Just be yourself," says Peter Falk to his wife in *A Woman Under the Influence*. "Which self?" she answers; "I can be anything." In this film Gena Rowlands plays a woman who, asserting herself against her environment, is engaged in a search for herself. But she knows that this self is not there as something finished or discoverable and that this self does not exist independently of or in abstraction from the expectations of the external world. In a famous scene with her husband and his fellow firefighters, who after a night spent struggling with a broken water main arrive in the morning at her kitchen table, she provocatively plays out, in ever faster succession, a large variety of roles and possible identities, from the caring housewife dishing out spaghetti, to the reserved introvert, to the teasing vamp. This functions not only as a parody of the thesis that the self is constituted by taking over roles. In asking "which self?" she appears to be trying to make her husband share the responsibility: he cannot make it that easy for himself. Simply "being oneself" is not possible, just as little as simply letting someone "be herself" is—within a network of relationships—possible.

The characters in John Cassavetes' films are radically relational, perfect examples of selves without a core and of constantly changing "selves in the making." What one could call their identity emerges only in the situations they are confronted with. These situations, too, are fluid; they always emerge—this is what is distinctive about these films—out of constellations that sometimes arise very suddenly. One of the typical features of Cassavetes' films, a sudden upending of a situation just as a new character enters the scene, is due to this. It is then more than the composition of the scene that changes, and sometimes it is completely irrelevant how the newly arrived character acts. With a new external composition of the scene, the internal composition of its participants also appears to change, virtually without mediating circumstances. The individuals moving within such constellations are not self-contained but, in an almost frightening way, radically relational. In the way in which they confront situations and people—in the way in which they expose themselves and are exposed—they have "fuzzy borders" that must always be contested.

2. INTRACTABILITY AND INWARDNESS

In what follows I will attempt to make my position more precise by engaging with some objections that can be raised against the conception of the self I have outlined, as well as against my reconstruction of the idea of self-alienation that is based on it. The first objection accuses this conception of being blind to the intractable dimensions of the self (those outside our command) that appear to go hand in hand with dissolving the self's being into a doing and with its fluidity and malleability. The second objection concerns the critique of inwardness. Here I will argue against intuitions that tie inwardness to the idea of a refuge that is taken to be crucial for the development of independence, or "obstinacy," over and against social demands.

(1) THE INTRACTABILITY OF THE SELF

The intuition underlying the first objection can be articulated as follows: we cannot do everything we want; there are conditions of our existence that are intractable and outside our command not only because there are external obstacles and constraints but also because something about us or in us prevents us from doing certain things or choosing certain ways of leading our life, and from having or realizing certain desires. Formulated differently, we have the feeling about some actions, desires, etc., that they simply do not "fit" us, even when we clearly want to do or have them. In such cases it seems right to say that someone is trying "to be something she is not": the compulsive character who cannot give up the idea of a wild bohemian existence, the Kreuzberg anarchist who carries around "deep inside" him the bourgeois ideal of an orderly life, or even the feminist who has a difficult time putting her conceptions of her roles into practice. Such persons are clearly incapable of wanting as they wish they could want. And when someone with such a life history finally makes it into "a house of her own," it is frequently remarked (more or less sardonically): now she has arrived, just where she belongs; now she is finally herself. These comments seem not only to indicate that there are limits to the malleability of who a person is; they also operate in one way or another with the assumption of a "being" that underlies a person's possible actions and that prescribes and limits her modes of existence.

The objection implicit in such reactions can be formulated as follows: the conception of the self sketched earlier in this chapter does not do justice to the ways our lives are subject to conditions not of our own making. Fixated on the idea of the power to have oneself and one's life at one's command, it is unable to capture the dimension of intractability that also constitutes our existence—the ineluctable commitments and the results of formative influences that we sometimes call character. According to this objection, the self is more substantial than it appears to be in my reconstruction, and the correct account of self-alienation is (more simply) that individuals are alienated from themselves when they are compelled to act contrary to these deep formative influences (or to their character or personality).

"VOLITIONAL NATURE" AND "GROUND PROJECTS" In discussing this objection I want to return to a position we examined in chapter 7, Frankfurt's theory of volitional nature, as well as introduce a further position, namely, Joseph Raz's claim that being loyal to certain "ground projects" is constitutive of a person's identity.[21] I examine these positions because I consider them to be the theoretically most sophisticated accounts of the intractability of the self (its being outside our command) and because one could claim that, if not genuinely essentialist positions, they are plausible reconstructions of what is persuasive about (or even indispensable in) such positions.

I have already presented Frankfurt's conception of a volitional nature in connection with the feminist who is at odds with herself (chapter 7). According to this view, there are things one feels ineluctably committed to ("one can't help caring about them") and also things one cannot bring oneself to want. (Frankfurt's example was the mother who cannot bring herself to give up her child.) This leads to defining a person's identity *ex negativo*: what constitutes someone is what is intractable in her, that which she cannot have at her command. The contours of the self, then, are determined externally or negatively by the limits of its own will or the limits of its power to bring something within its command, or to "dispose" of it. As we have seen, Frankfurt goes so far as to call the contours of the self defined in this way the "volitional nature" or "personal essence" of a human being. His argument's crucial assumption is that since it is these aspects, traits, and conditions that constitute us as a person, they *cannot* be at our disposal. The price of putting them at our disposal would be self-betrayal, the loss of one's own identity. They represent the conditions of possibility for having an identity. Joseph Raz's idea of ground projects follows a similar model: ground projects are the "core" projects and attachments that we cannot give up except at the cost of losing ourselves. They—our pursuing and promoting them—provide the basic orientation that guides us in leading our lives. Ground projects are, in other words, constitutive parts of what we are and of what constitutes us. Here, too, at issue are the essential foundations of our identity: ground projects are *grounding*—projects that ground our identity or on which our identity is founded.

Whereas my account of the self as "what one wants and does" does not seem to place limits in principle on the self's power to have itself at its command (or to "dispose" of itself), the conception of the self just examined emphasizes the self's limitations: it implies that we are conditioned and determined by factors that are in many respects ineluctable and not at our disposal. What constitutes us as determinate and particular persons, according to this view, is precisely what is outside our influence, necessary, and inaccessible to thought—the intractable commitments that we have without having chosen them and that we cannot have at our disposal or command. Both versions of this position imply that we are not simply what we do and want but are rather what—to a certain extent—we *must* do and want; we are that which *makes* us do and want. The self is then not fluid but solid, not, as the metaphor of cotton candy suggests, a transformative process without a core but a structure with an ineluctable foundation. David Velleman summarizes this position as follows: "Frankfurt conceives of the self as that to which a person must be true in order to be true to himself."[22] And this self, one might add, is *given* and not *made* (by us). Even if this position is not essentialist in the classical sense, its implication for the question of self-alienation is that we are alienated from ourselves when we act or are compelled to act contrary to this personal essence or when we act in a way that is disloyal to our ground projects.

Before turning to the question of whether it is plausible to assume such foundations of the self, I will first take a closer look at the nature of these foundations and determine more precisely the specific form of essentialism they entail. Two things must be taken into account here. First, the personal essence that Frankfurt means to capture is understood as the "essence of a *person*" rather than a definition of the "essence of *human beings*." This means that Frankfurt is interested here not in humans as creaturely beings and in the ways nature imposes conditions on them (even if this is not to be denied) but rather in *persons* who are characterized by the structure of their will—by the fact that in willing they relate to themselves. Volitional nature, then, is not "nature"—the argument does not appeal to our being constrained by the natural conditions of human life; it refers, instead, to a fact about the will. At stake is not the essence of human beings but the essence (or nature) of our *will* and the self-relation that is bound up with it. In a similar sense Raz, in focusing on what "grounds" us, is not seeking natural or biological foundations. He, too, is concerned with projects that constitute us and things we have committed ourselves to. If this is an essentialist position, it does not have the reifying character of the essentialist positions we criticized earlier. The essence at issue here refers to a dimension of intractability within the domain of what is at one's command. It consists in forms of intractable commitments about which we do not deny (as we do in processes of reification) that we ourselves have created them.

Second, talk of a volitional nature is characterized by an inner tension: it refers to something that is, on the one hand, *volitional*, on the other hand, *nature*. And while we normally think of a will as something we have at our disposal or command, this is not true of nature. Our volitional nature refers to something that we want but that we supposedly also *cannot help* but want. Raz's ground projects, too, refer to projects we have set for ourselves but that are nevertheless understood such that, once our commitments to them are there, they constitute who we are and therefore ground us.

"BEING TRUE TO ONESELF" In what sense is it plausible to assume that our identity has essential foundations of this type, to assume that certain commitments define us so that we would no longer be ourselves if we renounced them? Are there things, projects, and commitments to which we must remain true if we are not to lose ourselves? And is the self, then, less fluid than substantially fixed?

My answer, to go straight to the point, is: no. According to my interpretation, the question whether someone is "herself" is not about whether she remains true to certain projects and commitments but whether in passing through various fundamental commitments she is able to tell a coherent "appropriative story" of herself that can integrate the ruptures and ambivalences in her life history (including radical revaluations of her own values).[23] I remain true to myself not when I remain loyal to projects I once entered into but when I can integrate both my holding onto projects and my giving them up into a meaningful narrative about myself. This, as I will argue, calls into question two implications of Frankfurt's and Raz's positions: the specific form of continuity and the idea of the self's unity that both presuppose. To be sure, one must first get clear about what is intuitively plausible in these conceptions[24]—there seem to be essentialist elements in our everyday notions about the self that are not easily avoided—in order to be able to integrate the views bound up with them into my interpretation. There are two intuitions and a structural consideration that speak in favor of the ineluctability thesis:

(a) On the one hand, the intuition that sometimes one "simply cannot do otherwise" is compelling, and we might be tempted to characterize someone's personality in terms of these intractable dimensions that are outside our command. It seems right that there are commitments and projects of such fundamental importance to us that if we were to lose them we would feel we had lost our orientation in life. For the revolutionary whose revolution fails,[25] or the lover who loses her beloved, it is possible that the world and her own life become meaningless in the sense described by Frankfurt. The situation must appear all the more drastic when, instead of the revolution failing, one betrays it or when, instead of losing one's beloved, one breaks off the relationship oneself. Does one still know who one is when one does something of this sort? Does not a "betrayal" of this kind undermine the foundations of one's existence? In any case, such situations can indeed lead to existential crises if the commitments at issue are truly fundamental. Precisely when it is plausible to think of identifications and commitments as crucially important — "we are what we pursue and care for"[26] — it is natural to suspect a danger of losing oneself.

(b) A further quite basic thought also seems to be correct: in order for something or someone to have a particular identity (a particular character or form) it must have limits. Someone who could be anything (could want and do anything) is not merely eerily odd; she is in an important sense not really anyone. (Frankfurt calls such a person amorphous.) Under certain circumstances she impresses us as frighteningly empty. For this reason it is not completely incomprehensible when the helpless husband in Cassavetes' film *A Woman Under the Influence* reacts with alarm when his wife answers the encouraging advice "Just be yourself" with the comment "Which self? I can be anything." In this excessive freedom to be anything her husband senses the beginning of the dissolution of her personality.

(c) What is further correct about the ineluctability thesis—this is the structural argument—is that it is not evident how someone who was not already, and did not already want, something specific could determine herself as something or how someone who did not already have specific dispositions could be able to act. Frankfurt discusses this in his essay "On the Usefulness of Final Ends": Someone who has nothing—does not *already* have something—that is important to her has no starting point from which she could pose the question of how she should lead her life or what she should consider important. There is no neutral standpoint outside my desires and my already existing commitments. We do not disinterestedly decide "from the outside" and hence free of previously existing commitments what can become important to us. The crucial question is whether this is synonymous with the ineluctability of certain projects to which one previously committed oneself, whether for this reason these projects cannot be put up for renegotiation. This leads us to a version of the old question: how can one change and at the same time remain true to oneself?

I will argue that the conclusion that Frankfurt and Raz draw from the discussions sketched here is false. The model that invokes the idea of our deepest, ineluctable commitments depends, according to my claim, on substantializing commitments and projects in a way that depends on an inadequate understanding of the unity of the will. The supposed plausibility of this model arises from a confusion of two elements: the impossibility of taking up a standpoint outside already existing commitments is not to be equated with the ineluctability of a certain stock of constitutive commitments. When in my account I replace the substantial notion of a totality and continuity of the self with a processual version of the self as self-appropriation, I am attempting to do justice to the fact that we are enmeshed in deep identifications and to the requirements of a self-bestowed unity of the subject without, however, interpreting changes in personal orientation and ambivalences within such commitments as elements of self-alienation or loss of self.

LOSS OF SELF—DISCONTINUITY AND DISSOCIATION   It must first be explained how Frankfurt imagines the process of losing oneself that he speaks of. What does it mean to be destroyed as a person, as Frankfurt puts it,[27] through the loss of commitments or projects? And is it plausible to say that the loss of certain commitments *must* destroy us as persons? We must first consider what in such experiences is supposed to lead to the loss of self and how the structure of this loss of self is to be characterized.

(1) *Loss.* An essential feature of the model of the loss of self under discussion here becomes clear when one compares the complicated structure of self-*betrayal* with the simpler case of the *loss* of something one considers important. As I have indicated, the loss of essential life projects or of something one loves can lead to serious crises of orientation. We do not, however, assume that such a loss necessarily destroys a person's continuity because—formulated very briefly—in normal cases one at the same time "holds on internally" to what one has lost or, more accurately, holds on to and lets go of it at the same time. One mourns. As we know from psychoanalysis, successful mourning is marked by a balance between letting go of and holding on to the loved object.

In coping with a loss, a person's attachment to the object is transformed without being given up completely. For this reason both rigidly holding onto the object—being unable to acknowledge the loss—and giving it up immediately are problematic. Insofar as a painful loss can be overcome, the (psychological) continuity of the person throughout change is preserved by her integrating the experience of loss in a specific way.[28] In this respect she is in fact (in Frankfurt's sense) "no longer the same person" as the one who had a certain love or pursued a certain project. She is, however, someone whose identity and self-conception are marked by the experience of loss such that it could be said that what she has lost remains a part of herself in this negative form and is preserved in her identity. The question whether one is still oneself after a loss depends, then, on the conditions under which it is worked through, on how one relates to what has been lost (in a way that produces continuity), and not necessarily on the "objective" severity of the loss.

(2) *Self-Betrayal.* Much more complicated is the case in which the loss of a commitment or object comes about through our own break with it. When we *ourselves* betray what we love (and hence break with what constitutes us in Frankfurt's sense), precisely the element of "internally holding on to something" that can secure continuity in the case of a loss seems no longer possible. The object is then not simply gone—the loved one disappeared, the revolution no longer possible; rather, one has abandoned it oneself. What has to be worked through then is not only the loss of an object but—on a second level—the loss of one's own attachment to the object. Formulated schematically: in the one case the object is gone but the attachment continues to exist, and the task of the person who suffers the loss is to transform this attachment. In the other case (of alleged self-betrayal) the object is still present (the revolution is still possible, the loved one is still there), but the attachment to the object has been lost. Whereas, in one respect, one might consider this to be the easier case—in the end the attachment was dissolved voluntarily and as the result of one's own decision—on the other hand what takes place here is a serious transformation. Assuming the attachment in question belonged to the commitments, desires, and projects that constitute us in our "innermost selves," the dissolution of this attachment must, in fact, appear as a betrayal of oneself with the feared consequence: a loss of self.

On the other hand, is it not *I* who breaks with myself? And, if it is, why should I have betrayed myself in doing so? How is it even possible to betray oneself or to be untrue to oneself in Frankfurt's sense? My conjecture is that the plausibility of Frankfurt's talk of self-betrayal depends on two elements being run together such that the betrayer appears, at the same time and in the same respect, both to love and betray the revolution or loved one. Strictly speaking, though, this is not the case.

There are two possible ways of disentangling what appears here to be situationally (and motivationally) indissolubly bound together: either what has gone on is a (temporally occurring) *process of transformation*; then one would need to describe the structure of self-betrayal such that a *later* self has betrayed an *earlier* one (the counterrevolutionary that I now am betrays the revolutionary I once was).[29] In this case the crucial question is how to conceive of the relation between the earlier and later selves. The second possibility is that we have here a structural *ambivalence* or a mixed emotional state. I love something (the revolution or my loved one) and at the same time I do not love it. In that case I would have split myself into two parts in a certain respect, where one part betrays the other. Here, too, the crucial question is how we are to imagine the splitting of oneself into two parts and the relation between them.

In both cases the talk of self-betrayal implies a split into two selves: either a *discontinuity* between earlier and later selves or an ongoing *dissociation* of the self. The destruction of the person or the loss of self that supposedly accompanies the abandonment of constitutive attachments must be conceived of as follows: the person Frankfurt speaks of is destroyed because she is *no longer one* but is split into earlier and later (or two parallel) selves. Frankfurt can describe such a split completely without paradox (and without serious metaphysical problems) as a split in a person's "volitional unity." What I want and advocate as a revolutionary is incompatible with what I want and advocate as a counterrevolutionary; since my unity as a person, however, can be characterized only in terms of a unity of will, this volitional split splits me as a person. The dissolution of volitional unity means, then, according to Frankfurt, the dissolution of the person. Hence, if we want to criticize Frankfurt's account, we must call this idea of unity into question. As I noted earlier, I consider his tying the possibility of a person's unity exclusively to those situations in which we pursue and hold fast to a project with our "whole heart" to entail an overly substantialist picture of the self. And the idea that in cases of ambivalence or transformation a person splits into two parts (or two identities) goes hand in hand with a reessentialization of personal identity. Against this backdrop, the unity of a person can be understood only on the model of an undivided substance, and its continuity only in terms of something's remaining identical to itself.

One sees this—with respect to the case where the will is split in two contrary directions—in Frankfurt's discussion of a famous case of self-betrayal: Agamemnon, forced by a tragic conflict to betray either daughter or fatherland, is, after he has committed his betrayal, destroyed as a person. "Agamemnon at Aulis is destroyed by an inescapable conflict between two equally defining elements of his own nature: his love for his daughter and the love for the army he commands. . . . When he is forced to sacrifice one of these, he is thereby forced to betray himself. Rarely, if ever, do tragedies of this sort have sequels. Since the volitional unity of the tragic hero has been irreparably ruptured, there is a sense in which the person he had been no longer exists. Hence there can be no continuation of *his* story."[30]

This is counterintuitive as an interpretation of the epos, and it displays little insight into the nature of a tragic conflict. In fact, Agamemnon's story does continue, and precisely as the story of someone who has to cope with his betrayal and who remains scarred by it. The tragic hero is a personality characterized by having to endure an insuperable conflict. This means, though, that, just as with a simple loss, there can be a continuation of the story as *his* story insofar as he *appropriates* it, exactly as one does in the simpler case of loss and mourning. Agamemnon must integrate his abandonment of his loyalty to his daughter; he must accept it as a part of his will (which is then simultaneously willing and not willing). Here too, then, the element of holding onto the object is present without this implying a resolution of the conflict. (The conflict is tragic precisely because one holds onto both sides, because one does not give up one's loyalty to the one side while acting in favor of the other.)

BEING ONESELF AS SELF-APPROPRIATION The counter position to this substantializing or unifying conception of identity can be formulated as follows: identity is what perseveres in the balancing out of inner ambivalences or of (externally caused) conflicts and in securing continuity in the face of changing commitments. The integration of the self required here does not imply the resolution of all ambivalences and conflicts, and it is conceived of as a temporally extended process. The unity of the person that is achievable in this manner is not, then, given as a starting point but is a result of a process of integration or appropriation; at the same time, it is to be conceived of as a unity of qualitatively different elements, hence as a unity that is capable of encompassing internal tensions. (Incidentally, it does not follow from this that there is a self beyond or independent of these projects and commitments, something that remains identical to itself independently of them. So understood, the self, as something that "establishes relations among relations," is the agency responsible for "working through" the constellation of these commitments.)

In contrast to Frankfurt's conception of unity, this means I can be myself without being wholehearted in a substantial sense. This implies that I am also myself when I am *fundamentally ambivalent* with regard to important and constitutive attachments. (Otherwise, hardly anyone would have an identity if we assume that many if not most fundamental attachments—classically, those to one's parents—are marked by ambivalence.) What constitutes me (my identity) would consist, then, in the specific ways I engage with ambivalences or "balance" them.[31] One is threatened with the shattering of identity that Frankfurt sees in every loss of wholeheartedness only when this balancing is unsuccessful.

In contrast to the conception of continuity as "holding on to something" or remaining self-identical, it follows that someone can remain herself even if she has made fundamental about-turns with respect to basic aspects of her life, terminating important commitments or abandoning important projects. The self's continuity in such transformations depends not on steadily holding onto certain projects but rather on being able to integrate the succession of changes among projects or commitments. Neither the committed revolutionary nor the devoted lover necessarily betrays herself if she one day separates herself from her projects. The question is rather *how* one gives them up or *how* the process of transformation takes place. Crucial here is whether one can make sense of the process—the changes that have led from one condition to another— and integrate it into one's own life history or self-conception (as I characterized it in chapter 7, as a structure that is both constructed and reconstructed). If someone is unable to do this and experiences unbridgeable discontinuities, among which no connections can be made, that can be described as a form of self-alienation, as alienation from one's own past. By emphasizing the element of integration in this way, it is possible to take up a different position concerning the unitary nature of the self. Whereas Frankfurt's idea of (unalienated) identity is clearly oriented around a picture of a unitary and stable person rather than one who is characterized by ambivalences and radical breaks, my position focuses on the *process* of (self-)appropriation. What is important is not a substantial "totality" or constancy of identifications but the capacity to integrate and appropriate, that is, the accessibility of the conflicting parts and the mobility among them. Being able to make sense of, or to integrate, one's changes is in turn a complex process that, on the one hand, involves being able to give good reasons (to myself and others) for the changes in my position and, on the other hand, depends on the extent to which I can make sense of them emotionally and fit them into the overall economy of my desires and projects as it has developed in the course of my life history.

In his essay "The Experience of Time and Personality" Peter Bieri elaborates, in an especially clear manner, the active and constructive character of the creation of such a unity of the person (in the sense of creating the unity of a life history). In his account, too, identity is constituted as a history of appropriation. When he speaks of the creation of a "hermeneutic unity" of the person that is carried out in the form of a history of appropriation, he means, in the first place, that I am the one who *is able* to create the unity among the heterogeneous elements. In addition, he means that I must first *create* this unity in an active process, that it is not otherwise simply given. Personal identity as the result of a history of appropriation—the appropriation of myself in my life history—is in this sense an ideal that must be approximated actively.

> It is not sufficient, according to this ideal, that I simply *establish* vis-à-vis my past that certain things have happened to me. As a person I must attempt to *take possession* of them and to understand them as *parts of myself* such that they no longer appear *alien* to me. Described differently, this ideal says that I should attempt to bring a unity into my past life. In fact this past life already had a unity that came about without my assistance: the events of my history are causally dependent on one another and thereby form a causal unity. The unity at issue in the concept of appropriation is, in contrast, a unity that I myself must *create*. It arises from my need to understand my past. To the extent that I am successful in understanding my past, I bring unity into it. I would like to call this unity *hermeneutic unity*.[32]

The following points can be drawn out of Bieri's account for my critique of Frankfurt's position:

* First, from the conception of (self-)appropriation as an *active* achievement of the person who appropriates her life history there emerges an alternative to the more passive model of identification found in Frankfurt. The individual does not *find* her identifications as volitional necessities but creates them, relates to them, and only then makes them her own. What this

illuminates is the part individuals play in forming identifications—the fact that the commitments within which they move do not simply "happen" to them.

 ▓ Second, identity is conceived of as a *process*: there is no identity without the continually renewed appropriation of what one does and, along with this, the potential transformation of what one is. As Bieri says: "If we are successful in constructing a new hermeneutic unity of our past that is more integrative than the previous one, then our identity changes. This is a constant process, and this kind of change of identity is *essential* for persons, since this process reflects an effort to come closer and closer to the ideal of personhood: an appropriation of the past that is as complete as possible."[33] (As with the cotton candy that Perlmann speaks of, without this constant renewal a person's identity would collapse in on itself.) For the question of self-transformation and alienation it follows that holding on to ground projects and ideals (as Frankfurt also calls our ineluctable commitments) is not to be unalienated per se. On the contrary, when our ground projects and ideals are not part of a permanent process of appropriation, when volitional necessities or impossibilities remain in fact ineluctable, unquestionable, and not at our disposal, then identities are solidified and persons are rigidified in their loyalties; such persons are inflexible and therefore possibly alienated from themselves because the process of appropriation has come to a halt. In this sense Frankfurt is correct in objecting to the idea of the self's unlimited tractability (its being wholly within our command): "We are not fictitious characters, who have sovereign authors; nor are we gods, who can be authors of more than fiction. Therefore, we cannot be authors of ourselves."[34] On the other hand, the idea of a history of appropriation also implies the opposite position: in a certain respect we *must* be the authors of ourselves and we always already are our own authors precisely because in order to be someone we must appropriate our history. We must write, and continue to write, our history precisely because what we are is not already written down somewhere. Self-alienation, then, is a disturbance of this relation of appropriation and not the discontinuity of projects or ambivalence with respect to commitments.

 ▓ Third, it follows from Bieri's account that an antiessentialist conception of personal identity and the denial of an intractable, uncommandable substance do not necessarily lead to the will's being confused or directionless. The position adopted here (doubting the existence of an essential element of our existence) is not equivalent to the assumption that individuals must have a presuppositionless starting point or be capable of unlimited self-mastery. As Bieri notes: "it is important to see that the succession of changing histories of appropriation is the *only thing* that can answer the question 'Who am I?'.

There is no stable core of the person, no standpoint *outside* these histories from which I could ask: 'But who am I *really*—independently of these histories?'"[35] Applying this to our question about ground projects or volitional necessities, it follows that, on the one hand, there can be no personal essence, no something that constitutes us beyond our construction and interpretation of ourselves.[36] On the other hand, this by no means commits us to the claim that there must be a presuppositionless starting point or a disengaged self that is able to act freely outside already existing commitments or involvements.

With this I return to the confusion I referred to earlier. The fact that we always already have specific commitments and are always already involved with something does not imply that the self is intractable or outside our command, nor can it be inferred from this fact that we are substantially bound up with certain commitments or projects that constitute us (with volitional necessity). Of course, it is crucial to see that one can never stand completely outside such commitments without losing one's identity because that would mean standing outside one's own life. However, this only means, to again take up the image from chapter 7, that every transformation and reappropriation (even a radical one) is like Neurath's "rebuilding on the high sea" and that one cannot pull the ship onto land in order to replace all the planks at once.

The self is not given. It is always a self in the making, even if it cannot be designed from scratch but must instead—in an ongoing process of transformation—always be made out of something that already is something. To return to Neurath's ship: the idea that some planks are in principle irreplaceable is misleading. Or, to use Perlmann's image again, what is crucial for a person's continuity and unity is only that the web of cotton candy does not tear apart and that one can integrate the various changes or tensions into the narrative unity of a history of appropriation in which we always already find ourselves. This does not mean that something (like a single thread that connects everything together) must be preserved, but that one should be able to connect one thing with another in a meaningful way. A person's identity is threatened only when parts of the self can no longer be threaded together and not merely because it is spun with changing material. And, to return to the first of the intuitions mentioned earlier: it is possible that the threat of the thread breaking is especially acute when some commitments or projects are lost. This, however, is due—this is the key to preserving the intuition—to the kind of loss and how it is worked through (or the possibilities of working it through), not to the fact that there is a core of commitments and projects that constitutes us substantially and is outside our command.

(2) "A SELF THAT CAN RESIST AND OPPOSE": THE INNER CITADEL AS A PLACE OF RETREAT

The modern self . . . was born in a prison. It assumed its nature and fate the moment it perceived, named and denounced its oppressor.

—LIONEL TRILLING, *THE OPPOSING SELF*

The second objection I want to discuss is directed against the critique of the "inwardness conception" of the self that I developed previously in conjunction with my discussion of alienation. I claimed that there is no true self apart from its external manifestations, and the conception of the self that stood in the background of my discussion was one of not only a radically fluid but also a radically relational self, one that first develops *in* relations and therefore in its public articulations. Several objections can be raised to this position.

* Is it not clear that sometimes we can "come to ourselves" only by abstracting from the external world, that we sometimes need inwardness as a place of retreat in order to become aware of *who* we really are among all the things we are involved in and related to?[37] And is not the experience that our public, external manifestations can distort our innermost self a common and vivid one? Is the possibility of one's existence being distorted, deformed, and made alien by the public "other" not a real problem? Is not, then, the search Rousseau was driven by in his *Confessions* an understandable longing—the search for a pure, unfalsified self that, detached from its entanglement in the external world, lives "within itself"?

* Moreover, does not the thesis of "coming to oneself" and defining oneself in relation to others (which is common to all conceptions of the self as socially constructed) lead to an oversocialized model that is no longer able to accommodate the real tensions between individual and society? Is there really, as the socialization model appears to suggest, no presocial remainder, something that the individual cannot make publicly accessible and that does not result from her position in a public world? Formulated differently, are there no limits to be placed on the "individualization as socialization" thesis, especially when self-alienation is at issue? Or, as Diggins raises the question against pragmatist conceptions of the self, "how can one be true to one's self if the self has no ontological status apart from society and its discontents?"[38]

If one thinks of the gap between self and (social) world as a defining experience of modernity and understands modern individuality's objection to identifying the individual with her public functions and traditional roles (and subsuming her to them) as having an emancipatory dimension, then the (historical) function of the construct of inwardness is incontestable. And if, as MacIntyre portrays it, the ever intensifying split between inner and outer worlds was characteristic of bourgeois culture,[39] then we must take the appeal to the inner seriously as an objection. According to Lionel Trilling, the romantic conception of a "self that can resist and oppose" defends the claim of an individual who, in her individual uniqueness developed in the form of inwardness,[40] represents an opposing authority to that of society.

I will return to the problem of the sociality of individuals and limit myself at this point to examining the intuitions bound up in the construct of inwardness. Although I will argue that these intuitions can be understood as a placeholder for the (bourgeois individual's) desire for emancipation, I will also claim that they operate with a set of implausible assumptions. I believe—and this is all I want to go into briefly here—that the supposed plausibility of such objections (and the attractiveness of the outlined positions) rests at least partly on common confusions or misunderstandings. Finally—as I will show with the example of two characters from a novel of Henry James—the model of inwardness rests on an illusory idea of the pure self that forces it into precisely the defensive position it wanted to fight its way out of.

GENUINENESS AND INDEPENDENCE There are two ideas implicit in a positive appeal to inwardness: one is the assumption of *genuineness* (the idea of an "unfalsified" self), and the other is the assumption of a self's *independence*, understood as inner and therefore outside the external world's influence. In most contexts these two ideas go hand in hand with the claim that the self possesses a distinct ontological status independent of its social relations.

There are two objections I would like to bring against this position: first, in order to comprehend the possibility of such a pivot point for the self's obstinacy or resistance, it is not necessary to accord the self any independent ontological status. Second, the self's resistance, obstinacy, or independence in relation to social expectations of conformity and to the network of social practices and relations does not mark any pre- or extrarelational (or pre- or extrasocial) standpoint but rather a standpoint within these relations. (I go into this topic in more detail in the conclusion.)

Thus the claim that the individual develops in dependence on and confrontation with social relations and demands does not assume that these relations are free of tension. At the same time, the existence of a tension between individual and society does not imply that the former is independent of the latter. Not only can one claim that the individual, precisely in her obstinacy and resistance, derives her contours from this relation of tension; it is also the case that assuming such a discrepancy—a "self that can resist and oppose"— does not require the idea of an individual who is "inner" or independent of the external world. Thus one can conceive of a "resisting individuality" without thinking of obstinacy as something presocial,[41] but instead as a constellation of various sources, layers, and displacements. If individuality, though, is something that first emerges in such relations of tension, the charge of accommodationism (made against the claim of the self's sociality and relationality) is not tenable. The real conflict then does not turn on the question of the ineluctability of the *relation* in general. What is denied is not that individuals are resistant or obstinate but that the source of this obstinacy is to be found in the vacuum of an inner space that disavows a relation to the external world.

INNER LIFE AS INNER WORLD It is also the case that the intuition that one must sometimes withdraw in order "to come to oneself" does not necessarily lead to locating the true self in an inner space. One can partially withdraw from the world by distancing oneself from it, by (metaphorically speaking) creating a space in which one maintains a distance from certain influences and expectations. What is reflected on *in* this space, however, is still the world. In connection with this, David E. Cooper describes very compellingly Heidegger's rejection of the "introspective approach towards self-understanding": "He does not, of course, deny the need to pause and take stock of oneself; but this is the need, not for 'inner perception' but for awareness of the things, and my engagement with them, which constitute my 'environing world.' The shoemaker understands the man he is by seeing himself—replete with his sense of what matters to him and his ambitions for the future—reflected in the shoes he makes, the workshop in which he makes them, and the home in which he lives."[42] According to this, being able to withdraw from the world means reflecting on what one does in the world while abstracting from certain (or especially pressing) current expectations. It is still, however, always the world one deals with. The person who reflects in this way is still an individual who would not be conceivable without relations to and engagement with this world. Inwardness, when it claims to be worldless, is illusory. It would have no content.

It is wise, then, to regard the inner citadel as a metaphor. What one here "inwardly" keeps back from the world is still the world. What one reflects on here while momentarily suspending external influences can only be the world, oneself in one's relations to it. Inner life is an inner world. The individual is independent insofar as she can independently take a position with respect to the demands of the external world. And obstinacy does not develop in an unfalsified, unspoiled, and self-sufficient realm of one's own but rather as an obstinate (external) expression and obstinate dealing with the world.

THE SELF AND ITS SHELL (HENRY JAMES)   In a dialogue that one could almost read as a commentary on the views of his brother William concerning the "self in its widest sense," cited earlier, Henry James illustrates the conflict between a social and worldly conception of the self and a form of subjectivity oriented around a worldless inwardness. Isabel Archer, the young heroine of *The Portrait of a Lady*, receives what is supposed to be an introduction into life from her (only apparently well-disposed) motherly friend Serena Merle:

> When you've lived as long as I you'll see that every *human being has his shell* and that one must take the shell into account. By the shell I mean the whole envelope of circumstances. There's no such thing as an isolated man or woman; we're each made up of some cluster of appurtenances. What shall we call our "self"? Where does it begin? Where does it end? It overflows into everything that belongs to us—and then flows back again. I know a large part of myself is in the clothes I choose to wear. I've a great respect for *things*. One's self—for other people—is one's expression of one's self; and one's house, one's furniture, one's garments, the books one reads, the company one keeps—these things are all expressive.[43]

Disagreeing with Merle, Isabel Archer insists on an inwardness of character that cannot be reduced to external expressions and external qualities and attachments:

> I don't agree with you. I think just the other way. I don't know whether I succeed in expressing myself, but I know that nothing else expresses me. Nothing that belongs to me is any measure of me: everything's on the contrary a limit, a barrier, and a perfectly arbitrary one. Certainly the clothes which, as you say, I choose to wear don't express me; and heaven forbid they should. . . . My clothes express the dressmaker, but they don't express me.

To begin with it's not my own choice that I wear them: they're imposed on me by society.[44]

Merle's position corresponds to a conception of the self similar to the one I have discussed: the self expresses itself in external manifestations; it expresses itself and materializes itself as a "shell," consisting of the material and immaterial things with which one identifies and to which one relates, which, at the same time, does not remain external like a shell. These manifestations, the attachments and circumstances in which one finds oneself, are not detachable from the self but become part of it. They are therefore not constraints but conditions and they amount to "being determined" in a positive sense: they make someone into what she is. Isabel, on the contrary, insists that the self is ungraspable and immaterial, something for which everything that "belongs to it" can appear only as a completely contingent and hence meaningless characteristic and therefore only as a barrier and limit, as a falsification of a genuine "being oneself." Not only (contrary to Merle's position) do clothes make the self alien; tellingly, even language is characterized as alien and self-alienating. What exactly, though, *is* her self, if everything it could fasten onto and in which it could manifest itself is thought to be indifferent to it? The individual Isabel sees herself as eludes every definition. It expresses itself in nothing (in nothing manifest in the world) and cannot be expressed by anything. Here we have a perfect example of a conception of identity as inwardness. One can characterize James's position in relation to Isabel Archer's as follows: "To live, in the Jamesian sense, one must choose certain experiences and reject others; it is through such choices that we project a *social* identity. . . . Isabel, however, with her inflated American ideal of sincerity, refuses to accept any social identity that does not express her true spiritual being."[45] And this "true spiritual being" will reveal itself to be an illusion. The entire further development of events can be interpreted as a refutation of this ideal of sincerity. Henry James's implicit psychological position, as many examples show, involves a quintessentially relational conception of the self that is not only "embedded" in a static sense but is, beyond this, situational. Who his characters are can be expressed only by describing constellations of persons and situations.

Here, too (in Isabel's conception), insisting on the purely "inward" model of the self goes hand in hand with thinking of what is one's own in terms of resistance and independence in relation to society. The implicit view seems to be that what is one's own can be preserved or developed only by abstracting from external manifestations, from the impressions external things make on the individual, and from how the individual is expressed in them. Here too, then, the inwardness conception of authenticity is connected to the possibility of resistance and obstinacy. When Isabel Archer justifies her refusal to see herself as expressed by her clothes by appealing to their nature as a social convention—"it's not my own choice that I wear them: they're imposed on me by society"—she is making this kind of argument. As we have seen, this connection is not only not compelling; it is also illusory. The point is not merely that Isabel Archer cannot get by without wearing clothes. Even if she were to decide to dress completely carelessly or to treat certain forms of etiquette with indifference, she could not avoid expressing something in doing so; especially in the time and social stratum in which she lives, she would be expressing something whether she wanted to or not. "A self that can resist and oppose" must not only be one that is real, that is capable of shaping its reality, and that shapes itself in its involvement with reality; it must also, above all, be capable of reflecting on the relations that, for better or worse, it is caught up in. Learning this will be Isabel's fate. The conception of independence as inwardness founders on itself.

3. SELF-INVENTION AND THE MULTIPLICITY OF THE SELF

I'm not me.

—GENA ROWLANDS IN JOHN CASSAVETES'S FILM *OPENING NIGHT*

Whereas, in my discussion of Harry Frankfurt, I argued against a position that assumes too strong a unity of the self and seeks to tie the subject too closely to a basic core of its identity, my appropriative conception of the self also entails a critical distance to positions that want to completely dissolve both the unity and the conditioned nature of the self. In what follows I deal with approaches and themes—one can associate them, roughly, with postmodern or poststructuralist views—that, from the perspective of a critique of the subject, are oriented around the idea of a no longer identifiable—a fluid, multiple, or transformative—identity. Without being able to treat exhaustively the multifaceted discussion of the problem of subjectivity that has emerged above all from the work of Michel Foucault,[46] I will address some of the themes that have become important as a result of this debate: (1) the idea of self-*invention*,[47] in contrast to the traditional idea of *finding* oneself; and (2) the

idea of the *multiplicity*, plurality, and hybrid character of postmodern identities, in contrast to traditional ideas of the unity of the subject.

My claim is that the conception of self-appropriation goes beyond the
alternatives sketched here. Since self-*appropriation* is opposed to both the
model of self-*invention* and the model of *finding* oneself, my position shares
the critique of essentialism made by the Nietzschean poststructuralist camp
without, however, giving up on criteria for successful relations to self. And
since processes of appropriation always also involve an integration of diverse
and malleable elements, the appropriative model, as a conception of unity in
diversity, considers a unity in the self's relation to itself (one that must be first
somehow created) to be indispensable.[48]

(1) THE SELF AS A WORK OF ART—SELF-INVENTION VERSUS FINDING ONESELF

Already for Nietzsche, who can be regarded as the founding figure of the idea
of self-*invention*, the idea of creative self-formation stands in contrast to the
idea of *finding* oneself that underlies the search for the true self. Nietzsche
writes: "It is mythology to believe that we find our authentic self after having
left behind or forgotten this thing or that. In this way we unravel ourselves
back to infinity: instead, to *make ourselves*, to *shape* a form out of all elements—this is the task! Always that of a sculptor! Of a productive human
being!"[49] Clearly proceeding from the same distinction, the late Foucault formulates the point as follows: "From the idea that the self is not given to us, I
think that there is only one practical consequence: we have to create ourselves
as a work of art."[50] And Wilhelm Schmid, too, locates the alternative between
a substantially conceived "subject of identity" and what is to be reconceived
as the "subject of experience and experimentation" in a field of conflict that
adjoins the question of the authenticity of the self: "If there is no longer a
substantial subject, no longer a subject that exists as an unchanging ground
of our relation to self and world, then a space is opened up for a subject that
is to be artistically fashioned as something new: this subject is not 'authentic.'
This self-constitution is not a 'self-realization'—it has nothing to do with a
self that could be tracked down in some depth where it has lived on for itself
fully unknown."[51]

Thus creativity in relation to oneself takes the place of the ideal of authenticity. Yet this "self-production" does not only represent (as it is sometimes
polemically presented) an overcoming of the classical Enlightenment, hu-

manist project of emancipation; it also continues that project. Even if the ideal of self-creation has in the meantime "become an economic imperative"—as Diedrich Diederichsen notes in regard to a situation in which the idea of self-creation is increasingly interpreted in terms of plastic surgery[52]—at least for Foucault self-invention also represents a potential for resistance. Considered in this way, producing oneself is a strategy of the subject for not simply abandoning itself without resistance to formation through power (which at the same time constitutes it).

SELF-INVENTION VERSUS SELF-APPROPRIATION How, then, does this interpretation of the relation to self differ from the model of self-appropriation put forward here? And to what extent does it make a diagnosis of alienation impossible?[53]

If the idea of self-invention is contrasted with that of working through layers of masks, under which it is assumed that there stands a true self or the "subject as an immutable ground," then one can immediately see commonalities with the model of self-appropriation. The latter, too, envisages a "subject of experience and experimentation,"[54] and it, too, is explicitly concerned to avoid any appeal to an underlying self that "could be tracked down in some depth where it has lived . . . unknown." Both views agree, then, in their antiessentialism; in both cases the self is a "self in the making" that exists insofar as it produces itself in action.

At the same time, I want to elaborate two differences between the idea of self-production or self-invention and the thesis concerning the practical production and appropriation of the self:

The first difference between self-invention and self-appropriation consists in the fact that in the latter it is possible to identify criteria for successful processes of appropriation and hence also for disturbances in self-relations. The very point of the self-inventing "self as a work of art," in contrast, seems to be that here—in being oriented toward what is new and has never before been thought of, understood as something that conforms to no standard—such criteria are ruled out.

A second difference between the two approaches emerges in relation to what is prior to the constitutive process (invention or appropriation). If self-appropriation, as we have seen,[55] is a process in which finding and inventing, constructing and reconstructing, are equally primordial, then the process of appropriation always reckons with the existence of something prior that it takes over and transforms. This differs from the idea of self-invention since, in invoking a process of invention, it at least suggests a "creation out of nothing."

It is this difference I would like to go into first in order to return afterward to the question of normativity. The differences between the self-invention and self-appropriation models can be traced back essentially to the nature of the formative process (of the self) posited by each. The difference that comes into view then can be understood, roughly, as a difference between a demiurgic *process of production* and a *praxis that consists in carrying out actions.*

THE SELF AS DEMIURGE AND THE PRODUCTION PARADIGM OF THE SELF   There is a peculiar (and much discussed) tension in the work of some exponents of the idea of self-invention—a tension, namely, between the idea that there is no subject and an almost demiurgic idea of production, between a conception of the subject as a "grammatical error" (Nietzsche) or an effect of power (Foucault), on the one hand, and, on the other, the subject as an apparently omnipotent creator of a work of art (itself).[56] This idea of self-fashioning seems in some respects to go hand in hand with a voluntarism that exhibits traces of hubris. For where does the agent come from who is suddenly endowed with so much power to act that it can create itself as a work of art? Who creates the creator here? Or is it not only a *creatio ex nihilo* but a *creatio* without a *creator?*

Taken seriously, the analogy with a sculptor or a work of art that informs the idea of self-invention suggests the creation of something that did not exist previously and for which there is no "construction manual," no rules that govern its fashioning. What is at issue here, then, is not merely forming in general but a free and innovative forming of oneself. To say that the self invents itself is to say both that it invents itself as something *new* and that it is *free* and unhindered in this fashioning process.

Now the metaphor of a work of art raises several problems. First, insofar as a work of art is *invented*, it has no relation to something that was already there previously or that could determine or condition it. Second, someone who *creates herself as a work of art* approaches herself as material to be worked on; she is, then, simultaneously subject and object. Third, the self as a work of art is the result of a process of production, a product. Self-invention, then, is conceived of on the model of *poiesis*,[57] and this implies that the idea of self-production is bound up with an ultimately untenable paradigm derived from the metaphor of production.

THE SELF AS PRAXIS The difference between self-invention and self-appropriation can now be formulated using Aristotle's distinction between *praxis* and *poiesis*: whereas self-invention follows a "production paradigm" of the self, self-appropriation is conceived of as *praxis*.[58] The demiurgic idea of creation implicit in self-invention stands in contrast to an idea of self-appropriation in which one is practically, in performing actions, always already involved.[59] On the latter view, the self is less a work of art one makes oneself into than a practical-experimental process one is caught up in. This account has implications, on the one hand, for the self's relation to what exists prior to it (and hence for its conditioned nature) and, on the other hand, for its relation to intersubjectivity.

Since appropriation is not a creation out of nothing, there is always something previously there that is appropriated, simultaneously transformed, and in a certain respect first produced. If what previously exists is itself the result of a process of appropriation, then it is impossible to identify either the beginning or the end of such a process; there is no condition *outside* or *prior to* such a process that can be meaningfully identified. If the self, as I formulated it before, is at once given and made, then neither is it given, nor does it first come into being in the moment of its creation; it is, rather, a process of transformation that must always reckon with already given conditions. Self-appropriation means, then, self-formation without the omnipotence of the self-inventing demiurge.

This can also be seen in a further point: as the result of actions we carry out, we are (in Arendt's sense) always only coauthors of ourselves. Acting within a "web of actions," in relating to ourselves we are subject to the influence of others. We do not, like the self-inventing demiurge, exist alone.

This difference between the self as a result of a productive process and the self as a result of a praxis consisting in interactions with what is "other" also has implications for the question of normativity and hence for the question whether there can be criteria for the success of such processes. The "selves in the making" postulated by the model of appropriation become something by making themselves into that something; at the same time, they are not fully free in forming themselves but are confronted with both the obstinacy of their material (which, by the way, the sculptor, too, must reckon with) and the obstinacy of social processes. As selves in the making, they are subject to an inexhaustible process of interaction with others and with "the other" more generally. Appropriation, then, is neither a process of finding oneself nor a demiurgic fashioning but an experiment. Such an experiment, however, has conditions of success.[60] In contrast to demiurgic self-production, which finds its ideal in the lack of criteria and in being independent of all given conditions, in my model there are criteria of appropriateness and well-functioning.

Thus, from the fact that it is impossible to "find" oneself, my account does *not* conclude that it is also impossible to "miss" or "fall short" of oneself. Even in the absence of the possibility of finding oneself there can be success in the process of appropriation, which can be described as the success or lack of success in performing an action.

(2) "THE SELF THAT IS NOT ONE"—MULTIPLE IDENTITIES, HYBRIDITY, AND DISSOCIATION

In the discussion of postmodern identities there is a second topos that has achieved popularity beyond philosophical discourse in the narrower sense: that of multiple identities. Schmid formulates the task of a new conception of the self not based on the model of identity as follows:

> The firmly established form is to be broken through by transformation; the finite formation of the subject is to be burst open through infinite experience, which is always *experience of the other* in every sense of the word. This is how a subject characterized by mutability and malleability constitutes itself; a diverse self and hence *not a self of identity*: being always self-identical and the same hinders the penetration of the other and makes every change impossible. The subject of identity is no longer tenable today.[61]

The terms mentioned here can be heard over and over again in the flood of psychological and sociological debates concerning postmodern identities. They describe what is supposed to replace the old "subject of identity." Mutability, openness to experience, malleability, multiplicity: they characterize a self that is "*not one*," a subject that is capable of experiencing what is completely different from itself without thereby acquiring a firmly demarcated and definable identity. Like the demiurgic paradigm, a conception of the self characterized in these terms also seems to rule out any resumption of a discussion of alienation. Can a self that is essentially "an other" still be alienated from itself? At issue here is the unitary nature of the subject, the possibility of an individual being identical with herself in a way that could be contrasted with an alienating loss of self.

Now the purely conceptual problems with such a conception of identity and transformation are obvious. A self that has experiences is in a certain respect always "one," even if it becomes different (or "other") in its experiences with itself and the world. For if there were no subject that could integrate these experiences into its experience and history, thereby making them its own, one could not speak of experience at all. This is the case even when experience is conceived of as a "borderline experience" or a "transgression." Either a borderline experience changes the subject, in which case the subject—as something changed—remains "one" and is still a "subject of identity," even if this identity is flexible or mutable, or the subject does not remain "one," in which case it is unclear to what extent the subject has had an experience.[62]

The talk of multiplicity gets entangled in similar contradictions. Must not the various identities still be connected back to a bearer of these identities in order to be recognized or experienced as such? Do they not also depend on something that can integrate them? For this reason this much invoked multiplicity must either refer to different aspects of a person or to several identities that can be demarcated from one another. In the first case it would seem more appropriate to speak of a diversity of intersecting role identities or of ambivalences within a single person rather than of multiple identities. Genuine multiplicity, in which the orientations in question are comprehensive and mutually exclusive, would, in contrast, amount to a fragmentation of the person (as characterized by the clinical symptom of multiple personalities as opposed to the loose appropriation of the term in everyday usage). Then, however, we would no longer have transgressions and borderline experiences but rather (perhaps traumatic) experiences of which it could be said precisely that they make experience impossible. Such a subject would be, then, not diverse but threatened in its very existence. It is unclear how we are to imagine a multiple self that is no longer a "self of identity," and it is an open question how "penetration by the other" can be conceived without referring to something that undergoes change. Regarded in this way, the talk of a multiple self whose identity cannot be pinned down is inconsistent, or, in other words, these ways of speaking are unfortunate theoretical dramatizations of phenomena that can be grasped more adequately by other concepts. My thesis, then, is that abandoning this reference point—that of a unity-creating self that appropriates its various possible roles and dimensions, as well as its attitudes and desires, and works through and integrates conflicting experiences—has grave consequences. Whereas the position of Frankfurt we have discussed conceives of the continuity of the self too statically, abandoning any idea of a consistent relation to self in relation to our self-perceptions and self-interpretations is counterintuitive. The concept of appropriation captures much more adequately the phenomena in question, the flexibility and diversity of identities: conceived of as an act of appropriation, the self is, on the one hand, "not one" insofar as it consists of a multitude of dimensions that must be integrated. Since it constitutes itself in experiences it has with itself and the world, it is a self of change. And, inasmuch as processes of appropriation have an experimental and creative character, this self is unpredictable. On the other hand, as the bearer of such processes of appropriation, the self remains a reference point in relation to which the success or failure of such acts of integration can be seen (without them needing to bestow unity in a strong sense). Thus, even if one does not want to understand the self as an immutable substance and as something that is unitary and free of conflict (and even if one does not subject it to the teleological structure of a *Bildungsroman*), being able to integrate the various aspects and parts of oneself is a presupposition of every kind of (unalienated) identity. Appropriation means therefore appropriating oneself in a diversity of possible aspects and through a diversity of possible experiences.

Yet we cannot come to grips with the debates I have just discussed with conceptual considerations alone. For the talk of self-invention and of postmodern multiple identities has become an influential metaphor and has been absorbed in various ways into contemporary cultural critique. With this vocabulary it has been possible to articulate a position that, in distinguishing itself polemically from traditional models of identity, gives expression to the notion that subjects today develop their identities within diverse and sometimes contradictory constellations. Because of the echo this philosophical position has found in contemporary cultural critique, I would like, in concluding, to discuss this conception of the self by looking at a case in which a philosophical thesis (that of postmodern identities) seems to have taken on empirical reality, namely, the phenomena of shifting identities and of playing with identities that have emerged in the context of a new medium, the Internet.

(3) "LIFE ON THE SCREEN": A REALIZATION OF THE POSTMODERN SELF?

Become the person the chat-room thinks you are!

—CAR ADVERTISEMENT, NEW YORK CITY, 1999

In her book *Life on the Screen: Identity in the Age of the Internet* the North American psychologist Sherry Turkle puts forward a thesis that immediately seems intuitively compelling: the Internet produces not only a new social reality; it also enables new forms of identity to develop, which, for the first time, make it possible to grasp what postmodern or poststructuralist theories have for a long time proclaimed.[63] Here the postmodern situation is materialized. By her own account Turkle herself was never able to imagine concretely what poststructuralist theories had been talking about since the 1970s until, as a psychologist and "cybershrink,"[64] she encountered the sociological and psychological reality of new communications media such as the Internet: "Thus, more than twenty years after meeting the ideas of Lacan, Foucault, Deleuze and Guattari, I am meeting them again in my new life on the screen. But this time, the Gallic abstractions are more concrete. In my computer-mediated worlds, the self is multiple, fluid, and constituted in interaction with machine connections; it is made and transformed by language; sexual congress is an exchange of signifiers; and understanding follows from navigation and tinkering rather than analysis."[65]

One might see this as an inappropriately concrete application of a sophisticated theory. What is interesting, though, is that Turkle empirically investigates interactions and processes of self-presentation and self-formation on the Internet and that she has pursued these issues in several large-scale projects. Turkle claims that "the internet has become a significant social laboratory for experimenting with the constructions and reconstructions of self that characterize postmodern life" (180), and she has followed this "experiment" scientifically. From her analysis of interviews with Internet users, and her experiences in her Internet practice, we gain insight into what are undoubtedly new dimensions of social and psychological reality. These findings, though—this is my claim—do not support the thesis that the Internet allows for entirely new kinds of identity formation.

When Turkle writes about "life on the screen," she is not interested in those who use the Internet as an instrument—the way one uses a telephone book, for example, as an extensive pool of information where one can look things up quickly and efficiently. She is also not concerned with the enhanced possibilities of communication made available, for example, by e-mail. However much forms of communication might be transformed by these developments, such new practices remain within the domain of traditional forms of information exchange. What Turkle investigates, rather, are users who move within the Internet as within a virtual interactive space—that is, the world of virtual communities and Multi-User Domains (MUDs) in which users come into contact with one another anonymously or under multiple names and identities when participating in interactive games (often highly complex fantasy worlds with complicated rules, played over years), discussion forums, flirt chat rooms, or cybersex. For some of the users with whom Turkle conducted interviews—sometimes over many years—"online life" has become a second, virtual life in which important (sometimes even their most important) social contacts and experiences take place. This is exemplified by the well-put remark: "My real life is just another window. And usually not the best one."

According to Turkle, it is this life, in and with the MUDs, that leads to the creation of a postmodern self fundamentally different from the traditional self that is thought to be capable of greater and lesser degrees of authenticity.

> MUD's imply difference, multiplicity, heterogeneity, and fragmentation. Such an experience of identity contradicts the Latin root of the word *idem*, meaning "the same." But this contradiction increasingly defines the conditions of our lives beyond the virtual world. MUD's thus become objects-to-think-with for thinking about postmodern selves. . . . Traditional ideas about identity have been tied to a notion of authenticity that such virtual experiences actively subvert. When each player can create many characters and participate in many games, the self is not only decentered but multiplied without limit.
>
> (185)

Two problems at the center of Turkle's focus are of interest here: (1) How does the formation of the self take place in a medium that seems to impose fewer constraints on identity formation than the "real world" does? Whatever else may be said against the idea of the demiurgic self-creator, here it seems to be a reality: "In virtual reality, we self-fashion and self-create" (185). (2) How does playing with multiple identities proceed in a medium that offers more possibilities for this than (conventional) reality? "The internet . . . has contributed to thinking about identity as multiplicity. On it, people are able to build a self by cycling through many selves" (178).

The questions that arise for Turkle's claims in the present context are the following: what exactly is understood here (all too readily) as the creation of a self, and how does it relate to the talk of self-appropriation described previously? What are we to say about multiple selves? Are they in fact experienced as different selves or, instead, as various versions *of* a person who ultimately must integrate them and who may also fail to do so? And, finally, to what extent do such processes of identity formation really subvert the concept of authenticity?

I want to use some of the empirical examples discussed by Turkle to examine two hypotheses: first, that these patterns of identity formation are not entirely new or different from more traditional patterns; and, second, that they, too, cannot get by without a conception of authenticity.

The following utterance of a gamer who describes the advantages of her MUD life bears witness to the utopia of *unlimited self-creation*: "You can be whoever you want to be. You can completely redefine yourself if you want. You can be the opposite sex. You can be more talkative. You can just be whoever you want, really, whoever you have the capacity to be" (184). On the Internet, so the claim, one can be what and who one wants to be. There are, in the first place, completely banal reasons for this. Because of the medium's anonymity and immateriality, it is impossible to establish anyone's real identity (in the everyday sense). No one is in a position to point out the biological characteristics of the chubby man who appears in the MUD as an attractive young woman. The persons who encounter one another here are identified, first of all, only by unverifiable self-descriptions. The statement "You can be more talkative," however, follows a different logic. For, clearly, I can be more talkative in the MUD only if I actually talk more. Hence, if it is easier to make myself into a garrulous personality on the Internet than it is in the "real world," this can only be because my identity is less fixed on the Internet since no one is there who already knows me to be a shy wallflower.

Yet, even on the Internet, being able to play with identities depends on their being socially recognized. And this comes up immediately when users are asked what the possibility of choosing identities depends on: "It's easier to change the way people perceive you, because all they've got is what you show them." This reveals two aspects of life on the screen: first, the *lack of a context* for Internet identities—individuals appear here without a past and without a social setting; and, second, the *control* individuals have over how they express themselves. Now the logic behind the first aspect—the "new beginning"—is not particularly unusual, and it is by no means exclusive to the new medium. Anyone who has ever changed schools or started over in a new city is familiar with it. This, then, is not a qualitatively new phenomenon. The ease of changes and their lack of consequences merely make such experiences on the Internet more likely and available to everyone. The second point is perhaps more important: one has the chance to make oneself different from what one was before because one has control over all the dimensions of how one presents oneself externally; others do not see what they are not supposed to see. But this is not true without qualification: it seems likely that even here there are elements of one's own behavior (for instance, the language one uses) that involuntarily reveal things about oneself. Moreover, one must have (and employ) the capacity to chat in an entertaining way; otherwise one quickly acquires the reputation of being a bore, even in the MUD. The same holds for gender identity: this, too, the player must actually master to a certain extent. One does not, of course, need to have the primary or secondary sexual characteristics of a man or a woman in order to play the corresponding role on the Internet; one must, however, bring along a certain capacity for empathy and a precise observation of the role behavior of the respective gender in order to be recognized and accepted as a representative of that gender. This is not so easy, and users' covers are often blown, as evidenced by the apparently not infrequent "unmasking discussions" reported to take place. To be sure, others cannot see what I "really" am biologically, but this makes their *acceptance* of my (social) gender all the more important. I must be able to depict it plausibly.

On the Internet, individuals can indeed make of themselves what they want to, but this, too, needs to be qualified, as evidenced by a remark of one of Turkle's interviewees: "You can be . . . whoever you have *the capacity to be.*" This shows the utopia of free self-construction to be illusory and reveals its limits in two respects: first, here too I can make myself only into something that I already am in a certain respect; second, I can change my identity (even my cyberidentity) only if I am recognized in this role by others, namely, my fellow players. The conditions of this recognition may be easier to fulfill, and the possibilities for constructing my identity may be greater in many respects, but in general the conditions of creating identities on the Internet are similar to those that hold "outside."

Why, then, do participants generally regard the identities produced in MUDs as so real? Why is it so easy to think of the online world as its own reality,[66] as many players clearly do? This can be traced back to the intersubjective character of this media experience—which is in fact relatively new in kind—that is, to the fact that here one can become someone different not only in one's own fantasy (this has always been possible); rather, on the Internet one's self-construction can enter into an interactive process and acquire social reality through the reactions of others. Nevertheless, as indicated earlier, the omnipotence that characterizes private fantasy life also has its limits here. One could even claim that the more reality a game acquires, the weaker an individual's omnipotence becomes and the less control she has over what happens to her.[67] This suggests, however, that role conflicts exist also on the Internet and that here, too, one can become fixed in roles that no longer fit (or never really did). This would mean that problems of alienation can arise here too, even if they might be easier to eliminate than in "real life," simply by changing one's identity or leaving the game. But even the option of leaving is less straightforward than it appears: if one looks at the intensity with which players design their identities, form social networks, compete for status, furnish their virtual spaces as if they were homes, and even celebrate intricately planned weddings in the MUD, all this suggests that abandoning even these identities is not easy and can have psychological costs: anxieties over loss, longing, homesickness, a loss of orientation. Virtual identities can also be threatened. In this regard, Turkle is, in fact, dealing with a social laboratory; the "raw material" she experiments with, however, is not completely new.

Contrary to Turkle's own thesis, however, her interviewees' reflections at least touch on the question of the self's authenticity: "I feel very different online. I am a lot more outgoing, less inhibited. I would say I feel more like myself. But that's a contradiction. I feel more like who I wish I was."[68] Hence the practice of multiplying identities constantly raises the question of what one really is, and this question is connected in turn to an idea of unity that must be defined more precisely. As a twenty-six-year-old municipal employee explains: "I'm not one thing, I'm many things. Each part gets to be more fully expressed in MUD's than in the real world. So even though I play more than one self on MUD's, I feel more like 'myself' when I'm mudding."[69]

The "many things" he claims to be are understood in the very next sentence as "parts" and therefore as aspects of the one self that he is. Then, however, it seems that what we have here is less a real multiplicity than a richer and more diverse development of one's personality (very much in Schiller's or Marx's sense). This means, though, that there is an expansion of the self that must in turn be integrated. What takes place is not a multiplication of selves but playing with various aspects of an identity, a form of play that still always depends on the integrating act of the person who is playing.

Thus on the Internet it is possible to live out aspects of one's own personality that one cannot live out in everyday life; one is freer to try out different desires and orientations. This, however, represents not a discontinuity but a continuity with conventional experiences of the diversity and malleability of identity. This means that even in the case of Internet identities there are conditions for successfully integrating such experiences and cases of successful or unsuccessful integration. This, too, is impressively documented by Turkle's material. The self-experimentation described here is productive, then, only when individuals can understand these "selves" as parts and extensions of their personality, which can be seen in their effortlessly switching back and forth between various identities. Other cases come close to being pathological borderline experiences.

Thus neither of the two theses—the loss of authenticity as a reference point and the disappearance of traditional ideas of the self's unity—can be sustained, at least on the basis of the empirical material presented here. Nevertheless, new media do create greater room and more possibilities for interacting playfully with various identities. There are fewer limits placed on these possibilities: one can try out and broaden various aspects of one's own identity and ideal self-image with relatively few consequences. And evidence of the opportunities for the broadening of horizons and the deepening of one's ability to empathize can be seen in the reports of a self-professed macho man to the effect that, after having played a female role in a game for months, he now better understands how women feel when they are exposed to stupid pick-up attempts or are constantly taken to lack certain abilities.

My critical examination of Turkle's conclusions supports the claim that every plausible conception of self depends on assuming a unity and authenticity of agents (which needs to be defined more precisely). Moreover, the phenomena Turkle describes suggest a continuity between "new" and traditional relationships to self and world. That suggests in turn that questions of alienation and being oneself—of successful and unsuccessful self-relations in the context of one's existence—are still relevant for even postmodern identities.

10

LIVING ONE'S OWN LIFE: SELF-DETERMINATION, SELF-REALIZATION, AND AUTHENTICITY

WHAT IS THE OPPOSITE OF alienation? What positive criteria do we use to define the disturbances I have described as instances of alienation? And what does it mean to be able to live one's life as one's own in an unalienated fashion?

From the perspective developed here the answer to these questions is that alienation hinders a life of freedom. Only when we can experience our life as our own in a demanding sense are we free. Alienation refers to those processes and disturbances that hinder such an appropriation of our own lives. If alienation is understood as the opposite of positive freedom in this way—as the "central obstacle to 'real freedom'"[1]—then it is possible to draw conclusions from my account of alienation about the various dimensions of positive freedom.[2]

Does this approach, though, still capture the problem of alienation as an independent problem that can be distinguished conceptually from phenomena such as heteronomy and the loss of autonomy, on the one hand, and the threat to authenticity, on the other? Moreover, what exactly is the theoretical and practical payoff of this comparatively thin and formal take on alienation?

Whereas, in the preceding chapter, I argued for the *possibility* of reconstructing the concept of self-alienation, I must now show what this perspective *yields* and where it leads us. In order to do so we must first examine the relations between the concepts of self-determination, self-realization, and autonomy from the perspective of a theory of alienation. This is the task of the present chapter. Leading one's life as *one's own* in a robust sense presupposes various conditions, and it is precisely these conditions that the concept of alienation addresses.

My principal claim here is that alienation is not coextensive with heteronomy. The capacity *to have oneself at one's command* or to be *accessible* to oneself in what one does, which we have contrasted with various forms of self-alienation, depends on more than self-determination. It presupposes the possibility of reflectively determining oneself *as something*, of relating to something in an affective and identificatory way, and of being able to *appropriate* that something. This capacity is realized in relating to projects and forming projects in the world, as a kind of realizing one's own capacities in the world. Hence the perspective of self-alienation leads via a *formal* concept of self-determination to a *material* conception that points in the direction of what might be called *self-realization*. The conception of self-realization that emerges for this perspective is distinct from rival—for example, romantic— ideas of authenticity in that here self-realization is conceived of as a capacity that can be realized only in relation to the social and material worlds.

Thus, the first section of this chapter illuminates the relation between alienation and heteronomy. Here I will re-examine the examples of the first four chapters with an eye to the distinction between heteronomy and alienation in order to draw conclusions from this about the relation between autonomy and alienation.

In the second section I articulate a conception of self-realization that coheres with the constellation of ideas I have set out and that forms the background of the analyses I have provided thus far. When self-realization is understood as the capacity to give oneself reality in the world in a self-determined way, it is possible to see important differences to contemporary ideas of romantic authenticity, as I criticize them in the third section by engaging with the views of Richard Rorty.

1. SELF-DETERMINATION AND SELF-ALIENATION

Can one be self-determined and still be alienated from oneself? Or, conversely, can one lead a heteronomous life that is not alienated? In what relation do heteronomy and alienation stand to each another? I have claimed that self-alienation is not to be equated with heteronomy. And yet there is no unalienated self-relation without self-determination.[3]

The problem under discussion here can be formulated as follows: when one is alienated from oneself, one is not *determined by a foreign will*, yet it is not *one's own* will that one follows. One lives then—in Kantian terms—in accordance with neither a *foreign law* nor *one's own*. How is this to be understood? In order to clarify this apparently paradoxical description of alienation I will return once again to the examples previously discussed.

(1) When the suburban academic stumbled into his new life, he did not subject himself to a foreign will. What was crucial for understanding the phenomenon illustrated by his case was seeing that the process had taken on a *dynamic of its own* and that his practical situations had become *reified*. To put this in terms of the concepts borrowed from Tugendhat (according to which self-determination means posing the practical question "what should I do?"): if the academic's situation is to be understood as reified, this is not because the practical question is answered by someone other than himself; rather, it is not even posed. For the possibility of regarding something as a potential object of a decision precedes the question of *who* decides or what should guide one's decision. Being able to perceive a space for action in which the practical question is possible is a precondition of being able to raise and answer this question oneself. Alienation does not consist—as heteronomy does—in practical questions being answered *by others* but in the *masking of practical questions*. Someone who allows herself simply to drift in her life does not only not live a self-determined life; she does not really *live* it at all.[4]

(2) The appropriation of roles addressed in the second example also goes beyond the problem of heteronomy. Although the role-player has only an instrumental relation to her activities, it is still prima facie she who decides them. Even when she acts in accordance with a foreign law (what her roles demand), more than throwing off this foreign rule is required if she is to make her actions her own in an unalienated way. Here the *quality* of a possible appropriation of a role depends also on identification, her expressive capacity, and her involvement in what she does. Hence—here, too—it is not that the inauthentic role player can only follow others in answering practical questions; she has problems raising them at all.

(3) In the case of the feminist who is divided against herself, we also see that making decisions *oneself* is not sufficient for living a life that is one's own. Rather, one must be able to make decisions that one can also understand as one's own and be guided in them by desires and impulses with which one can identify. Even though in H.'s case the will that conflicts with her own is prima facie also her own, she still feels that she is ruled by an alien power. In

this case the boundary between a foreign law and one's own runs throughout the person herself. Someone who is divided against herself does not live her own life, since it is not at all clear *who* is really living it. For her there is not one answer to the question "What should I do?" but multiple, contradictory answers that seem to belong to different persons. Self-determination, then, presupposes identifying with oneself. This in turn depends, as I have argued, on a form of self-accessibility, which reveals that there are forms of self-rule in which a person is nevertheless alienated from herself. Someone who is rigid is the master of herself and her own desires—perhaps too much, however.[5] From the perspective of the problem of alienation the question arises not only *whether* but also *how* one rules oneself.

(4) Finally, the case of Perlmann shows that we can also not say of someone who does not care about her life, who accepts what happens to her with indifference and disinterest, that she leads a self-determined or autonomous life. If indifference means not having desires, aspirations, or interest in the world, then to what extent is a participatory, formative relation to the world a necessary condition of being self-determined? Perlmann's problem is not that he cannot *himself* determine what he does; his problem is that he cannot determine himself *as anything*. And it is precisely this situation that hinders him from experiencing his life as his own. Hence here, too, it is not *someone else* who answers his life's practical questions; for someone to whom both the questions and the answers seem meaningless, no questions arise at all.

The conclusion of my investigation up to now can be summarized as follows: leading one's own life means pressing ahead in one's life with projects that one pursues in a self-determined fashion, that one makes *one's own* in doing so, and that one can *affectively identify* with. This, first, brings our relation to the world into the picture since it implies that one experiences the world and what one does in it as meaningful. Second, it yields a complex understanding of what it is to be *one's own master* in relation to oneself, that is, master over one's own desires and decisions. Third, it raises the issue of *how* projects are pursued, which I will return to in connection with the concept of self-realization. In order to be able to pose the practical question "What should I do?" I must (a) see the question as such and be able to identify it as a possibility, (b) be interested in it (and in answering it), and (c) be in agreement with myself (as the one who poses the question). From the perspective of a theory of alienation, these are what could be called the material conditions of realizing autonomy.

ETHICAL AUTONOMY

Recent discussions of ethical (or personal) autonomy—which I want to sketch by looking briefly at the most influential positions—address many of the same problems I have discussed here. Starting from the idea that autonomy is not something one simply has but something one must acquire and realize, these discussions aim at a more contentful, sometimes even a perfectionist conception of autonomy.

S. I. Benn, for example, understands autonomy as an ideal. Whereas *autarchy* is characterized by a very basic independence of choice and decision that requires only that minimal conditions of cognitive and practical rationality be met, *autonomy*, in contrast, designates an ideal of a self-determined life that goes beyond these minimal conditions. The autonomous person is the "author of her own personality" and therefore the author of her own life in a broader sense than someone who is merely independent.[6] Whereas someone who is conventional in a merely autarchic way uncritically or unreflectively accepts the world's demands, the autonomous author of her own life critically examines what she does in the context of an experimental and reflective conduct of her life. With this idea, Benn opens up the question of what makes something "a law of one's own," but in so doing he remains focused on the problem of conventionalism and hence on the unexamined influence of others.

In Gerald Dworkin's and John Christman's conceptions of autonomy (which share with Frankfurt's the idea of a reflective self-relation characterized by two levels), the requirement that one identify with one's own desires plays a crucial role in defining successful self-determination.[7] Here, too, unexamined desires and outlooks do not serve as valid standards for defining self-determined actions; here, too, the crucial question is which of one's own orientations can be considered really one's own. Autonomy, on this account, depends on the capacity to evaluate critically and reflect on one's desires as well as on taking the responsibility for them that corresponds to this reflection. This capacity can be threatened by manipulation, social conditioning, or psychic disintegration, which means that these positions also take an interest in uncovering the influences that undermine autonomy. Thus Gerald Dworkin's "full formula for autonomy" reads: "A person is autonomous if he identifies with his desires, goals, and values, and such identification is not influenced in ways which make the process of identification in some way alien to the individual."[8] Dworkin defines what makes the process of identification alien to the individual in terms of a process of reflection (not, then, in terms of content but with a view to the *process* of will formation): this reflection must be free of manipulation and coercion.

John Christman conceives of the conditions of autonomy similarly in focusing on the nonmanipulative formation of preferences: "Self-mastery means more than having a certain attitude towards one's desires at a time. It means in addition that one's values were formed in a manner or by a process that one had (or could have had) something to say about."[9] The limitation of these discussions, however, lies (as we saw in chapter 7) in the fact that—because "one's own" desires are conceived of exclusively as those that come about in the absence of manipulation or interference by others—successful identification with oneself comes down, in the end, to the absence of manipulative influences and so is defined purely negatively. Identifying with oneself, then, amounts to the absence of distorting influences, but its positive features are not articulated. For this reason it is all too easy for these positions to remain focused on the problem of conventionalism and the influence of others, such that this influence is taken to be the principal source of heteronomy.

Finally, Joseph Raz develops a conception of personal autonomy that (insofar as it is relevant for my discussion) also emphasizes the contrast with "drifting": "Personal autonomy contrasts with a life of no choices, or of *drifting through life* without ever exercising one's capacity to choose."[10] As we have seen, these claims do not follow immediately from the concept of autonomy itself. This means that Raz's is a very broad, contentful, perfectionist conception of autonomy that—just as in the cases previously discussed—is difficult to understand as the symmetrical opposite of heteronomy and that points in the direction of a theory of self-realization. Put differently, Raz's conception also presupposes a concept of alienation. When Raz defines autonomy as the capacity to be the author of one's own life—to give it a shape and meaning—he is not only claiming that the autonomous person must independently and actively shape her life. In addition, she must presuppose that *something matters* in her life. The insight that autonomy depends on having meaningful options at one's disposal is an important component of a critique of the diluted, liberal conception of autonomy,[11] though it is precisely how the concept of autonomy should be enriched that is contested. For this reason any account that takes up such a conception of autonomy also faces the task of explaining the relation between autonomy and its realization.

One can understand this connection with the help of the following Hegelian theme (which I set out already in the introduction): the capacity for self-determination depends, first, on a capacity for reflection that, in the process the *Philosophy of Right* calls the "purification of the drives," liberates the free will from its determination by nature and thereby from the compulsion involved in merely reacting to what is already given. Second, it depends on a carrying out of what one wills in which the will makes itself real. Against the background of the concept of formation, or *Bildung* (as Hegel understands it in §187 of his *Philosophy of Right*), the will's being realized in the world appears as the "material side" of self-determination (and as its concretization). Determining oneself, then, must mean determining oneself *as* something. If self-determination for Hegel is not located in the mere preferences of the freedom of *Willkür* (the will in its capacity to choose) but is conceived of, rather, as a process of liberation in which what is first merely given is made into one's own, then this process of working away what is alien must at the same time be understood as an appropriation of the world. The fact that this appropriation is conceived of as practical activity is made manifest in the concept of *Bildung*: in restructuring the world, individuals form themselves. They form themselves in and with the world; they come "to themselves" only in relations to the world.

In what follows I set out in more detail the conception of self-realization that has lurked in the background of my previous discussion; the basic contours of this conception should already be reasonably clear. Self-realization, as I have spoken of it here, is not the realization of one's own given, underlying self; instead, it involves realizing oneself in the pursuit of one's projects and thereby—in this identificatory relation, in carrying out one's actions and in appropriating the world—giving reality to oneself. Although I cannot provide a comprehensive account of self-realization here, I will concentrate on two of its aspects that are crucial for a theory of alienation: the connection between self-realization and self-determination and the relation to the world that is presupposed by the model of self-realization presented here.

2. SELF-REALIZATION AND APPROPRIATION OF THE WORLD

An individual cannot know what he is until he has made himself a reality through action.

—G. W. F. HEGEL, *PHENOMENOLOGY OF SPIRIT*

The conception of self-realization that emerges from my reflections here differs, on the one hand, from a widespread view according to which focusing on self-realization is part of a culture of narcissism (Christopher Lasch),[12] the stance of self-centered individuals obsessed with realizing themselves without concern for the needs and rights of others. On the other hand, the antiessentialist model of appropriation set out earlier implies that self-realization must aim at something other than inner growth or development, teleologically conceived. The concept of self-realization I will develop here follows in a tradition that, as Adorno puts it, is not focused on the "cultivation of the individual, who, like a plant, needs to be watered in order to bloom": "For all these thinkers [Kant, Goethe, and Hegel] the subject does not come to itself through the narcissistically self-related cultivation of its being-for-itself but rather through *externalization, by devotedly abandoning itself to what is not itself.*"[13] Various questions arise, then, in conjunction with the concept of self-realization: what is it that realizes itself when we speak of *self*-realization? In what sense must we (or the self) *realize* ourselves, and *how* does that occur? In response to these questions I will offer only a few brief remarks:

My analysis thus far suggests an idea of self-realization as the individual's realization *in the world* or mediated by the world. In this sense, self-realization does not consist only in the development of one's capacities. Rather, mediated by these capacities and potentials, self-realization is a process of actively appropriating the world. Hence, self-realization is to be understood not as a realization of *something* nor as a kind of inner growth or development (as, for example, in humanist psychology) but as a way of being active. One does not realize *oneself*; one realizes oneself *in what one does*. We realize ourselves insofar as, through this externalization, we emerge out of the "night of possibility" into the day of reality (Hegel).[14]

Realizing oneself in an activity refers to a specific way of being active. We do not realize ourselves in everything we do. How, then, are we to identify those activities or ways of being active in which we realize ourselves? It would be misleading to think this is merely a matter of how important or demanding an activity is. An activity becomes a candidate for self-realization because of its inherent structure. In order to be able to realize oneself in an activity, so my claim, two conditions must be met, which Friedrich Kambartel summarizes as follows: "We realize ourselves in actions that we do *for their own sake*, on the basis of "*our own*" decision, namely, on the basis of a decision we insightfully make in relation to our life."[15] Kambartel refers to two related aspects of self-realization. First, activities in which we are able to realize ourselves must be *self-determined*: in order to be able to realize *myself*, I must be able to set my own ends.[16] Second, acts of self-realization must have ends of a certain kind: those we pursue *for their own sake*.

The first condition might seem banal. On the one hand, it excludes activities in which I am determined or coerced by others (or by what is "other" more generally) from the domain of activities in which I can realize myself: "Surely we can say of someone who leads her life in such a way that she merely follows alien and, in particular, objectified demands and expectations that she misses or falls short of herself."[17] One the other hand, the supposed connection between self-determination and self-realization can serve to demarcate the modern conception of self-realization from premodern conceptions of "fulfilling one's essential purpose" or of a meaningfully fulfilled life. Thus, realizing oneself in one's activities cannot simply be equated with carrying out activities that are objectively meaningful, rich in meaning, or full of significance. An activity can be meaningful according to external criteria, or even significant in a sense that transcends the individual, but if one has not explicitly made this meaning *one's own* one does not realize oneself in that activity but something else instead—for example, an idea.[18]

The second dimension of self-realization requires more explanation: the *noninstrumental* or intrinsic character of activities in which one can realize oneself. The idea that an activity can be an end in itself derives from Aristotle's distinction between two kinds of activity: those done for their own sake and those done for the sake of something else. My claim is that we realize ourselves in an activity to the extent that we can do it for its own sake, that is, to the extent that it is not merely the means to another end. (This is Tugendhat's point when he reformulates the idea of alienated labor in terms of Aristotle's concept of intrinsic value: "an activity is alienated to the extent that one *does not* or *cannot* do it for its own sake as well.")[19] This implies that the distinction between self-realization and alienation can be described as a distinction between intrinsically and instrumentally valuable relationships or ways of life. This is also the meaning behind Kambartel's claim that one misses or falls short of oneself (or of the goal of self-realization) not only when one cannot set one's ends *oneself* but also when one determines (by oneself!) all one's activities—and ultimately, then, one's life as a whole—exclusively as *means to an end*. We can speak of self-realization only when we do the things that make up our life for their own sake, or more precisely, when we orient our life as a whole around ends that we pursue for their own sake.

It is never possible to completely avoid action grounded in means-end reasoning (action aimed at achieving external ends). It is likely that the attainment of every end is preceded by chains of actions in which not every individual link has intrinsic value. Even in playing the piano, something I do for its own sake, I must do finger exercises that I perform only because of their relation to the external end (external to the exercises themselves) of acquiring the technical skills to play a Beethoven sonata. The possibility of self-realization, however, is threatened precisely when one gets caught in a teleological circle, a situation in which one does one thing only for the sake of another without ever connecting them to a final end, that is, to an end where one can no longer ask the question for what purpose I am doing this? When this characterizes an entire life, the result is a fatal structure: "We then understand our action and our current life as a *means* to the end of another action and life, in which only there are we really ourselves."[20] Hence, although instrumental action is always a part of the pursuit of life goals, it is meaningful only if it passes over into an action that leads to a goal that is not itself another means to an end but is pursued for its own sake.

Why, though, is an activity—and, correspondingly, oneself in doing it— alienated if this activity does not carry its end within itself? If something is a mere means, one is indifferent to it; it is replaceable. In connection with the problem of alienated labor, Andreas Wildt elaborates this point as follows: "What . . . is a mere means is something to which the agent is indifferent in a certain respect; it could be replaced by any other equally suitable means without any loss."[21] Self-realization rests on a noninstrumental relation to our own activities, and it is achieved in activities that we understand as more than merely instrumentally valuable. Thus self-realization, too, can be understood as a concept that addresses the carrying out of actions; it provides no content- ful or substantial guidelines for leading a good life—it, too, is not a question of *what* but of *how* something is realized or of how we realize ourselves in carrying out our activities.

3. SELF-ALIENATION AND UNIQUENESS

Starting from the assumption that, in order to make their self-determination real, persons must "give themselves reality" in the world, we arrived at a con- ception of self-realization that is not limited to understanding it merely as realizing individual uniqueness but that, instead, ties it to the world. If we get clear on the implications of this conception of self-realization, we see that we must distinguish between worldless and worldly conceptions of self-realization. In the one case, self-realization means realizing *oneself*, realizing oneself as a unique individual; in the other case it means realizing *oneself in something*, that is, through activity in or contact with the world. (Following Theunissen, these two options can be contrasted as Hegelian and post-Hegelian versions of self-realization.)[22]

In what follows I criticize one of the most influential contemporary "worldless" accounts of self-realization or authenticity.[23] I am referring to models of romantic authenticity in which self-realization is understood as the realization of individual uniqueness or originality.[24] According to the conception of self-realization I develop here, "living one's own life"—living in an unalienated fashion or realizing oneself in one's life—precisely does not mean, in the first place, realizing oneself as a unique individual in the sense found in romantic conceptions of authenticity. I do not mean to deny or criticize individual uniqueness (in order, say, to subordinate the individual to the universal); I merely want to make the idea of such uniqueness less "dramatic." An individual's uniqueness, so my claim, cannot be *directly* grasped, striven for, or intended. Individual uniqueness is merely a by-product of realizing oneself in the world in a self-determined way. In what follows I limit myself to discussing Richard Rorty's position, perhaps the most interesting contemporary version of romantic individualism.[25] Rorty's position seems to me especially sophisticated in the way it brings together liberalism, romanticism, and postmodernism, and it allows us to see particularly clearly where disagreements with the approach favored by a theory of alienation lie.

AUTHENTICITY AND ORIGINALITY (RORTY)

Rorty identifies the possibility of being oneself, or of leading a life that is really one's own, with the idea of individual uniqueness: realizing oneself as an individual means making oneself into an "original" that cannot be mistaken for others. The greatest "horror"[26] for the (romantic) individual lies in having to acknowledge that she is a mere copy: "One will not have impressed one's mark on the language but, rather, will have spent one's life shoving about already coined pieces. So one will not really have had an I at all. One's creations, and one's self, will just be better or worse instances of familiar types."[27] Having a self of one's own means, then, being unique. The unique life is above all different from all present and previous lives lived by others; what must be realized is something novel, something for which there is neither a predecessor nor a standard. Rorty makes Harold Bloom's "strong poet," who succeeds in finding a new language, into the paradigm of individuality.[28] Individuality means being able to live idiosyncratically.

Rorty proposes a model of aesthetic, experimental self-production, which can be understood as a contemporary, antiessentialist version of a romantic conception of authenticity that does not appeal to the idea of inwardness. He combines the romantic cult of genius with an idea from Nietzsche: authenticity is a matter of creating and forming, not of *finding*, one's individuality.

Rorty's crucial move in developing his account of authenticity is to attempt to mitigate the possible antisocial consequences of such a radical conception of individuality (from indifferent withdrawal to an openly elitist amoralism) by arguing forcefully for separating the private from the public and the individual from the universal. The development and living out of idiosyncratic fantasies is understood as a private, and precisely not as a political, experiment. Authenticity is a question of "private autonomy." According to Rorty, this separation between public and private is necessary so that both spheres can develop and exist alongside each other without either harming the other. The experimental life projects pursued in private spaces of refuge can be idiosyncratic precisely because they (must) remain private. What Rorty seeks to avoid with his account is carrying over the idea of authenticity to political communities. The everyday business of *common* life within political communities is to be governed by the procedural rules of liberal institutions; perfectionist aspirations to individual self-realization belong in the realm of private life experiments. Rorty characterizes the figure of the romantic intellectual who succeeds in living out the separation between public and private identities as follows:

> Such an intellectual finds her moral identity—her sense of her relation to most other human beings—in the democratic institutions which she inhabits. But she does not think that her *moral* identity exhausts her self-description. For she does not think her conduct toward other human beings is the most important thing about her. What is *more* important is her *rapport à soi*, her private search for autonomy, her refusal to be exhaustively describable in words which apply to anyone other than herself. This is the search summed up in Blake's exclamation: "I must create my own system. Or be enslaved by another man's."[29]

In criticizing Rorty's model of authenticity, I am less interested in the social or moral implications of his position, his much discussed relativism or his refusal to seek an ultimate foundation for moral universalism. I am concerned instead with the plausibility of the model of authenticity that underlies his position. Hence I will criticize two aspects of Rorty's account: the self-referentiality that follows from the worldlessness of his account and the alleged private character of individual life experiments.

UNIQUENESS AND INTERESTS

Is it a lack of originality that prevents us from living our life as our own? Does our search for private autonomy fail when we cannot grasp ourselves as unique? Ernst Tugendhat has criticized the conception of individuality as uniqueness as follows:

> Someone who autonomously raises the qualitative identity question "What kind of a person do I want to be?" will *in fact* arrive at results that allow him to appear unique; but if he turns his uniqueness into a problem and makes it his *aim*, an inappropriate factor is thereby introduced into the practical question of truth. Instead of simply directing the question to how matters actually stand and what the best possibility would be for my existence and that of others, the issue now would be how I can distinguish myself from others; that is, there would be a concern about one's "distantiality," which Heidegger correctly (in my view) ascribed to inauthenticity.[30]

Martin Löw-Beer takes up this claim—that uniqueness does not provide a meaningful perspective from which to answer the question of how one would like to live—in his essay "Are We Unique?" and uses it to argue against Rorty's idea of self-development within private life experiments. This idea, he claims, is "too thin": "No one is satisfied merely because he is original. Individuality cannot consist in the goal of being essentially different from everyone else; an individual cannot be content merely in knowing that 'she is not a copy.' We do not understand how this alone can be fulfilling. It would have to be shown, against Rorty, that he has incorrectly explained why the development of their individuality matters to human beings."[31] I would like to reinforce this claim: what makes Rorty's description of individuality thin, among other things, is his neglect of the fact that individuality develops only in relation to, or in engaging with, something and that for this reason individuals can realize themselves only in relating to the world.

The young academic with whom I began my analysis is not alienated from himself because his life resembles those of many others—because he is a "mere copy"—but rather because he is not present in his life in a specific way. Conventions may have in fact played a role in making his life rigid, but this is not identical with the process of rigidification as I have analyzed it.

Even the role behavior of chapter 6, cannot be interpreted in this way: those who conform to roles are not inauthentic because they are copies but because they have no real—but merely an instrumental—interest in what they do. Here, too, conformism is an effect or consequence but not the cause. By the same token, uniqueness, when it appears, is a consequence and by-product of taking a real interest in something, a result of letting oneself get caught up in the problems that arise in conjunction with the projects one pursues. Even what is novel originates as an unintended consequence. If authentic role-playing can be distinguished from inauthentic role-playing by the degree to which the pregiven role templates are individually appropriated and modified, this reshaping of roles is not undertaken for the sake of novelty. If an example of unalienated role behavior is a seminar where a genuine discussion breaks out in which bearers of various roles are swept away with enthusiasm, this is because the participants in the discussion exhibit engagement with the topic and interest in it. The modifications of the roles that result from this—and this is characteristic of the situation described—emerge involuntarily. With respect to expressing oneself or "finding one's language," what is most important is whether one *really says* something rather than whether one says anything particularly new.[32] That, however, depends on whether one finds a language that does justice to the *problems* with which one is confronted. In the case of clichés, too, what is disturbing is not that everyone uses them but that they are useless and are not (or are no longer) suited to expressing experiences adequately. What matters is expressing *something* rather than *oneself*, and we express *ourselves* successfully to the degree that we succeed in doing the former.

From this perspective, self-realization is a matter of being present in one's life and taking interest in what one does, of being engaged and wrapped up in the world in a self-determined and authentic fashion. Self-realization is not simply not being a copy. Rorty's idea of how individuality is realized is so strangely thin because it relies on a self-referential conception of individuality and therefore remains peculiarly empty. In contrast, the model of self-realization I have sketched claims that we have access to ourselves only via the world and that we develop in interacting with the things in relation to which we form ourselves. Rorty's individuality is worldless by comparison. If Rorty's unique individual also enters the world—as a creator—what matters is clearly not the world but the individual. In this respect Carl Schmitt's critique of romantics and their "occasional relation to the world" also applies to Rorty: "Romanticism is subjectivized occasionalism. In other words, in romanticism the romantic subject treats the world as an occasion and an opportunity for his romantic productivity."[33] What is interesting here is how the self-referentiality of Rorty's model turns into what Tugendhat has discussed in reference to Heidegger's idea of distantiality (*Abständigkeit*): someone who aims directly at originality in developing her individuality shows herself to be bound to others negatively since she can prove her own uniqueness only in her distance to others. But then individuals who, in searching for authentic expression and a language of their own, seek to escape the conformism of the "They" are in fact indissolubly bound to it. The "strong poet" turns out to be an "other-directed character." The point here is that self-referentiality precisely increases dependence on others because it has no standard outside this relation to others. The requirements placed on one's own actions do not come from the world; their standards of success do not come from engagement with it. Precisely because romantic subjectivity takes the world only as an "occasion" does it remain bound to it in its negative dependence.

ARE INDIVIDUAL LIFE-EXPERIMENTS PRIVATE?

How, then, does Rorty's separation of public from private, of a public moral identity from private, idiosyncratic autonomy, hold up in the face of this critique and the conception of self-realization I have proposed here? Is this separation tenable? Is the distinction he relies on generally useful? Once again, I do not want to approach these questions directly; instead, I want to ask about the plausibility of the idea of idiosyncratic self-creation in private life experiments itself. Here I differ from Rorty in my conception of what an experiment is and how it functions.

How are we to imagine such life experiments, the private, idiosyncratic creation of a unique identity? Take someone who passes through a number of different forms of life in which she not only tries out very different interests and activities but also experiences very different kinds of relationships and "scenes."[34] What is being experimented with here, how is it experimented with, and what is the occasion of the experiment? Here, too, it seems to me that—in contrast to the idea of purely aesthetic experimentation—what is crucial is the orientation one has toward the object in question (in this case, one's own life) and hence toward the question of how one should lead one's life and as *what* one should determine oneself in it. We enter into such experiments not for the sake of experimentation itself but in order to solve problems (even if only boredom or rigidification) that emerge from a particular way of life. Someone who tries out new kinds of relationships by living in "open relationships" and bringing up children within extended, nontraditional families does so out of dissatisfaction with existing models, that is, on the basis of experiences she has with herself and in her life.[35] What is lived here, when properly understood, are experiments. If someone seeks to find the right form of life in this way, however, the "liquefaction of everything pregiven and achieved" is a *means*.[36] Thus this liquefaction is not an end in itself, even if the process of exploration turns out to be endless. On this view, life experiments are to be understood as forms of experimental problem solving and not as experiments for the sake of experimentation.

This conception of experimentation has two implications: first, here too the originality or uniqueness of the experiment is merely a by-product; the solution to a certain problem might in fact be unique, unparalleled, and unrepeatable because it is relevant only to a particular situation that cannot be reproduced or because it is a new solution for a new problem. A life experiment understood in this way does not, however, *aim* at originality. Second, what one does in such experiments is not without standards: their standards lie in the thing itself. An experiment is successful when a form of life "works" in a certain respect. When one solves problems experimentally, one seeks the correct and appropriate solution to a problem. Such a solution makes a claim to being the appropriate solution to a given problem until further experimentation proves otherwise. This means that the solution makes a validity claim and is open to criticism. One endorses one's form of life as a solution at least to the specific situation one is reacting to. Precisely when one "liquifies" forms of life, one reflects on them, supports them with reasons, and is more or less accessible to arguments—at least if one has really "liquified" the given standards and practices in question.[37]

The private, idiosyncratic life experiments that Rorty has in mind differ, then, from those that can succeed or fail in the sense sketched earlier with respect to their validity claims: it is not only that the former need not make sense to others; they *should not* make sense to others since they seek to be neither a copy nor a prototype. This way of living experimentally is private, then, because no claims or proposals emerge from it for living together socially.

My skepticism regarding this view is based on the idea that whether or not a form of life makes sense is something that must be demonstrated. To locate its success precisely in the fact that it does not make sense to others seems to me absurd and marked by distantiality in the sense I have described. Conversely, it is difficult to see how it is possible for someone who is capable of a certain degree of reflection not to raise any validity claims in what she does, not even for herself. It is not only that we depend on the recognition of others to ensure the success of a certain form of life and that private forms of life easily pass over into the shared domain. The most important reason for my skepticism is the following: if the separation of private autonomy from the public domain serves not only to protect the public from private idiosyncrasies but also to afford individual self-realization (or self-formation) a protected space in which it can develop, this seems to me to appeal (contrary to Rorty's own intentions) to an ideal of individuality as something that develops naturally. Once again, individuality would then be something that blossoms in secret and flourishes best when it remains free of external influences. But the problem, then, is not only that one remains negatively related to others—and thereby dependent on them—in one's "concern for distantiality." Only a public discussion of forms of life opens up the possibility of shaping them. Only in relation to "universality" is it possible to think about relationships in which, for better or worse, one is already enmeshed. In this sense one not only never lives "one's own life" alone; one also does not live it privately as one's own. One's *rapport à soi*, when understood as a relation to self mediated by the world, is not so easily separated from one's conduct toward others. Yet relationships we are caught up in without being able to shape them are alienated.

CONCLUSION: THE SOCIALITY OF THE SELF, THE SOCIALITY OF FREEDOM

The human being is a zoon politikon in the most literal sense: he is not only a social animal, but an animal that can become an individual only in society.

—KARL MARX, *FIRST VERSION OF CAPITAL*

WHAT FOLLOWS FROM THE POSITIONS I have developed here concerning individuals' relations to the social relationships, practices, and institutions within which they lead their lives?

My concluding remarks follow directly on my critique of Rorty. Although for Rorty authenticity is emphatically not to be realized at the cost of others, it also does not depend on them in a significant sense. His enclosure of romantic aspirations within a domain of self-realization that he conceives of as individualistic and private provides no space in which a theory of alienation—with its claim that alienation from self and alienation from society are equally primordial—could gain a foothold. For if it is precisely being embedded in a shared vocabulary, a shared language, and shared social practices that threaten authentic individuality, then the question of whether and how individuals can "refind themselves" in social institutions—institutions in which they merely pass by alongside one another with more or less ease—ceases to makes sense. Self-realization is understood as taking place beyond the realm of the social, and the necessity of entering into relations with others is understood as a threat to an undisturbed "being oneself."

These considerations lead us back to the ambiguity I attributed in part 1 to Rousseau and the very beginning of the modern discussion of alienation: alienation appears either as alienation *by* the social world or *from* the social world, *by* or *from* others, and ultimately as alienation *by* or *from* the universal.

Depending on which standpoint one takes here, the possibility for authenticity or self-realization is to be sought either in a domain *beyond* the practices, roles, and institutions shared with others or *in* this domain itself.[1]

My reconstruction of the concept of alienation has aimed to show that it is only by relating appropriatively to the social practices that determine our lives and not by (to use Hegel's terms) abstractly negating them that an unalienated relation to self is possible. If, as I have argued, the self emerges only in relation *to something*—if it emerges only as the permanently rearranging result of a process in which the world is appropriated—this world is always a social world. Being involved in the world—the fact that individuals are interwoven in a network of social meanings within which they act and on the basis of which they understand their actions—is ineluctable. If the cases I have discussed have shown that self-alienation is also alienation in and from the social world, then the problem, understood as a disturbed relation to self and world, can be solved only in, not beyond, the world of social practices.

"THE ACTION OF THE ONE IS THE ACTION OF THE OTHER"

■ If in the case of role behavior (chapter 6) individuals form themselves in and through their roles, then the dichotomy of the self and its roles as well as the boundary between inner and outer are called into question: the individual and her roles are formed as part of the same process, and these roles change in being appropriated. The individual becomes alienated from herself in becoming alienated from her roles and vice versa. If authenticity can no longer be sought in a fictitious place outside social expectations and roles, then overcoming alienation means not overcoming the sociality that roles represent but appropriating and transforming them. This also means that overcoming alienation requires the availability of social roles and institutions that make identification and appropriation possible.

■ My analysis of the powerlessness of the academic who ends up in the suburbs (chapter 5) did not focus solely on the conventional character of his form of life, on the fact that in this form of life he developed into a "mere copy" (as Rorty and Bloom would say). I argued, instead, that this was only a symptom or consequence of the fact that practical questions had remained masked. In accordance with this, his recovering the power to have his life at his command appears not as a turning away from what is shared with others but as a real appropriation of a form of life that is always shared with others.

   ■   The ineluctably social character of even the attitudes we have toward ourselves and our own desires is vividly illustrated in the case of the feminist who is internally divided and at odds with herself (chapter 7). The conflict she carries on with herself cannot be understood without referring to the social meaning and interpretation of her actions. Whether she wants to or not, she moves within a constellation in which social ascriptions, role expectations, and established social practices regarding gender affect not only relations among individuals but also individuals' relations to themselves. Here too, though, the solution to her problem requires not simply being liberated from others—not abstracting from every formative influence or from the social meaning of her actions and desires—but rather the capacity to establish relations to these things and hence (here, again) to appropriate the constellations created by them.

   ■   Insofar as Perlmann's indifference (chapter 8) can be interpreted as a phenomenon of alienation, we see that in order to assure his own existence he needs a relation not only to what is "other" in general but to other persons as well. Things we love, identify with, and strive for are what they are only against the backdrop of shared, socially shaped meanings. Being involved in projects presupposes the existence of other human beings. One could not understand what a competent father is, or even what a good musician or a good hermit is, if there were no social institutions or roles defining parenthood, musical virtuosity, or religious absorption. Thus identifying with projects—even when they seem to be completely idiosyncratic—always occurs in connection with a social world that is shared with others, even when this takes the form of distancing oneself from that world.[2]

Hence the advice to block out social interpretations and to live not "in the opinion of others" but "in oneself" (as Rousseau formulated it) is problematic in all these cases. A self-relation formed by denying or abstracting from the influence of others is illusory. As we have seen, self-accessibility always presupposes being able to understand oneself in one's socially formed traits; having oneself at one's command always means being able to move freely in relations that go beyond the individual.

In investigating what it could mean to "find oneself in one's own actions" we found that actions that are one's own are never merely privately one's own; they are always actions of others as well—influenced by them and interwoven with them in various ways. Thus we can find ourselves in them only if we learn to understand ourselves as part of a social context that equally makes possible, shapes, determines, and limits our self-conceptions. A life of one's own, then, is something that emerges not in abstracting from but in appropriating a shared life; individual particularity can be achieved not by turning away from but only by individually appropriating a shared vocabulary.

Understood in this way, the problem of alienation leads us to the question of the nature of our relations to social practices and institutions and to an account of the demands we should make on them as the social conditions that make self-determination and self-realization possible. Someone is alienated, I have claimed, if she cannot react to her own given conditions. Since the sociality of our existence belongs among these conditions, the alternative between freedom and alienation is decided by how and to what extent we succeed in making this sociality *our own*.

SOME IMPLICATIONS

In conclusion, I would like to outline some implications of my account:

First, the thesis that we must relate to our given social conditions does not aim at collectivistically merging the individual into the community or at asserting the priority of the community over the individual. If we can individuate ourselves only in society, as Marx claims, this means that, even when we assert ourselves as individuals, we are determined and shaped by the social character of our existence. From this, however, it does not follow that we can develop a successful relation to self only if we are, as it were, "fused together" in communal forms of life; what follows, rather, is merely that recognizing the fact that "we are associated" belongs to the conditions of freely having one's own existence at one's command.[3] Insofar as what matters here is taking up a relation, the latter is always a relation between differentiated things. Thus social alienation does not mean (as is frequently assumed) the loss of community but rather the incapacity to establish *relations* to others in one's actions.

Second, not only does *appropriating* social practices and institutions include transforming and shaping them; it is also the case that the question of what the ineluctable conditions of one's own existence are may not be answered by an appeal to essentialist arguments. Even solidarity (as the opposite of social alienation) is, as I argued with respect to the individual's self-relation, simultaneously given and made. The appropriation of relations that go beyond the individual is at once constructive and reconstructive; it reacts to the "fact of connectedness" just as it creates it.[4]

Third, while I considered the cases of alienation presented here from the perspective of how the subject is constituted, the corresponding analysis and evaluation—of how institutions are constituted—remains to be carried out. How must institutions be constituted so that individuals living within them can understand themselves as the (co-)authors of those institutions and identify with them as agents? What would social institutions look like that could be understood as embodiments of freedom? In opposition to contemporary worries about the loss of meaning in modern society, it is these questions that must be answered if we are to discover resources for finding meaning, understood as an identificatory relation to what one does.

NOTES

Translator's Introduction

1. Portions of this introduction are taken from a review of Jaeggi's book that I wrote shortly after it was first published; *Notre Dame Philosophical Reviews* (http://ndpr.nd.edu), July 2, 2007.
2. Hegel, *Phenomenology of Spirit*, 119, 121.
3. "It is a great obstinacy—the kind of obstinacy that does honor to human beings—that they refuse to acknowledge . . . any [authority] that has not been justified by thought. This obstinacy is the distinctive characteristic of the modern age." Hegel, *Elements of the Philosophy of Right*, 2 (translation amended).

Preface and Acknowledgments

1. Schaff, *Alienation as a Social Phenomenon*, 3. Shlomo Avineri similarly notes that alienation has become the "most popular of Marx's phrases." Avineri, *The Social and Political Thought of Karl Marx*, 2.
2. For the philosophical discussion see, among others, Anderson, *Value in Ethics and Economics* and Radin, *Contested Commodities*. See also Jaeggi, "Der Markt und sein Preis."
3. Thus in December 1999, in covering the militant protests in Seattle against economic globalization at a meeting of the "World Trade Organization," a commentator in *Newsweek* noted: "There does seem to be a common *sense of alienation* among a surprising number of Americans. Dan Seligman, head of The Sierra Club's trade office, defines the new mood as a feeling of 'loss of control' in a world of rapid change and turbocharged global capitalism." "The New Radicals" (emphasis added).
4. Boltanski and Chiapello, *The New Spirit of Capitalism*.
5. For the ambivalences of such developments see Honneth et al., *Reification*.

6. See Misik, *Genial dagegen*, which also provides an interesting synopsis of contemporary cultural phenomena that respond to the problem of alienation, from the critique of commercialization of a rock band like Wir sind Helden to the theater of René Pollesch.

7. See also Axel Honneth's reconstruction of the idea of reification in terms of a theory of recognition: Honneth, *Reification*.

8. I have treated this thesis in detail in the last chapter of my study of Hannah Arendt; see Jaeggi, *Welt und Person*.

9. Within critical theory, alienation critique aligns itself with aspects of Hegelian social philosophy in opposition to liberal Kantian or justice-oriented theories.

10. Ursula Wolf, for example, discusses the objection that with regard to ethical questions "many humans today find life to be so meaningless, fragmented, and apathy-inducing that the question of the good life in general is no longer compelling." Wolf, *Das Problem des moralischen Sollens*, 176.

11. See Honneth, "Pathologies of the Social," 4, 28–29.

12. See Lohmann, *Indifferenz und Gesellschaft*. Lohmann impressively articulates this dimension of Marx's position by investigating the strands of alienation critique in his work (and its transformations) against the backdrop of challenges posed by systems theory.

13. With this I do not mean phenomenology in a methodologically strict sense but rather merely a procedure that is oriented toward phenomena.

1. "A Stranger in the World"

1. Israel and Maass, *Der Begriff Entfremdung*.

2. Habermas, *Erläuterungen zur Diskursethik*, 48.

3. MacIntyre, *Marxism*, 23.

4. I borrow the expression "experiential content" from Negt and Kluge, *Öffentlichkeit und Erfahrung*. It refers to concepts that make experiences possible and that, in turn, give life to those same concepts.

5. As Raymond Geuss says, all interesting philosophical concepts are "impure." Raymond Geuss, *Glück und Politik*, 56.

6. See the "Translator's Introduction."

7. Schacht, *Alienation*, 116.

8. Nicolaus, *Hegels Theorie der Entfremdung*, 27.

9. Theunissen, *Selbstverwirklichung und Allgemeinheit*.

10. There is no disagreement on this among interpreters of Rousseau. Thus, Hans Barth describes Rousseau as a theoretician of alienation "avant la letter." Barth, *Wahrheit und Ideologie*, 105. And, according to Bronislaw Baczko: "The Hegelian-Marxian term [alienation] corresponds precisely to the condition for which Rousseau has no name but which he constantly describes." Baczko, *Rousseau*, 27.

11. Rousseau, *The Discourses*, 124.
12. Ibid., 187.
13. Frederick Neuhouser brings this out very decisively in his interpretation of Rousseau. Neuhouser, *Foundations of Hegel's Social Theory*, 55–81.
14. For the discussion of atomism in social philosophy, see Taylor, "What's Wrong with Negative Liberty," 211–229.
15. I am speaking here of Hegel's treatment of alienation as a problem of contemporary society. His philosophical concept of alienation, on the other hand, exhibits the following structure, which informs Marx's concept as well: alienation is the self-alienation of Spirit that is unable to recognize its own products as such. On this level the concept of alienation is not necessarily intended as pejorative or even normative. See Nicolaus, *Hegels Theorie der Entfremdung* regarding the various dimensions of Hegel's theory of alienation.
16. Löwith, *From Hegel to Nietzsche*, 135–39.
17. The 1844 Manuscripts first appeared in the *Marx-Engels-Gesamtausgabe* in 1932 and were enthusiastically welcomed at the time by Herbert Marcuse, who regarded them as revealing at last the philosophical foundations of Marx's critique of political economy and theory of revolution.
18. Lukács, *History and Class Consciousness*.
19. Lukács himself made comments to this effect in 1967: "To assess the impact of the book at that time, and also its relevance today, we must consider one problem that surpasses in its importance all questions of detail. This is the question of alienation, which, for the first time since Marx, is treated as central to the revolutionary critique of capitalism. . . . Of course the problem was in the air at the time." Lukács, *History and Class Consciousness*, xxii. He explicitly points out the close connection between his view and the existentialist discussion of alienation in mentioning here both the appearance of Heidegger's *Being and Time* (1927) and the French postwar discussion, as well as in noting that "the alienation of man is a crucial problem of the age in which we live and is recognised as such by both bourgeois and proletarian thinkers, by commentators on both right and left" (ibid., xxii).
20. It is logical that Habermas's grand-scale attempt to refound critical theory and reformulate it using the paradigm of communicative action leads to a reconstruction of the theory of reification: thus the thesis of the colonization of the life-world transforms one of the central intuitions of critical theory since Marx.

2. Marx and Heidegger

1. Goldmann, *Lukács and Heidegger*, 31.
2. Fromm, *Marx's Concept of Man*.

3. Marx, "Economic and Philosophic Manuscripts." For a detailed and very instructive interpretation of these writings, cf. Wildt, *Die Anthropologie des jungen Marx.*

4. In discussing Marx, Charles Taylor speaks of a "Promethean expressivism," highlighting the fact that Marx attempts to reconcile (as Taylor describes the problem) the need for expression, which constantly comes into conflict with the modern disenchantment of the world, with the modern emphasis on form-giving power. This expressivism is Promethean because it is not about expressing a (given) cosmic order or a divine will but about being able to express oneself through products created by humans; see, in this regard, Taylor, *Hegel*, 559 and preceding.

5. Marx, "Economic and Philosophic Manuscripts," 3:278–279.

6. I allude here to Daniel Brudney's interpretation of the communist form of association as "structural friendship." Brudney, "Die Rechtfertigung."

7. Marx, "Economic and Philosophic Manuscripts," 3:276.

8. One could argue that this broadening of the Kantian prohibition against instrumentalization to include relations to self—that is, an ethical interpretation of that prohibition—is what makes the convergence of domination and meaninglessness possible.

9. "If the product of labor does not belong to the worker, if it confronts him as an alien power, then this can only be because it belongs to some human being other than the worker. If his activity is a torment to him, it must be a pleasure and joy of life for someone else." Marx, "Economic and Philosophic Manuscripts," 3:278. Here alienation is traced back to a relation of domination, which, viewed more broadly, shows itself to be a relation of structural domination.

10. For a detailed and critical discussion of Marx's theory of alienation and the idea of wealth employed in it, see Lohmann, *Indifferenz und Gesellschaft.*

11. Brudney, "Die Rechtfertigung," 395–423.

12. Labor is understood, in Aristotelian fashion, as the distinctively human activity insofar as it is not exclusively determined by natural necessity or the call of nature. Thus it is possible to locate what Marx calls the distinctive feature of human labor not only in the fact that human labor is planned rather than guided by instinct but also in the fact that the human being "forms objects in accordance with the laws of beauty." We should interpret in a similar manner his claim that in alienated labor the worker is animal in his human functions and human in his animal functions: "What is animal becomes human and what is human becomes animal." Marx, "Economic and Philosophic Manuscripts," 3:275.

13. To the extent that this paradigm conceives of the world only as an externalization of the self, Hannah Arendt's critique of Marx, mentioned earlier, is not

entirely unjustified. I discuss this in detail in chapter 5 of Jaeggi, *Welt und Person*.

14. The most detailed discussion of these problems can be found in Lange's extremely instructive study: Lange, *Das Prinzip Arbeit*.

15. Geuss, *The Idea of a Critical Theory*, 14.

16. Heidegger's own reference to the concept of reification is proof that it makes sense to bring him into the present discussion:

> It has long been known that ancient ontology works with "thing-concepts" and that there is a danger of "reifying consciousness." But what does this "reifying" signify? Where does it arise? Why does Being get "conceived" "proximally" in terms of the present-at-hand *and not* in terms of the ready-to-hand, which indeed lies *closer* to us? *Why* does this reifying always keep coming back to exercise its dominion? What *positive* structure does the Being of "consciousness" have, if reification remains inappropriate to it?
>
> Heidegger, Being and Time, 487.

For the points of contact between the problems of alienation and reification in Lukács and Heidegger, see Goldmann, *Lukács and Heidegger*.

17. This implies a conception of world different from that of traditional philosophy or traditional ontology (the philosophy of consciousness), as well as a different understanding of what the tradition understands as a "subject" that relates to the world.

18. Rentsch, *Martin Heidegger*, 122.

19. According to Heidegger's conception, the mode of present-at-hand characterizes both natural science's understanding of the world and our everyday understanding, which fails to make clear the ready-to-hand character of the things with which it deals and naively posits a separation between itself and the world.

20. Heidegger is not here merely espousing the claim that the subject creates or constitutes the world. "We are simultaneously master and slave of the world," i.e., we understand ourselves on the basis of a world that at the same time is not simply there or given.

21. Heidegger, *Being and Time*, 84.

22. Ibid., 57.

23. Merker, "Konversion statt Reflexion."

24. Ibid., 217.

25. Sartre, *Being and Nothingness*.

26. Barbara Merker conceives of this as a difference between ontic and ontological dimensions, which she understands as "two different ways in which being can go wrong that nevertheless stand in a grounding relationship to one another": "'ontological confusions', such as, for example, existence's [*Existenz*]

interpretation of itself as substance, and 'ontic failures,' which are characterized by a lack of autonomy, authenticity and appropriateness." Merker, "Konversion statt Reflexion," 217.

27. Heidegger, *Being and Time*, 93.
28. Ibid., 151.
29. This is a matter of dispute in the Heidegger literature. In this regard, see the debate about the pejorative and constitutive interpretations of the "They," carried
on, among others, by John Haugeland, Robert Dreyfus, and Robert Brandom.
30. Heidegger, *Being and Time*, 165.
31. Ibid., 164.
32. Habermas, *Erläuterungen zur Diskursethik.*

3. The Structure and Problems of Alienation Critique

1. Fromm, "Zum Gefühl der Ohnmacht," 189.
2. See Michael Theunissen's Hegel interpretation, according to which "relations
of indifference are merely veiled relations of domination." Theunissen, *Sein
und Schein*, 362f. Lohmann takes up this thesis in his study of Marx: Lohmann,
Indifferenz und Gesellschaft.
3. Brudney, *Marx's Attempt to Leave Philosophy*, 389.
4. Wood, *Karl Marx*, 3.
5. See Honderich, "Alienation," 21.
6. Richard Bernstein, for example, regards precisely this ambiguity as the strength
and potential of Marx's theory of alienation, which, following Hegel, attempts
to overcome the dichotomy between "is" and "ought": "In his own way Marx
is attacking the 'myth of the given'—the idea that we can sharply distinguish
that which is immediately given to us in cognition from what is constructed,
inferred, or interpreted by us." Bernstein, *Praxis and Action*, 72.
7. See Williams, *Ethics and the Limits of Philosophy*. Williams discusses these
thick concepts in the context of his proposal for overcoming the distinction
between facts and values (among other places: 129, 143, and following).
8. Furth, *Phänomenologie der Enttäuschungen*, 45.
9. See Althusser's thesis of the epistemological break: Althusser, *For Marx.*
10. Marcuse, *One-Dimensional Man*, 11.
11. Ibid., 12.
12. Tugendhat, "Antike und Moderne Ethik," 46.
13. For an overview of the discussion of subjective and objective criteria for quality
of life, see Gosepath and Jaeggi, "Standards der Lebensqualität."
14. Martha Nussbaum is probably the most prominent exponent of such a position. See, among others, Nussbaum, *Creating Capabilities.*

15. Marx saw very clearly the historicity of human nature due to our ability to shape ourselves and our world. For this reason the question of whether Marx's social philosophy is perfectionist is more difficult to answer than it at first seems.

16. I do not want to say anything conclusive here about the question—unresolved and always topical—of whether it is possible to ground a theory of human nature and thereby provide an "anthropological" foundation for social philosophy. My project pursues a different course. For the different options for grounding social philosophy, see Honneth, "Pathologies of the Social," 3–48.

17. Foucault, "The Ethics of the Concern for Self," 282.

18. Butler, *The Psychic Life of Power*, 28.

4. Having Oneself at One's Command

1. I use "metaphysical" here in the (admittedly limited) pejorative sense, as it has gained currency in the contemporary literature. In this sense it refers (if also sometimes vaguely) to "ultimate values" that are justified in relation to transcendental sources, as opposed to the world of appearances.

2. See the "Translator's Introduction" for an explanation of the phrase "having oneself at one's command."

3. Tugendhat, "Antike und Moderne Ethik," 50.

4. Ibid., 55.

5. Ibid.

6. As, for example, in Steinfath, *Orientierung am Guten*.

7. Tugendhat, "Antike und Moderne Ethik," 55 and following.

8. In this context Steven Lukes's way of relating the concept of alienation to Marx's theory is instructive:

> Of course, Marx attributed a number of ills to capitalism: among them class domination and exploitation, waste of resources and energies, irrationality, inefficiency, poverty, degradation, and misery. "Alienation," however, captures those factors—particularly acute under capitalism—that constitute unfreedom, and whose abolition would constitute human emancipation. The other ills I have mentioned are, of course, not unrelated to unfreedom, but alienation captures the central obstacles to "real freedom."
>
> Lukes, *Marxism and Morality*, 80f.

9. Berlin, *Four Essays on Liberty*, 131.

10. In this context see Raymond Geuss's extremely instructive attempt to sort out this set of problems: Geuss, "Auffassungen der Freiheit."

11. Pippin, "Naturalness and Mindedness," 194.

12. Here, in this section, I borrow from views I have developed elsewhere. See Jaeggi, "Aneignung braucht Fremdheit."

13. It is well known that for John Locke the process of appropriation, understood as the mixing of something with the "labor of one's own hands," is the basis and legitimization of property.

14. Theunissen, "Produktive Innerlichkeit," 23.

15. Raz, *The Morality of Freedom*, 394.

Living One's Life as an Alien Life

1. See Anna Kusser's account of the paradox of an "essence-based critique": "a person who does not correspond to the human essence precisely does not exhibit the essential properties of a human being. Although she does not realize the human essence, she somehow already partakes of this essence—it is 'her' essence as a human being to which she does not correspond." Kusser, *Dimensionen der Kritik von Wünschen*, 55.

2. In this context it is not so important whether this essential core is conceived of on the romantic model, where what is realized is a distinctively unique individual nature, or on the Aristotelian model, where what is realized is a telos of human nature.

3. Jameson, *Postmodernism*.

4. I am alluding here to Heidegger's analysis of equipment (*das Zeug*) in *Being and Time*.

5. Regarding this, see Margolis's description of the cosmic self as one of the leading cultural concepts of modernity: "This self is the essential quality of the person, the center of feeling and worth that each of us has at the core of our being. It is knowable and we approach it in an attitude of discovery. This self cries out for expression." Margolis, *The Fabric of Self*, 4.

6. Baumann, *Die Autonomie der Person*, 12.

7. Tugendhat also emphasizes the central importance of this question. Tugendhat, *Self-Consciousness and Self-Determination*.

5. *Seinesgleichen geschieht*

1. I am alluding here to Erich Fromm's characterization of alienation as a "feeling of powerlessness," "Zum Gefühl der Ohnmacht," 189.

2. One could object: if he is not unhappy and is even proud, how can he then be *alien* in his life? But these things seem to me separable. The feeling of alienness is not necessarily an expression of unhappiness, nor does it necessarily lead to it. One could claim at most that very strong feelings of happiness almost

automatically go together with a degree of involvement that makes feelings of alienness improbable.

3. As Hannah Arendt formulates this point, it is "the function, however, of all action, as distinguished from mere behavior, to interrupt what otherwise would have proceeded automatically and therefore predictably." Arendt, *On Violence*, 30–31.

4. Tugendhat, *Self-Consciousness and Self-Determination*, 188.

5. For this reason, for example, adolescents whose states of mind are attributed to hormonal changes are right in feeling offended: in interpreting their behavior in this way one not only denies their individual uniqueness but also ascribes to them a certain powerlessness—and a corresponding lack of responsibility—in relation to their own reactions and feelings.

6. Transsexuals are a different case. Here it is not a matter of bodily *processes* and their control but of a thoroughgoing sense of being alien in one's own body.

7. Put differently, of course events such as renting a house, entering into a marriage contract, and shopping on Saturdays are in themselves actions or chains of actions and not events. Thus it is already a metaphorical way of speaking when one says that these things appear as "events over which one has no influence" or as "a quasi-natural process." Here, however, the contradiction lies precisely in (subjectively) experiencing an action as a mere event.

8. This does not, of course, mean that such an agent would not be responsible in a moral or legal sense.

9. Tugendhat, *Self-Consciousness and Self-Determination*.

10. The connection to Heidegger's analysis of "fallenness" is obvious; see part 1, chapter 2.

11. I am presupposing here the following minimal definition of heteronomy [*Fremdbestimmung*]: I am heteronomous, or determined by something alien to me, when someone or something influences me in such a way that I end up following her (or its) will instead of my own. In this definition "someone or something" can be anonymous (e.g., a law or a convention), and influence admits of various degrees, up to and including outright coercion. There must always, however, be a foreign will that affects one's own will, a "foreign law" that stands in opposition to "one's own." Something that has a dynamic of its own does not have in this sense a foreign will or foreign law. Perhaps one can also define heteronomy more broadly, but I think it undesirable to blur the distinction between a situation in which someone leads me to do something that she wants rather than I and the situation described earlier—that is, between a situation in which someone is (heteronomously) determined by something foreign (or alien) and one in which one is not determined at all.

12. Raz, *The Morality of Freedom*, 371 (emphasis added).

13. It should be remembered that what is important in this example is not that conventions take the place of what is one's own and represent, as it were, a foreign law.

14. This is not the same thing as social convention, but there is an aspect of conventions that elucidates especially well one of the crucial mechanisms that lead to this kind of rigidification, namely, a restriction of the possibilities of action, a limiting of alternatives.

15. This, too, does not from the outset have anything to do with conventions or with the fact that the guidelines for how to live come from others. What is important is not that I have the same apartment furnishings as others but that it is the furnishings themselves that prescribe how I am to live. Even if both aspects frequently occur together, unconventional forms of life can also rigidify in the sense described here without thereby becoming conventional. I treat the problem of conventionality in more detail in the following chapter in connection with a discussion of social roles and role behavior.

16. Tugendhat discusses the decentering of one's own subjectivity as a demand that follows from precisely the fundamental "egocentricity" of our relation to the world. Tugendhat, *Egozentrizität und Mystik*.

17. I am speaking here only of the conditions that one *can* — in principle — have at one's command. That there are also conditions under which one leads one's life (beginning with bodily conditions) that are in principle not subject to our command is a different point.

18. Hannah Arendt, who always emphasizes our inability to control the consequences of our actions and understood this to be an essential feature of action (in contrast to the activities of producing and laboring), speaks in this context of a "web" in which our actions are always already immersed; see Arendt, *Vita Activa*.

19. One might think here of one aspect of the previously described situation: the child. It is improbable that parents could anticipate all the changes this new situation brings with it. Such a decision is, for this reason, also always a decision to "take things as they come."

20. Plessner, *Das Problem der Öffentlichkeit*, 15.

21. This is an allusion to Heidegger's analysis of the "They" in which it is said of most of what happens that "it was no one." Hannah Arendt gives this phenomenon a social-critical twist, calling it "rule by nobody"; see chapter 2.

22. A penetrating example of not being present in a situation is provided by Gisela Elsner's description of a mother who falls into a depression after the birth of her child: the screaming, demanding creature appears to her to be an incomprehensible monster; his signs of life dismay her. In dealing with the child, she is recognizably beside herself; she is too little present in her behavior for

her to respond to his demands organically, as it were—to respond as though each of her actions followed "of its own" from the others. She observes herself from the outside in complete dismay; her reactions falter in every detail. She constantly does the wrong thing, which makes the situation even more difficult and menacing. This seems to me a good example because it contrasts with the picture of "happy mothers," who master new and unexpected situations precisely because they identify with them, are present *in* the situations, and for that reason are able to respond from inside them. It also demonstrates that this is not an ability one can take for granted, that it is not at all instinctual. Elsner, *Abseits.*

23. I tend to regard posing the "question of meaning" in a fundamental way as always a symptom of crisis. This question can be answered only when it is connected back up to something concrete. Hence, as Freud already noted, it is hard to avoid a "suspicion of meaninglessness" in relation to the question of meaning.

24. I return to the problem of experimentation and a comparison of these two types of experiment in part 3, chapter 10.

25. For reasons already mentioned, accessibility seems to me to be a better concept than transparency because it emphasizes the practical character of this dimension of self-experience.

26. Hence the ethical importance of processes of self-deception for leading a life. For this, see Löw-Beer, *Selbsttäuschung.*

27. The normalizing effect of such horizons of experiences manifests itself not only in the fact that one cannot violate the convention but also in the fact that one must *either* follow it or violate it.

6. "A Pale, Incomplete, Strange, Artificial Man"

1. Plessner, *Das Problem der Öffentlichkeit,* 13.
2. "We are puppets, our strings pulled by unknown powers; there is nothing, nothing that we ourselves do." Büchner, *Dantons Tod,* 100.
3. Regarding "Homo Sociologicus," see Dahrendorf, *Homo Sociologicus,* 58.
4. *Authentic* in this sense means genuine, recognized, original, or unfalsified. Thus under the keyword of *authenticity* in subject catalogs of libraries one also finds titles such as "Testing the Authenticity of Precious Metals."
5. The person most responsible for role theory's prominence in sociology may have been Erving Goffman, with his analyses in *The Presentation of Self in Everyday Life,* though it was Dahrendorf's book, cited in note 3, this chapter, that introduced role theory to Germany. The concept of a role seems to have been omnipresent, above all in the sociology of the 1950s and '60s, such that

nearly all dictionary entries for the term *role theory* begin with reflections on the reasons for the concept's pervasive influence, and—whether they evaluate it positively or negatively—they trace its influence back to the concept's intuitive plausibility and relevance to everyday life. In addition to its usage in sociology narrowly defined, the concept of a role also became, via "symbolic interactionism," the central category of social psychology and theories of socialization. For an overview of role theory in sociology, see Claessens, *Rolle und Macht* and Joas, *Die gegenwärtige Lage der soziologischen Rollentheorie;* for the questions discussed in (early) theories of socialization, see Krappmann, *Soziologische Dimensionen der Identität.* In what follows I am concerned with the topic of roles only insofar as it has implications for a theory of alienation.

6. Dahrendorf, *Homo Sociologicus,* 18.

7. Ibid., 12.

8. Of course, metaphors of the drama and of roles (still relevant today in the talk of society as a production or spectacle) have been used for a long time to describe the relation between individual and society; the idea that the world is a stage is present already in the sixteenth century, as seen in Shakespeare's famous dictum "all the world's a stage." This way of speaking takes on a pejorative character, however, only against the backdrop of the ideal of authenticity described here.

9. Dahrendorf, *Homo Sociologicus,* 58.

10. Ibid., 9.

11. See also Lionel Trilling:

> We nowadays say "role" without taking thought of its original histrionic meaning: "in my professional role," "in my paternal, or maternal role," even "in my masculine, or feminine, role." But the old histrionic meaning is present whether or not we let ourselves be aware of it, and it brings with it the idea that somewhere under all the roles there is Me, that poor old ultimate actuality, who, when all roles have been played, would like to murmur "Off, off your lendings!" and settle down with his own original actual self.
>
> Trilling, *Sincerity and Authenticity,* 10.

12. Cited in Margolis, *The Fabric of Self,* 90.

13. With regard to defining authenticity as a kind of individuality and uniqueness that transcends social roles, see also Charles Taylor's account: "As [the ideal of authenticity] emerges, for instance with Herder, it calls on me to discover my own original way of being. By definition, this cannot be socially derived but must be inwardly generated;" Taylor, *The Ethics of Authenticity,* 47.

14. Wilshire, in his very interesting book *Role Playing and Identity,* is, to my knowledge, the only one to shed light on the problems of the concept of a role in both

spheres. Against a "transcendental-pragmatic" background, he first develops a theory of the drama and then a theory of identity in order to question, finally, the application of the role metaphor to offstage identity. He criticizes, among other things, the relative shallowness of the assumptions that sociological role theory uses in its analysis of theater, which it then uses as the basis for the analogy to offstage identities.

15. See Jean-Paul Sartre's example of the waiter in *Being and Nothingness*. What he means though (and this is how the paradox is resolved) is that "being" is to be understood here not as "essence" but as "existence." "I *am* a waiter" means "I exist as a waiter and could also be something else"—in contrast to the attribution "that *is* a stone."

16. This was heard from a participant in a conference on autonomy. In fact, many people spontaneously answer the question of when they are themselves with "at home." But why should it be that, in taking off one's street clothes, one automatically arrives at one's authentic self? Is not the clearly engaged student, for example, deceived when she assumes that at home (in this case, at her parents' home) she is more herself than in the university seminar, even if at her parents' home she can talk about everything under the sun but not about philosophy, her great interest? Should we not rather suspect that there are in both places parts of her self that she can act out to different extents?

17. Goffman, *The Presentation of Self in Everyday Life*, 253.

18. Ibid., 252–253.

19. One can see this also in the difficulty of producing unconventional behavior outside role behavior. It is not only that, when immediacy is cultivated, it itself easily becomes a studied pattern of behavior but also that, as a whole, such attempts appear to result almost necessarily in the establishment of new conventions.

20. See also Richard Sennett, who develops Plessner's ideas into a diagnosis of the present. Sennett, *The Fall of Public Man*.

21. The phrase *productivity thesis* points to parallels to the contemporary discussion of social constructivism inspired by poststructuralism that I referred to in part 1.

22. Plessner, "Soziale Rolle und menschliche Natur," 238.

23. Plessner develops a critique of the idea of community based on precisely the values of distance and of mediation that are given voice to here; Helmuth Plessner, *The Limits of Community*. For a productive use of Plessner's concept of personal identity, see Richter, *Grenzen der Ordnung*.

24. Plessner, *Das Problem der Öffentlichkeit*, 19.

25. Ibid.

26. Ibid.

27. Even if "romantic" here is used very loosely, Plessner understands his position in opposition to a form of alienation critique that he understands as a remnant of romanticism: the "idea of human self-alienation" is for him "a magic word of undiminished evocativeness," a "remnant of romanticism that burdens our relation to what is public, devalues it, and turns it into an annoyance;" Plessner, *Das Problem der Öffentlichkeit*, 12.

28. Simmel, "Soziologie," 144.

29. My appeal to Simmel is admittedly one-sided since he is thoroughly ambivalent with respect to this point. As Undine Eberlein argues, there is a tension in Simmel between a "sociologistic" conception of the individual as an "intersection of social circles" and his later, philosophical conception of the subject as an "individual law," which criticizes his earlier position and opposes to it the idea of an "unsocialized remainder." Eberlein, *Einzigartigkeit*, 31.

30. See Diggins, *The Promise of Pragmatism*.

31. See Rousseau's Letter to D'Alembert, who in his encyclopedia article on Geneva had proposed the establishment of a theater: "I do not like the need to occupy the heart constantly with the stage as if it were ill at ease inside of us." Rousseau, *Politics and the Arts*, 16.

32. This might well be the main point common to all theories of intersubjectivity from Fichte (via Hegel) to Habermas and Honneth.

33. Sartre, *Being and Nothingness*, 263.

34. Ibid., 264.

35. Honneth, "The Struggle for Recognition," 158–167. Honneth criticizes this implication of Sartre's analysis by reinterpreting the phenomenon of being seen. To Sartre's reductionist account he opposes a description that is rich in content with the "internal normative warp and weft of social interaction." Ibid., 163. On the basis of this—with a view to the more complex theory of intersubjectivity that originates in Hegel and Fichte—one can diagnose (and criticize) in Sartre a reduction of intersubjectivity to self-assertion.

36. Sartre, *Being and Nothingness*, 259.

37. That this ambiguity appears in his analysis but is not thought through to a less negativistic solution is due to the fact that in the end Sartre remains trapped in a negative conception of freedom—even in the *Critique of Dialectical Reason*, where he abandons his methodological individualism and reflects on the conditions of collective action. I cannot go into further detail here with respect to my claim that in totalizing the suspicion of reification he falls back into an ideal of authenticity that contradicts his own theory; for a discussion of Sartre as well as a number of other authors that can be classified as belonging to a negativistic strand of recognition theory, see Jaeggi, "Anerkennung und Ver-

dinglichung." For an orienting discussion of this negativistic strand and a critique of reconciliation-based theories of recognition from (among others) the perspective of social theory, see Celikates, "Wo bleibt der 'Kampf' im Kampf um Anerkennung?"

38. Heidegger's analysis of the "They" can also be interpreted in this way. It is possible to find a way out of the tension between the "They" as a transcendental structure and its pejorative character only if we understand authenticity as something that can be pursued—gradually—only within the "They."

39. George Herbert Mead has a similar understanding of the relation between the conventionality and originality of roles:

> In a society there must be a set of common organized habits of responses found in all, but the way in which individuals act under specific circumstances gives rise to all of the individual differences which characterize the different persons. The fact that they have to act in a certain common fashion does not deprive them of originality. The common language is there, but a different use of it is made in every new contact between persons; the element of novelty in the reconstruction takes place through the reaction of the individuals to the group to which they belong.
>
> Mead, *Mind, Self and Society*, 198.

40. This is the basis of Goffman's analysis; Dreitzel has evaluated this insight in considerable detail in Dreitzel, *Die gesellschaftlichen Leiden*.

41. Dreitzel, *Die gesellschaftlichen Leiden*, 331.

42. Ibid.

43. Ibid. From the account of alienation as a lack of distance from one's roles emerges a conception of self-alienation that is compatible with Marx's, insofar as it involves the alienation of a being that is always already social from itself as a social being: "one can say that the loss of distance from one's roles is synonymous with what Marx described as self-alienation." Ibid. See, in opposition to this, Jutta Matzner's critique of role theory: "If Dahrendorf praises Marx for having the right instinct with respect to the concept of a role—and, indeed, understood as a role in a play, as something its bearers can take off—he nevertheless misses the significance of the character's mask: the 'personal individual' does not lie hidden under the mask as an unalienated remainder. He transcends existing society; the mask can be taken off only with the negation of class society." Matzner, "Der Begriff der Charaktermaske," 136.

44. See the "Translator's Introduction."

45. Dreitzel, *Die gesellschaftlichen Leiden*, 331.

46. Dewey, *Experience and Education*, 26.

47. Ibid., 36.

48. Taking the example of a computer hacker or a laboratory scientist: why should we consider someone who works on a single project with great energy and interest as limited and alienated, even if in pursuing her project she neglects many aspects of life that seem important to us? (Think of the caricature of the hacker: pimply, bleary-eyed, consuming chocolates and cola while sitting in front of the computer screen while avoiding people and light.) Even the most obvious one-sidedness of activities and capacities does not necessarily mean a restriction of experience in the sense of an inhibiting of further experiences. Whether or not very specific interests can open up further dimensions of the world is something that must be determined case by case.

49. Benn, A *Theory of Freedom*, 202.

50. Georg Simmel, 5. "Kapitel: Über die Kreuzung sozialer Kreise," S. 100–116, in *Über soziale Differenzierung Soziologische und psychologische Untersuchungen* (Leipzig: Duncker & Humblot, 1890).

51. See Goffman's comments about the "obstinacy" that develops in the cracks and on the margins of roles: "Without something to belong to, we have no stable self, and yet total commitment and attachment to any social unit implies a kind of selflessness. Our sense of being a person can come from being drawn into a wider social unit; our sense of selfhood can arise through the little ways in which we resist the pull. Our status is backed by the solid buildings of the world, while our sense of personal identity often resides in the cracks." Goffman, *Asylums*, 320.

52. This can be applied to Winnicott's talk of true and false selves. The false self of someone who laughs when she thinks one ought to find something amusing, of someone who is interested in something that she thinks one ought to be interested in, and so forth, does not *screen off* an existent "true self" (as Winnicott misleadingly describes it at first); rather, it hinders its development. For Winnicott, the true self develops when the mother empathically "reflects" her child and thereby provides him with an image of himself. The false self, on the other hand, develops when the unempathic mother does not reflect the child but, instead, confronts him with her own defenses. The child then identifies with her defenses. "Since the child necessarily identifies with the picture that his fellow creatures construct of him in fantasy interactions, he develops an emergent self-consciousness out of a constitutive alienation that Winnicott conceives of as a 'false self.'" This means that here, too, there are not two things, as it were, a true and a false self; rather, the false, alienated self develops in place of the true self. Thus, insofar as the false self "screens off" something, it hinders it in its development; see Mertens, *Handbuch psychoanalytischer Grundbegriffe*, 672.

53. Simmel, "Zur Philosophie des Schauspielers."
54. Simmel elaborates this idea of a particular law by likening it to the moral law: "And this ideal is one whose demands are so strong, so objectively above all mood and arbitrariness—one could say: so elevated above the mere reality of the actor—that it is like a moral norm, which comes to the human being from his objective situation but can demand of him only the particular moral achievement his personality can and must yield in this situation, an achievement that would perhaps be completely different for a different personality under the same circumstances." Simmel, "Zur Philosophie des Schauspielers," 425.
55. Ibid.
56. Ibid., 428.

7. "She but Not Herself"

1. This is how Harry Frankfurt describes the alienated person in "Freedom of the Will," 22.
2. I want to speak here of the "center" or "margins" of a personality in a completely everyday and nontechnical sense. These concepts refer simply to more or less important desires and projects, things that are invested with more or less significance by the person in question and are therefore more or less central to the life of that person. This leaves open the possibility that apparently trivial things are of significance or can come to be recognized as such. This view emphatically does not decide the question of whether there is a core stock of desires or projects that makes up a person's identity; this question will be discussed later.
3. It is possible that nearly all behaviors have an explicable meaning in the sense at issue in Freud's account of the "psychopathology of everyday life." I do not want to rule this out here. Our case, however, deals with a situation of explicit conflict in which the meaning is not implicit but has already become explicitly clear.
4. Charles Taylor, "What Is Human Agency?" in *Human Agency and Language*, 15–44.
5. Psychoanalysis defines ambivalence as the "simultaneous existence of contradictory tendencies, attitudes or feelings in the relationship to a single object—especially the coexistence of love and hate." Laplanche and Pontalis, *The Language of Psycho-Analysis*, 26.
6. With regard to the relation between tragic conflicts and problems of alienation, it can be said that desires must first be *one's own* in order to be able to come into a tragic conflict with each other. Someone who is indifferent knows no

tragic conflicts, nor does someone who is governed by alien desires. In order to fall into tragic inner conflicts one must first identify with one's desires. For this reason, too, abolishing alienation is not the same as resolving conflicts.

7. That an ambivalent conflict sometimes ends such that the desire that has been merely rejected is (re)interpreted into an alien desire depends on the psychological dynamic of such situations. Such instances are not cases of rationalization, nor are they the effect of a "normative power" that comes from the facticity of one's own life history. Once someone has made the decision to deny a particular desire in favor of a competing one, further developments can lead to a situation where it appears in retrospect that no other decision was conceivable. In this sense the denied desire, which, figuratively speaking, marks a crossroads, at some point (if everything goes well) no longer belongs to one's own life. This understandable process, however, can also become problematic: imagine someone who lives purely in her present desires and projects and retrospectively blocks out past rejections or failures completely. This represents a curious lack of depth that—like alienation from one's own past—might be counted among the symptoms of self-alienation.

8. Geuss, "Auffassungen der Freiheit," 6.

9. For the relation between emancipation and freedom, see Obermauer, "Freedom and Emancipation."

10. Frankfurt, "Freedom of the Will," 11–25.

11. Ibid., 12.

12. For our purposes this cannot yet be a sufficient description of the problem, if only because agreement can go in either direction, that is, by adapting first order desires to second or vice versa. I will return to this issue.

13. This marks an interesting parallel to Hegel's theory of the will as developed in his *Philosophy of Right*. As in his account of the "purification of the drives" (Hegel, *Elements of the Philosophy of Right*, §19), here one takes a position in relation to one's own desires, out of which arises an evaluation of those desires that is characteristic of the structure of human freedom and personality. Just as in Hegel's argument against the freedom of *Willkür*, I am not free simply when I do what I want. Rather, I am free—in a normatively more robust sense— when I am able to do what I want on the level of my *second order volitions*. If I can identify with one of my desires and am in a position to act effectively on it, I possess, according to Frankfurt, all the freedom I could want. However, with regard to the question as to what the process that makes a desire into my own consists in, Hegel's and Frankfurt's accounts diverge.

14. This should by no means be understood to mean that in general addicts are not persons. The wanton—someone who has never actually developed higher-level desires in any respect—is, empirically speaking, an extremely improbable

case. Most addicts represent one or another version of the unwilling addict. One could even claim that self-reproach and self-detachment paired with denial make up a constitutive part of the symptom. Of those, on the other hand, who assertively affirm their addiction, Frankfurt's model would have to claim that they have a second order volition to be an addict. Thus they are persons, even when we consider their stance imprudent. On the other hand—and this speaks in favor of Frankfurt's account—it is not accidental that in some phases of addictions we say that someone is in danger of abandoning herself—that is, of losing herself as an acting, deciding, responsible person.

15. Hegel, *Phenomenology of Spirit*, 49.
16. Frankfurt, "Identification and Externality," 58–68.
17. Ibid., 63.
18. Not being able to identify with oneself would mean, then, that I reject what I am because it does not correspond to the demands I place on myself or to the ideal I have of myself. To be sure, I do not want to be what I am (I do not, for example, want to be someone who always procrastinates in writing my lectures); I can, however, be easily identified (by myself as well as by others) as someone to whom, again and again, that very thing happens. It could be, then, that my ideal corresponds less to myself than my actual behavior does. If so, it would be inappropriate to say that I am alien to myself in these characteristics. There would then be behaviors and characteristics of mine that I reject that I must also, like it or not, identify with and recognize as belonging to me.
19. Frankfurt, "Identification and Externality," 65.
20. Ibid. In this sense Frankfurt also says: "The distinction between internal and external passions is not the same as the distinction between what is and what is not 'real' in the sense of a person's ideal image of himself." Ibid., 64.
21. Ibid., 66.
22. Ibid., 68.
23. Ibid.
24. Frankfurt, "On the Necessity of Ideals," 114.
25. Ibid., 115.
26. Frankfurt, "Autonomy, Necessity, and Love," 138.
27. Frankfurt, "On the Necessity of Ideals," 108–116.
28. It would be misleading, however, to speak here of something like a third order volition since that would suggest the possibility of further levels—and with it an infinite regress in the order of desires—which is precisely what the idea of volitional necessities is supposed to rule out.
29. Frankfurt, "Autonomy, Necessity, and Love," 136.
30. Ibid., 137.
31. Frankfurt, "Autonomy, Necessity, and Love," 137.

32. Ibid.

33. This is where one sees the important difference to Hegel's "purification of the drives." Charles Taylor's critique of Frankfurt also starts from the nature of willing or choice as Frankfurt understands it: by expanding second order volitions into "strong evaluations," Taylor introduces an element of justified evaluation. For this see also Kusser, *Dimensionen der Kritik von Wünschen*, who accuses Frankfurt (already at the level of first order desires) of ignoring the practical justification of desires and of ending up with a "decisionistic undermining of practical rationality." Ibid., 149. She makes these claims against the background of her own alternative proposal for an "epistemic critique of desires," which I cannot discuss in detail here.

34. The image of rebuilding on the high sea comes from Otto Neurath. In such a rebuilding, even if one ends up replacing every individual plank of the ship with a new one, they cannot all be replaced at once.

35. Christman, "Autonomy and Personal History."

36. The account of optimal conditions developed by Geuss in response to the question of how false interests can be identified claims that, given the malleability of desires and interests and their dependence on the conditions of life, persons' "'real' interests" are those "they would have formed in 'optimal' (i.e., beneficent) conditions." Geuss, *The Idea of a Critical Theory*, 50. These favorable conditions exclude, at the very least, extreme privation and gross ignorance, but Geuss does not go into further detail in defining them.

37. Geuss, *The Idea of a Critical Theory*, 50.

38. Ibid., 54.

39. Charles Taylor, "Self-Interpreting Animals," in *Human Agency and Language*, 45–76.

40. Löw-Beer, "Rigidität."

41. Glover, *I*, 152.

42. As we will see in chapter 10, Taylor's use of the concept of articulation elaborates this point in an interesting way. I will also further discuss the topos of self-invention in that chapter.

43. Of course, this is far from a complete account of the complex debate about truth and interpretation; here I am concerned only in a very limited manner with parallel themes that illuminate aspects of self-conceptions relevant to the topic of alienation.

44. And this is precisely where illusions do not succeed, or only at the price of drastically diminishing or violating the basic standards of rationality.

45. I would like to thank Martin Löw-Beer very much not only for allowing me to read his manuscripts on the subject of rigidity but also for our extremely instructive discussions about both his work and mine. Löw-Beer, "Rigidität."

46. Sennett, *The Uses of Disorder*, 9.

47. In this respect Alexander Mitscherlich's thesis concerning the "inability to mourn" analyzes a problem of alienation.
48. I am here following by way of analogy the reflections Charles Taylor has made in connection with the critique of needs. For this see Taylor, "What's Wrong with Negative Liberty," in *Human Agency and Language*, 2:223–224, and following.

8. "As If Through a Wall of Glass"

1. Mercier, *Perlmann's Silence*, 10–11.
2. Ibid., 73.
3. The Perlmann I deal with here has been stylized for my purposes and is not completely identical with the character of the novel. In the novel, for example, there is in fact a new interest, a Russian manuscript, that Perlmann gradually falls under the spell of.
4. In part 3, chapter 9, I return to the other question, concerning the circumstances under which a process of radical self-transformation can also lead to forms of alienation and how much and what kind of continuity is necessary for an unalienated self-conception.
5. Mercier, *Perlmann's Silence*, 73–74.
6. Nagel, *The View from Nowhere*.
7. Ibid., 214.
8. Ibid., 218.
9. Here I can only briefly touch on this thesis and the problem of the meaning of life without entering into the rich and complex discussion of it in the literature. The suspicion that the question of the meaning of life is meaningless does appear to match a pattern of argumentation that—from Hegel to Heidegger—is also prevalent in arguments against epistemological skepticism. See Fehige, Meggle, and Wessels, *Der Sinn des Lebens*, a very useful reader on the meaning of life, which includes literary texts and essays as well as classical texts from the (recent) philosophical literature.
10. Nagel, *The View from Nowhere*, 214.
11. James, *The Principles of Psychology*, 279.
12. James himself provides the nicest example of how malleable the boundary between inner and outer is (and of how this malleability depends also on social and historical factors) when he claims that, presented with the choice between a body that is unsightly but perfectly dressed and a beautiful one that is carelessly neglected, everyone would, of course, make the same choice—and then immediately assumes that everyone would choose without hesitation the well-dressed but ugly body. James, *The Principles of Psychology*, 280. I doubt that this choice would be so obvious for everyone today.

13. Ibid., 279.

14. Ibid., 281.

15. This image of the inner citadel was used by Isaiah Berlin in his essay on negative and positive freedom. John Christman—giving it a positive twist—then used it for the title of his book, and he has precisely this dimension of withdrawal and self-determination in mind. See Berlin, *Four Essays on Liberty* and Christman, *The Inner Citadel.*

16. Thus, Adorno, for example, describes the stance of indifference in the "false life" as unavoidably ambivalent: "Thinking men and artists have not infrequently described a sense of being not quite there, of not playing along, a feeling as if they were not themselves at all, but a kind of spectator. . . . 'What does it really matter?' is a line we like to associate with bourgeois callousness, but it is the line most likely to make the individual aware, without dread, of the insignificance of his existence. . . . Spellbound, the living have a choice between involuntary ataraxy—an aesthetic life due to weakness—and the bestiality of the involved." Adorno, *Negative Dialectics*, 363–364. To be sure, the ambivalence described here is unavoidable, a forced ambivalence due to a necessary dilemma in a world that as a whole is taken to be a "false state of things." Ibid., 11.

17. For an encyclopedic account of the various forms of indifference in the cultural history of the West, see Geier, *Das Glück der Gleichgültigen*. Geier explicitly carries out his study under the assumption that indifference is a phenomenon of ambivalence.

18. Hegel, *Vorlesungen über die Geschichte der Philosophie* II, 290.

19. Löw-Beer, "Rigidität."

20. Frankfurt, "On the Usefulness of Final Ends," 88.

21. At this point Frankfurt makes an interesting objection to his own position: are there not practices of indifference that do not lead to an obliteration of the person?

> Is it self-evident that caring about nothing means having a bad life? Certain Eastern systems of thought actually appear to recommend it. Their adherents are encouraged to strive toward a condition in which the will is annihilated—in which one no longer exists as a volitional agent. They acknowledge, however, that annihilating the will requires a sustained program of rigorously disciplined effort. . . . Thus, even for those to whom the most important thing is that nothing should be important to them, caring about that involves extensive volition and action.
>
> Frankfurt, "On the Usefulness of Final Ends," 88

Hence the reply to this objection is that wanting no longer to have a will is also an endeavor of the will. And in the "Eastern" practices Frankfurt alludes to, presumably the attentiveness he is concerned with is sharpened rather than dulled.

22. Hegel, *Vorlesungen über die Geschichte der Philosophie* II, 293.

23. As Hegel expresses it in the *Phenomenology of Spirit*.

24. This idea of appropriative transformation is already crucial for the constitution of the free will. In this regard the introduction to the *Philosophy of Right* is relevant insofar as it can be read as a kind of history of socialization in which subjects develop into persons. Subjects become persons when they "put their will into something" and in so doing are recognized as free beings. This will, however, must first achieve the status of a free will by passing from the negative freedom of *Willkür* (of the arbitrary, or choosing, will) to a "free will that wills the free will." This process of formation, which Hegel calls the "purification of the drives," consists in a process of "working away" what is alien, which includes one's own desires as they appear prior to this appropriative transformation. The point here is that the will that is merely *Willkür* is not really free since it lets itself be determined by unformed desires.

25. Wood, *Hegel's Ethical Thought*, 45.

26. This comparison comes from Geuss, "Freedom as an Ideal."

Alienation as a Disturbed Appropriation

1. See Tugendhat, "Antike und Moderne Ethik," as well as my detailed account in chapter 3.

9. "Like a Structure of Cotton Candy"

1. The contrast between psychological and metaphysical definitions can be found in Jonathan Glover, who, after reviewing and endorsing Derek Parfit's rejection of a metaphysical foundation of the unity of the person in the first part of his book, inquires in the second part into the conditions and effects of identity in the psychological sense; Glover, *I*, 106.

2. The term *core model* here includes positions that from other points of view would need to be distinguished, for example, positions that posit a given essential purpose (and function) of human beings or those based on the romantic idea of an inner temperament unique to each individual. One can situate these positions historically, as before and after the loss of an "objective essential purpose" of the human being.

3. Hegel, *Elements of the Philosophy of Right*, §1.

4. Silverman and Farocki, *Von Godard sprechen*, 28.

5. Nietzsche, *On the Genealogy of Morals*, p. 45.

6. The most detailed and instructive discussion of the various sources of Taylor's conception of expression, which harks back not only to Herder but also to Hegel and can be traced back to Augustine, can be found in Rosa, *Identität und kulturelle Praxis*, 149.

7. Charles Taylor, "What Is Human Agency?" in *Human Agency and Language*, 15–44, 36.

8. Ibid., 36.

9. Rosa, *Identität und kulturelle Praxis*, 149.

10. Cited ibid., 152.

11. Here, however, one can see an internal inconsistency or ambivalence in Taylor's approach, as Holmer Steinfath argues in a review of Taylor's *Sources of the Self*. This ambivalence is

    expressed, on the one hand, in his commitment to a teleological strain of thought that is influenced by a romantic expressive conception of human nature and still shows traces of a questionable essentialism. On the other hand, however, becoming oneself, as a process of interpretation that cannot be reduced to a process of giving objective reality to something that is latently given, is made into an in principle never-ending process of reflection that breaks open the closed character of the Aristotelian model and thereby accounts for a specifically modern experience.

    Steinfath, "In den Tiefen des Selbst," 106.

12. Taylor, "What Is Human Agency?" 38.

13. Steinfath, "In den Tiefen des Selbst," 106.

14. See here the detailed discussion of the existentialist critique of the core self in Cooper, *Existentialism*, especially chapter 6.

15. Sartre, *Existentialism and Human Emotions*, 32.

16. Christman, "Autonomy and Self-Reflection," 13.

17. I use *relationality* here to denote the relation to others and to what is "other" more generally; that is, it refers to sociality, on the one hand, and to relations to the world of things, on the other.

18. I borrow this expression from Carney, *The Films of John Cassavetes*.

19. Cooper summarizes the existentialist critique as follows: "If consciousness is 'plunged into the world of objects' and the 'ego is . . . outside, in the world,' then it will be there, and not in the inner recesses of a 'soulthing' that I find myself." Cooper, *Existentialism*, 97.

20. Hegel, *Phenomenology of Spirit*, 240.

21. Raz, *The Morality of Freedom*.

22. Velleman, "Identification and Identity."

23. Bieri, "Zeiterfahrung und Personalität."

24. Velleman, who in his previously cited paper critically examines Frankfurt's essentialism, gives a psychological explanation of this: the idea of a volitional nature or a personal essence is attractive because of the underlying idea of wholeheartedness, the idea that we are really ourselves when we commit ourselves to something completely, unconditionally, and without ambivalence. The attractiveness of this model—for which at the same time there is not a single plausible example—rests on wishful thinking on our part. We would like to be such persons, but deny the ambivalences that far more accurately characterize our lives, and we thereby give up the possibility of productively integrating these ambivalences into our self-conceptions. I agree with the general direction of this critique, but my argument takes a different path.

25. I use the apparently outmoded example of revolution not for nostalgic reasons but in order to have an example of a strong and emotionally charged project that for once does not come from one's personal life, as do most of Frankfurt's examples.

26. Cooper, *Existentialism.*

27. Frankfurt, "Freedom of the Will," 21.

28. Psychoanalysis recognizes two ways one can fail in coping with a loss: a melancholic-depressive form, marked by autoaggression, and a narcissistically disturbed form that abandons the object. Successful mourning, in contrast, is characterized by a selective introjection of the loved one in which parts of the loved one are taken over into one's own person. The constancy of the object is, then, a precondition of successful mourning.

29. Empirically, of course, the transition will involve many vicissitudes; what one does in one moment one can regret in the next; one can still hang on to the revolution with a part of one's soul while already betraying it at the same time. And so on.

30. Frankfurt, "Autonomy, Necessity, and Love," 139.

31. How exactly this tolerating of ambivalence functions would obviously need to be described more precisely. Here one can again refer to psychoanalysis (especially to the work of Melanie Klein), for which tolerating ambivalence is a criterion of maturity and a central part of growing up. Not being able to tolerate ambivalence is, on the other hand—as in borderline personality disorder—a sign of serious psychic disturbance.

32. Bieri, "Zeiterfahrung und Personalität," 273.

33. Ibid.

34. Frankfurt, "The Faintest Passion," 101.

35. Bieri, "Zeiterfahrung und Personalität," 273.

36. Of course, one can attempt to identify characteristic *stances* that persons adopt with respect to changing projects (the seriousness or dogmatism with which

the revolutionary pursues revolution or counterrevolution, the devotion with which the lover loves). These are then precisely no longer ground projects in Raz's sense nor constitutive commitments without which, according to Frankfurt, we are no longer true to ourselves.

37. Here I treat inwardness (or the objection made in its name) not as a philosophical concept in a strict sense but as a cultural model that has been influential in many ways.

38. Diggins, *The Promise of Pragmatism*, 37.

39. MacIntyre, *Herbert Marcuse*, 10: "This intensifying rift between the inner and the outer was characteristic of bourgeois culture. As it intensifies, there was an intensified need to express in terms of the 'inner' what could not longer find a place in external social life."

40. Trilling, *Sincerity and Authenticity*, 29. For an understanding the concept of uniqueness in romantic individualism, see Eberlein, *Einzigartigkeit*. I speak here of "romantic conceptions of inwardness" in the sense intended by Trilling without being able to do justice to the multifaceted richness of the historical period called romanticism. Richard Rorty uses the term in the same way when he characterizes the "romantic intellectual."

41. Glover, *I*.

42. Cooper, *Existentialism*, 97.

43. James, *Portrait of a Lady*, 187.

44. Ibid., 187.

45. Hofmann, *Selbstkonzepte der New Woman*, 216. Hofmann's own interpretation, however, seems to me completely mistaken. She takes Isabel's outlook to be a masculine conception of the self, in contrast to a reified feminine conception, represented by Merle, that sees women as unstable, dependent, and empty to such an extent that they can attain stability and permanence only through material props. On her interpretation, Isabel's conception of inwardness is emancipatory, whereas in my view the novel deals with and brings to light precisely the dialectic of this sort of emancipation and the illusory character of the conception of self that goes with it.

46. For a systematic discussion, see Saar, "Selbstkritik."

47. The idea of self-invention is inspired mostly by Nietzsche and has been in vogue for a long time with a wide variety of thinkers (of which Foucault, Rorty, and Alexander Nehamas are only the most well known). Dieter Thomä speaks in this context of an "inflation of concepts like 'self-making,' 'self-fashioning,' and 'self-creation,' the fascination with which is perhaps due to the fact that they seem to connect a sober skepticism with respect to facts with an effusive feeling of creativity." Thomä, *Erzähle dich selbst*, 3.

48. On the problem of such a unity, see Pollmann, *Integrität*.

49. Nietzsche, *Nachgelassene Fragmente*, 361.
50. Foucault, "On the Genealogy of Ethics," 262 (emphasis added).
51. Schmid, "Uns selbst gestalten," 50.
52. Diedrichsen, "Supergirls biologische Hardware."
53. It is obvious that I cannot go into this debate in as much detail as it deserves. That would involve, among other things, distinguishing various conceptions of self-invention and examining, in discussion with Foucault, the decidedly contested question of the ethical significance of an "aesthetic of existence" and the relation between the critique of power of his middle period and the "ethics" of his late period.
54. Schmid, "Uns selbst gestalten," 50–62.
55. See especially my remarks concerning the achievement of a self-conception in chapter 7, and my comments on the concept of appropriation in the first section of this chapter.
56. Undine Eberlein points out that this tension exists already in Nietzsche and can be traced through to later poststructuralist appropriations of it: the tension between a "farewell to the subject," on the one hand, and the demiurgic character of the "paradigm of self-production," on the other. Eberlein, *Einzigartigkeit*, 43.
57. Judith Butler also understands self-constitution for Foucault "as a type of *poiesis*." Ibid., 26.
58. Highly simplified, Aristotle distinguishes *poiesis*, the creation of a product guided by technical knowledge, from *praxis*, action whose goal lies in the performance of the action itself and not in some external result.
59. In fact, this is a much more apt description of Foucault's account of the self-practices of an aesthetic of existence than of the Nietzschean demiurge. Undine Eberlein (in *Einzigartigkeit*) distinguishes here between the demiurgic model and a "basket-weaving" model of existence.
60. See chapter 10 for the difference between a romantic-aesthetic model of experimentation and the one I use here, which borrows from the pragmatist conception of an experiment. I also criticize here the idea of the new and the lack of standards.
61. Schmid, "Uns selbst gestalten," 50 (emphasis added).
62. This objection also holds against Foucault's talk of dissolving the subject through experience. The claim, directed against phenomenology, that experience as he conceives of it serves to "tear the subject away from itself such that it is no longer itself or such that it is driven to its destruction and dissolution" is inconsistent. If, as Foucault emphasizes, "an experience is something you come out of changed," then he must presuppose a bearer or a subject of this change. Foucault, *Remarks on Marx: Conversations with Duccio Trombadori*. New York: Semiotext(e), 27.

63. Turkle, *Life on the Screen.*
64. Sherry Turkle became known for having set up one of the first psychological "practices" in the Internet from which, in addition to her research projects conducted at MIT, the bulk of her empirical material comes.
65. Turkle, *Life on the Screen* , 15.
66. I cannot go into the questionable nature of this idea here, which would require a discussion of the conception of reality that underlies it. In this regard, however, see the critique articulated from a phenomenological standpoint by Lucas D. Introna: "Every cyber-traveler will eventually have to deal with the fact of being always already in the world." Introna, "On Cyberspace and Being."
67. One can draw interesting conclusions from this regarding the reality or unreality of such worlds that do not rely on a naive conception of reality. Interestingly enough, the criterion for reality then turns out to be something like intractability.
68. Turkle, *Life on the Screen,* 179.
69. Ibid., 185.

10. Living One's Own Life

1. Lukes, *Marxism and Morality*, 80.
2. Raymond Geuss notes that the concept of positive freedom comprises, in a mostly unordered way, all that makes up the (positive) capacity "to be one's own master" or "to live one's own life." In a kind of cartography, Geuss includes power, self-determination, authenticity, and self-realization among the elements of positive freedom. Geuss, "Auffassungen der Freiheit."
3. In part 1 I pointed to this as the central feature of the problem of alienation in modernity.
4. One might call this phenomenon structural heteronomy; it is not clear, though, what that means without further explanation. I am less concerned here with terminology than with the structure of the phenomenon.
5. Löw-Beer, "Rigidität."
6. Benn, *A Theory of Freedom*, 155.
7. Dworkin, *The Theory and Practice of Autonomy* and Christman, *The Inner Citadel.*
8. Cited in Christman, *The Inner Citadel,* 7.
9. Ibid., 346. See also Christman, "Liberalism and Positive Freedom." The conditions for an autonomous development of preferences are developed in detail in Christman, "Autonomy and Personal History."
10. Raz, *The Morality of Freedom,* 371.

11. For example, the idea of meaningful options helps us to distinguish a genuine value pluralism from the false one that characterizes a world that, in spite of all its diversity, is "one-dimensional."

12. Christopher Lasch, *The Culture of Narcissism* (New York: Norton, 1979).

13. Adorno, *Critical Models*, 164 (emphasis added).

14. Hegel, *Phenomenology of Spirit*, 242.

15. Kambartel, "Universalität als Lebensform," 24 (emphasis added).

16. For the view that there is not an obvious connection between self-fulfillment and autonomy, see Gewirth, *Self-Fulfillment*, 37–40.

17. Kambartel, "Universalität als Lebensform," 22.

18. An example of meaningful activities that are not self-determined is provided by Tarkowski's film *Andrei Rublev*, which describes the complicated and elaborate process of casting a bell in a village during the Middle Ages. The labor process here is nearly ritualistic: religious, meaningful, and collectively carried out. And the creator (or constructor) of the bell understands his activity not only as a kind of worship; he also requires for it, so it is suggested, something like divine, mystical inspiration. But since, at the same time, there is no free space for individuals to relate to this labor—because they do not lead self-determined lives in today's sense—it seems inappropriate to me to call their labor an act of self-realization. What is realized in such labor is a higher idea, not the laborer.

19. Tugendhat, *Self-Consciousness and Self-Determination*, 189.

20. Kambartel, "Universalität als Lebensform," 24.

21. Wildt, *Die Anthropologie des jungen Marx*.

22. Theunissen, *Selbstverwirklichung und Allgemeinheit*.

23. I intentionally use the general concept of worldlessness to express that what is at issue here is relations to others and to the "other" more generally, namely to the "environment" (*Umwelt*) and to the "with-world" (*Mitwelt*: Heidegger), and that in my opinion both threaten to be lost in the self-referential character of the position discussed here.

24. This is a somewhat vague use of the term *romantic*, but it is found in Rorty himself, who characterizes his position as that of a "romantic intellectual."

25. Eberlein, *Einzigartigkeit*.

26. Rorty cites Harold Bloom, who speaks of the "the strong poet's anxiety of influence" and of his "horror at having to acknowledge that he is only a copy or replica." Rorty, *Contingency, Irony and Solidarity*, 24.

27. Ibid.

28. Ibid.

29. Rorty, "Moral Identity and Private Autonomy," 193.

30. Tugendhat, *Self-Consciousness and Self-Determination*, 261.

31. Löw-Beer, "Sind wir einzigartig? 132.

32. That originality and novelty are mere byproducts seems obvious to me in the domain of literature and art. A novel that aims first and foremost at originality will seldom be of great aesthetic quality.

33. Schmitt, *Political Romanticism*, 17.

34. If I understand it correctly, Rorty's model does not exclude such collective experiments since *private* is not synonymous with *isolated*; rather, the former means only that what one does makes no public claims to being intersubjectively valid or that these life projects are not universalizable.

35. The film *Zusammen!* by Lukas Moodysson (2000) wonderfully illustrates this in looking back at the communes of the 1970s and the various problems such experiments generate. In so doing it is extremely fair in showing the rigidifications and the potential for self-deception of both conventional and unconventional models.

36. Menke, *Reflections of Equality*, 136.

37. It is an odd but perhaps not accidental coincidence—and of great contemporary relevance—that liberals' emphasis on the impossibility of grounding idiosyncratic forms of life goes hand in hand with a renewed conventionalism. This suggests that a public discussion of forms of life—in which truth claims are made—contributes more to promoting unconventional forms of life than merely fostering their coexistence alongside one another.

Conclusion

1. With respect to this question the traditions sketched—starting with Rousseau, through Hegel and Marx on the one hand, and through Kierkegaard and Heidegger on the other—take opposing positions.

2. In conjunction with his discussion of G. H. Mead's view that the "cooperative possibilities of action marked out by roles are . . . the only possible offers of meaning," Ernst Tugendhat develops the claim that "a critique of socially given cooperative activities from the standpoint of their meaning would always be conceivable only on the basis of a model of a better society—or in any case this is Mead's conception. Such a critique cannot be developed from the perspective of an activity that is not socially related; the latter is not a possible source of meaning at all." Tugendhat, *Self-Consciousness and Self-Determination*, 244.

3. Amengual, "Gattungswesen als Solidarität," 345–368.

4. I develop this in detail in Jaeggi, "Solidarity and Indifference."

WORKS CITED

Adorno, Theodor W. *Critical Models*. New York: Columbia University Press, 1998.
——. *Minima Moralia: Reflections from Damaged Life*. New York: Verso, 2006.
——. *Negative Dialectics*. London: Routledge, 2006.
Althusser, Louis. *For Marx*. Trans. Ben Brewster. London: Verso, 2005.
Amengual, Gabriel. "Gattungswesen als Solidarität." In *Ludwig Feuerbach und die Philosophie der Zukunft*, ed. Hans-Jürg Braun, Hans-Martin Sass, Werner Schuffenhauer, and Francesco Tomasoni, 345–368. Berlin: Akademie, 1990.
Anderson, Elizabeth. *Value in Ethics and Economics*. Cambridge: Harvard University Press, 1993.
Arendt, Hannah. *On Violence*. New York: Harcourt Brace Jovanovich, 1970.
——. *The Human Condition*. Chicago: University of Chicago Press, 1958.
Avineri, Shlomo. *The Social and Political Thought of Karl Marx*. Cambridge: Cambridge University Press, 1968.
Baczko, Bronislaw. *Rousseau: Einsamkeit und Gemeinschaft*. Vienna: Europa, 1970.
Bartels, Martin. "Selbstbewußtsein als interessegeleiteter Vollzug: Der psychoanalytische und der existenzial ontologische Beitrag zum Selbst bewußtseinsproblem," PhD diss., Heidelberg, 1971.
Barth, Hans. *Wahrheit und Ideologie*. Frankfurt: Suhrkamp, 1974.
Baumann, Peter. *Die Autonomie der Person*. Paderborn: Mentis, 2000.
Beckett, Samuel. *The Unnamable*. London: Calder and Boyers, 1975.
Benhabib, Seyla, Judith Butler, Drucilla Cornell, and Nancy Fraser, eds. *Feminist Contentions: A Philosophical Exchange*. London: Routledge, 1994.
Benn, Stanley I. "Freedom, Autonomy, and the Concept of a Person." *Proceedings of the Aristotelian Society* 76 (1975–1976): 109–130.
——. *A Theory of Freedom*. New York: Cambridge University Press, 1988.
Berlin, Isaiah. *Four Essays on Liberty*. London: Oxford University Press, 1969.

Bernstein, Richard. *Praxis and Action: Contemporary Philosophies of Human Activity.* Philadelphia: University of Pennsylvania Press, 1971.

Bieri, Peter. "Zeiterfahrung und Personalität." In *Zeit, Natur und Mensch,* ed. Heinz Burger, 261–281. Berlin: Spitz, 1986.

Boltanski, Luc, and Eve Chiapello. *The New Spirit of Capitalism.* Trans. Gregory Elliott. London: Verso, 2005.

Brinkmann, Rolf Dieter. *Keiner weiß mehr.* Reinbek: Rowohlt, 1970.

Brudney, Daniel. "Die Rechtfertigung einer Konzeption des guten Lebens beim frühen Marx." *Deutsche Zeitschrift für Philosophie* 50, no. 3 (2002): 395–423.

——. *Marx's Attempt to Leave Philosophy.* Cambridge: Harvard University Press, 1998.

Büchner, Georg. *Dantons Tod.* In *Werke und Briefe,* ed. Karl Pörnbacher. Munich: Hanser, 1988.

Butler, Judith. *Kritik der ethischen Gewalt.* Frankfurt: Suhrkamp, 2003.

——. *The Psychic Life of Power.* Stanford: Stanford University Press, 1997.

Carney, Ray. *The Films of John Cassavetes.* Cambridge: Cambridge University Press, 1994.

Celikates, Robin. "Wo bleibt der 'Kampf' im Kampf um Anerkennung?" Unpublished MS, 2004.

Christman, John. "Autonomy and Personal History." *Canadian Journal of Philosophy* 21, no. 1 (1991): 1–24.

——. "Autonomy and Self-Reflection." Unpublished MS, 1999.

——. *The Inner Citadel.* New York: Oxford University Press, 1989.

——. "Liberalism and Positive Freedom." *Ethics* 101, no. 2 (1991): 343–359.

Claessens, Dieter. *Rolle und Macht.* Munich: Juventa, 1974.

Cooper, David E. *Existentialism: A Reconstruction.* Oxford: Blackwell, 1990.

Dahrendorf, Ralf. *Homo Sociologicus.* London: Routledge and Kegan Paul, 1973.

Dewey, John. *Experience and Education.* New York: Simon and Schuster, 1997.

Diedrichsen, Diedrich. "Supergirls biologische Hardware." *Süddeutsche Zeitung,* May 6/7, 2000.

Diggins, John Patrick. *The Promise of Pragmatism: Modernism and the Crisis of Knowledge and Authority.* Chicago: University of Chicago Press, 1994.

Dreitzel, Hans Peter. *Die gesellschaftlichen Leiden und das Leiden an der Gesellschaft.* Stuttgart: Enke, 1968.

Dworkin, Gerald. *The Theory and Practice of Autonomy.* Cambridge: Cambridge University Press, 1988.

Eberlein, Undine. *Einzigartigkeit: Das romantische Individualitätskonzept der Moderne.* Frankfurt: Campus, 2000.

Elsner, Gisela. *Abseits: Roman.* Reinbek: Rowohlt, 1984.

Fehige, Christoph, Georg Meggle, and Ulla Wessels, eds. *Der Sinn des Lebens.* Munich: Deutscher Taschenbuch, 2000.

Fink-Eitel, Hinrich. *Michel Foucault: Zur Einführung.* Hamburg: Junius, 1990.

Foucault, Michel. "The Ethics of the Concern for Self as a Practice of Freedom." In Michel Foucault, *Ethics: Subjectivity and Truth*, ed. Paul Rabinow, 281–302. New York: New Press, 1997.

——. *Mikrophysik der Macht.* Berlin: Merve, 1976.

——. "On the Genealogy of Ethics." In Michel Foucault, *Ethics: Subjectivity and Truth*, ed. Paul Rabinow, 253–280. New York: New Press, 1997.

——. *Remarks on Marx: Conversations with Duccio Trombadori.* New York: Semiotext(e), 1991.

Frankfurt, Harry. "Autonomy, Necessity, and Love." In Harry Frankfurt, *Necessity, Volition, and Love*, 129–141. Cambridge: Cambridge University Press, 1999.

——. "The Faintest Passion." In Harry Frankfurt, *Necessity, Volition, and Love*, 95–107. Cambridge: Cambridge University Press, 1999.

——. "Freedom of the Will and the Concept of a Person." In Harry Frankfurt, *The Importance of What We Care About*, 11–25. Cambridge: Cambridge University Press, 1988.

——. "Identification and Externality." In Harry Frankfurt, *The Importance of What We Care About*, 58–68. Cambridge: Cambridge University Press, 1988.

——. *The Importance of What We Care About.* Cambridge: Cambridge University Press, 1988.

——. *Necessity, Volition, and Love.* Cambridge: Cambridge University Press, 1999.

——. "On the Necessity of Ideals." In Harry Frankfurt, *Necessity, Volition, and Love*, 108–116. Cambridge: Cambridge University Press, 1999.

——. "On the Usefulness of Final Ends." In Harry Frankfurt, *Necessity, Volition, and Love*, 82–94. Cambridge: Cambridge University Press, 1999.

Friedman, Marilyn, Larry May, Kate Parsons, and Jennifer Stiff, eds. *Rights and Reason: Essays in Honor of Carl Wellman.* Dordrecht: Kluwer Academic, 2000.

Fromm, Erich. *Marx's Concept of Man.* London: Continuum, 2004.

——. "Zum Gefühl der Ohnmacht." In Erich Fromm, *Gesamtausgabe* 1:189–206. Stuttgart: Deutsche Verlags-Anstalt, 1980.

Furth, Peter. *Phänomenologie der Enttäuschungen: Ideologiekritik nachtotalitär.* Frankfurt: Fischer, 1991.

Geier, Manfred. *Das Glück der Gleichgültigen: Von der stoischen Seelenruhe zur postmodernen Indifferenz.* Reinbek: Rowohlt, 1997.

Geuss, Raymond. "Auffassungen der Freiheit." *Zeitschrift für philosophische Forschung* 49 (January–March 1995): 1–14.

——. "Freedom as an Ideal." *Proceedings of the Aristotelian Society*, suppl. vol. 69 (1995): 87–100.

——. *Glück und Politik: Potsdamer Vorlesungen*. Berlin: Berliner Wissenschafts-Verlag, 2004.

——. *The Idea of a Critical Theory: Habermas and the Frankfurt School*. Cambridge: Cambridge University Press, 1981.

Gewirth, Alan. *Self-Fulfillment*. Princeton: Princeton University Press, 1998.

Glover, Jonathan. *I: The Philosophy and Psychology of Personal Identity*. London: Allen Lane, 1988.

Goffman, Erving. *Asylums*. New York: Anchor, 1961.

——. *The Presentation of Self in Everyday Life*. New York: Doubleday, 1959.

Goldmann, Lucien. *Lukács and Heidegger: Towards a New Philosophy*. London: Routledge and Kegan Paul, 1977.

Gosepath, Stefan, and Rahel Jaeggi. "Standards der Lebensqualität." Bad Neuenahr-Ahrweiler: Europäische Akademie zur Erforschung der Folgen wissenschaftlich-technischer Entwicklungen, 2002.

Habermas, Jürgen. *Justification and Application: Remarks on Discourse Ethics*. Cambridge: MIT Press, 1993.

Hegel, G. W. F. *Elements of the Philosophy of Right*. Edited by Allen W. Wood. Trans. H. B. Nisbet. Cambridge: Cambridge University Press, 1991.

——. *Phenomenology of Spirit*. Trans. A. V. Miller. Oxford: Oxford University Press, 1977.

——. *Vorlesungen über die Geschichte der Philosophie* II. In *Werke* 19, ed. Eva Moldenhauer and Karl Markus Michel. Frankfurt: Suhrkamp, 1986.

Heidegger, Martin. *Being and Time*. Trans. John Macquarrie and Edward Robinson. London: SCM, 1962.

Hofmann, Stefanie. *Selbstkonzepte der New Woman in George Eliots Daniel Deronda und Henry James' The Portrait of a Lady*. Tübingen: Narr, 2000.

Honderich, Ted. "Alienation." In *Oxford Companion to Philosophy*, ed. Ted Honderich, 21. Oxford: Oxford University Press, 1995.

Honneth, Axel. *The Struggle for Recognition: The Moral Grammar of Social Conflicts*. Cambridge, Mass.: MIT, 1996.

——. *Reification: A New Look at an Old Idea*. New York: Oxford University Press, 2012.

——. "Pathologies of the Social: The Past and Present of Social Philosophy." In Axel Honneth, *Disrespect: Normative Foundations of Critical Theory*, 3–48. Cambridge: Polity, 2007.

——. "The Struggle for Recognition: On Sartre's Theory of Intersubjectivity." In Axel Honneth, *The Fragmented World of the Social*, ed. Charles W. Wright, 158–167. Albany: State University of New York Press, 1995.

——, Judith Butler, Raymond Geuss, Jonathan Lear, and Martin Jay. *Reification: A New Look at an Old Idea*. Oxford: Oxford University Press, 2008.

Introna, Lucas D. "On Cyberspace and Being: Identity, Self and Hyperreality." *Philosophy in the Contemporary World* 4 (1997): 16–25.

Israel, Joachim, and Hans-Joachim Maass. *Der Begriff Entfremdung: Zur Verdinglichung des Menschen in der bürokratischen Gesellschaft.* Reinbek: Rowohlt, 1985.

Jaeggi, Rahel. "Aneignung braucht Fremdheit: Überlegungen zum Begriff der Aneignung bei Marx." *Texte zur Kunst* 46 (June 2002): 60–69.

——. "Anerkennung und Verdinglichung." Unpublished MS, 2004.

——. "Der Markt und sein Preis." *Deutsche Zeitschrift für Philosophie* 47, no. 6 (1999): 987–1004.

——. "Solidarity and Indifference." In *Solidarity in Health and Social Care in Europe*, ed. Rudd ter Meulen, Wil Arts, and Rudd Muffels, 287–308. Dordrecht: Kluwer, 2001.

——. *Welt und Person: Zum anthropologischen Hintergrund der Gesellschaftskritik Hannah Arendts.* Berlin: Lukas, 1997.

James, Henry. *Portrait of a Lady.* London: Penguin, 1997.

James, William. *The Principles of Psychology.* Cambridge: Harvard University Press, 1981.

Jameson, Frederic. *Postmodernism; or, The Cultural Logic of Late Capitalism.* Durham: Duke University Press, 1991.

Joas, Hans. *Die gegenwärtige Lage der soziologischen Rollentheorie.* Frankfurt: Athenäum, 1973.

Kambartel, Friedrich. "Universalität als Lebensform." In Friedrich Kambartel, *Philosophie der humanen Welt*, 14–26. Frankfurt: Suhrkamp, 1989.

Kerber, Harald, and Arnold Schmieder, eds. *Handbuch Soziologie.* Reinbek: Rowohlt, 1984.

Krappmann, Lothar. *Soziologische Dimensionen der Identität.* Stuttgart: Klett, 1972.

Kusser, Anna. *Dimensionen der Kritik von Wünschen.* Frankfurt: Athenäum, 1989.

Laing, Ronald D. *Das geteilte Selbst.* Munich: Deutscher Taschenbuch, 1987.

Lange, Ernst Michael. *Das Prinzip Arbeit: Drei metakritische Kapitel über Grundbegriffe, Struktur und Darstellung der "Kritik der politischen Ökonomie" von Karl Marx.* Frankfurt: Ullstein, 1980.

Laplanche, Jean, and Jean Bertrand Pontalis. *The Language of Psycho-Analysis.* Trans. Donald Nicholson-Smith. London: Karnac, 1988.

Lohmann, Georg. *Indifferenz und Gesellschaft: Eine kritische Auseinandersetzung mit Marx.* Frankfurt: Suhrkamp, 1991.

Löw-Beer, Martin. "Rigidität." Unpublished MS, 2001.

——. *Selbsttäuschung.* Freiburg: Alber, 1990.

——. "Sind wir einzigartig? Zum Verhältnis von Autonomie und Individualität." *Deutsche Zeitschrift für Philosophie* 42, no. 1 (1994): 121–139.

Löwith, Karl. *From Hegel to Nietzsche.* New York: Anchor, 1967.

Lukács, Georg. *History and Class Consciousness: Studies in Marxist Dialectics.* Trans. Rodney Livingstone. London: Merlin, 1971.

Lukes, Steven. *Marxism and Morality.* Oxford: Clarendon, 1985.

MacIntyre, Alasdair. *Herbert Marcuse: An Exposition and a Polemic.* New York: Viking, 1970.

——. *Marxism: An Interpretation.* London: SCM, 1953.

——. *Marxism and Christianity.* Notre Dame: University of Notre Dame Press, 1984.

Marcuse, Herbert. "Neue Quellen zur Grundlegung des Historischen Materialismus." In Herbert Marcuse, *Schriften* 1. Frankfurt: Suhrkamp, 1978.

——. *One-Dimensional Man.* London: Routledge, 1994.

Margolis, Diane Rothbard. *The Fabric of Self.* New Haven: Yale University Press, 1998.

Marx, Karl. "Economic and Philosophic Manuscripts." In Karl Marx and Friedrich Engels. *Karl Marx Friedrich Engels Collected Works* 3:229–348. New York: International, 1975.

——. *First Version of Capital.* In Karl Marx and Friedrich Engels. *Marx Friedrich Engels Collected Works* 28. New York: International, 1986.

——. *The Grundrisse.* Translated by David McLellan. New York: Harper and Row, 1971.

Matzner, Jutta. "Der Begriff der Charaktermaske bei Karl Marx." *Soziale Welt* 15, no. 2 (1964): 130–139.

Mead, George Herbert. *Mind, Self and Society.* Chicago: University of Chicago Press, 1967.

Menke, Christoph. *Reflections of Equality.* Trans. Howard Rouse and Andrei Denejkine. Stanford: Stanford University Press, 2006.

Mercier, Pascal. *Perlmann's Silence.* Trans. Shaun Whiteside. New York: Grove, 2011.

Merker, Barbara. "Konversion statt Reflexion: Eine Grundfigur der Philosophie Martin Heideggers." In *Martin Heidegger: Innen- und Außenansichten*, ed. Forum für Philosophie Bad Homburg, 215–243. Frankfurt: Suhrkamp, 1989.

——. *Selbsttäuschung und Selbsterkenntnis.* Frankfurt: Suhrkamp, 1988.

Mertens, Wolfgang, ed. *Handbuch psychoanalytischer Grundbegriffe.* Stuttgart: Kohlhammer, 2000.

Meyerson, Diane. "On Being One's Own Person." *Ethical Theory and Moral Practice* 1, no. 4 (1998): 447–466.

Misik, Robert. *Genial dagegen: Kritisches Denken von Marx bis Michael Moore.* Berlin: Aufbau, 2005.

Musil, Robert. *The Man Without Qualities*, vol. 1: *A Sort of Introduction and The Like of It Now Happens.* Trans. Eithne Wilkins and Ernst Kaiser. New York: Coward-McCann, 1953.

Nagel, Thomas. *The View from Nowhere*. Oxford: Oxford University Press, 1986.

Negt, Oskar, and Alexander Kluge. *Öffentlichkeit und Erfahrung*. Frankfurt: Suhrkamp, 1972.

Neuhouser, Frederick. *Foundations of Hegel's Social Theory: Actualizing Freedom*. Cambridge: Harvard University Press, 2000.

"The New Radicals." *Newsweek*. December 12, 1999.

Nicolaus, Helmut. *Hegels Theorie der Entfremdung*. Heidelberg: Manutius, 1995.

Nietzsche, Friedrich. *Nachgelassene Fragmente 1880–1882*. In *Kritische Studienausgabe* 9, ed. Giorgio Colli and Mazzino Montinari. Munich: Deutscher Taschenbuch, 1988.

——. *On the Genealogy of Morals*. Trans. Walter Kaufmann. New York: Random House, 1989.

Nussbaum, Martha. *Creating Capabilities: The Human Deveopment Approach*. Cambridge: Belknap Press of Harvard University Press, 2011.

Obermauer, Ralph. "Freedom and Emancipation in T. W. Adorno and C. Castoriadis." PhD diss., New School for Social Research, 2002.

Pippin, Robert. "Naturalness and Mindedness: Hegel's Compatibilism." *European Journal of Philosophy* 7, no. 2 (1999): 194–212.

Plessner, Helmuth. *Das Problem der Öffentlichkeit und die Idee der Entfremdung*. Göttingen: Vandenhoeck and Ruprecht, 1960.

——. *The Limits of Community: A Critique of Social Radicalism*. New York: Humanity, 1999.

——. "Soziale Rolle und menschliche Natur." In *Gesammelte Schriften* 10. Frankfurt: Suhrkamp, 1985.

Pollmann, Arnd. *Integrität*. Bielefeld: Transcript, 2005.

Radin, Margaret Jane. *Contested Commodities*. Cambridge: Harvard University Press, 1996.

Raz, Joseph. *The Morality of Freedom*. Oxford: Clarendon, 1986.

——. "When We Are Ourselves: The Active and the Passive." In Joseph Raz, *Engaging Reason*, 5–21. Oxford: Oxford University Press, 1999.

Rentsch, Thomas. *Martin Heidegger, Das Sein und der Tod: Eine kritische Einführung*. Munich: Piper, 1989.

Richter, Norbert. *Grenzen der Ordnung*. Frankfurt: Campus, 2005.

Rorty, Richard. *Contingency, Irony and Solidarity*. Cambridge: Cambridge University Press, 1999.

——. "Moral Identity and Private Autonomy: The Case of Foucault." In Richard Rorty, *Essays on Heidegger and Others: Philosophical Papers* 2, 193–198. Cambridge: Cambridge University Press, 1991.

Rosa, Hartmut. *Identität und kulturelle Praxis: Politische Philosophie nach Charles Taylor*. Frankfurt: Campus, 1998.

Rousseau, Jean-Jacques. *The Discourses and Other Early Political Writings.* Trans. Victor Gourevitch. New York: Cambridge University Press, 1997.

——. *Politics and the Arts: Letter to M. D'Alembert on the Theatre.* Ed. and trans. Allan Bloom. Ithaca: Cornell University Press, 1968.

Saar, Martin. "Selbstkritik." PhD diss., Johann-Wolfgang-Goethe Universität, 2004.

Sartre, Jean-Paul. *Being and Nothingness.* Trans. Hazel E. Barnes. London: Routledge, 1969.

——. *Existentialism and Human Emotions.* Secaucus, NJ: Lyle Stuart, 1985.

Schacht, Richard. *Alienation.* Garden City, NY: Doubleday, 1970.

——. *The Future of Alienation.* Urbana: University of Illinois Press, 1994.

Schaff, Adam. *Alienation as a Social Phenomenon.* Oxford: Pergamon, 1980.

Schmid, Wilhelm. "Uns selbst gestalten: Zur Philosophie der Lebenskunst bei Nietzsche." In *Nietzschestudien* 21 (1992): 50–62.

Schmitt, Carl. *Political Romanticism.* Trans. Guy Oakes. Cambridge: MIT Press, 1986.

Sennett, Richard. *The Fall of Public Man.* New York: Knopf, 1977.

——. *The Uses of Disorder: Personal Identity and City Life.* New York: Knopf, 1970.

Silverman, Kaja, and Harun Farocki. *Von Godard sprechen.* Berlin: Vorwerk 8, 1998.

Simmel, Georg. *Goethe.* Leipzig: Klinkhardt and Biermann, 1923.

——. "Soziologie." In *Gesamtausgabe* 11. Frankfurt: Suhrkamp, 1992.

——. "Zur Philosophie des Schauspielers." In *Gesamtausgabe* 8. Frankfurt: Suhrkamp, 1983.

Steinfath, Holmer. "In den Tiefen des Selbst." *Philosophische Rundschau* 38 (1991): 103–111.

——. *Orientierung am Guten.* Frankfurt: Suhrkamp, 2001.

Taylor, Charles. *Philosophy and the Human Sciences: Philosophical Papers 2.* Cambridge: Cambridge University Press, 1985.

——. *Human Agency and Language: Philosophical Papers 1.* Cambridge: Cambridge University Press, 1985.

——. *The Ethics of Authenticity.* Cambridge: Harvard University Press, 1991.

——. *Hegel.* Cambridge: Cambridge University Press, 1975.

Theunissen, Michael. "Produktive Innerlichkeit." *Frankfurter Hefte extra* 6 (December 1984).

——. *Sein und Schein: Die kritische Funktion der Hegelschen Logik.* Frankfurt: Suhrkamp, 1978.

——. *Selbstverwirklichung und Allgemeinheit: Zur Kritik des gegenwartigen Bewusstseins.* Berlin: De Gruyter, 1981.

Thomä, Dieter. *Erzähle dich selbst: Lebensgeschichte als philosophisches Problem.* Munich: Beck, 1998.

Trilling, Lionel. *The Opposing Self.* Oxford: Oxford University Press, 1980.

———. *Sincerity and Authenticity*. Cambridge: Harvard University Press, 1971.

Tugendhat, Ernst. "Antike und Moderne Ethik." In Ernst Tugendhat, *Probleme der Ethik*. Stuttgart: Reclam, 1986.

———. *Egozentrizität und Mystik: Eine anthropologische Studie*. Munich: Beck, 2003.

——— *Self-Consciousness and Self-Determination*. Trans. Paul Stern. Cambridge: MIT Press, 1986.

Turkle, Sherry. *Life on the Screen: Identity in the Age of the Internet*. London: Weidenfeld and Nicolson, 1996.

Velleman, J. David. "Identification and Identity." Unpublished MS, 1999. Online at http://country.rs.itd.umich.edu/-velleman/Self/ld&ld.html.

Wildt, Andreas. *Die Anthropologie des jungen Marx*. Hagen: Fernuniversität, 1987.

Williams, Bernard. *Ethics and the Limits of Philosophy*. Cambridge: Harvard University Press, 1985.

Wilshire, Bruce. *Role Playing and Identity: The Limits of Theatre as Metaphor*. Bloomington: Indiana University Press, 1982.

Wolf, Ursula. *Das Problem des moralischen Sollens*. Berlin: De Gruyter, 1984.

Wood, Allen W. *Hegel's Ethical Thought*. Cambridge: Cambridge University Press, 1990.

———. *Karl Marx*. London: Routledge and Kegan Paul, 1981.

INDEX

Abständigkeit (distantiality), 213

Abstract independence, 147

Actions: as action of other, 217–19; as alien power, 57; consequences of, 61–64; independent existence of, 51–67; inhibition of, 126–28; scope of, 67

Activism, as form of life lifestyle, 61

Actor, 96–98

Addicts, 238*n*14

Adolescents, 229*n*5

Adorno, Theodor W., 242*n*16

Agamemnon (fictional character), 175

Alienated labor, 224*n*12

Alienation: as appropriation relation, 36–37; autonomy influenced by, xxii; concept of, 3, 26–27; critical theory defined by, vii; critique of critique of, 27–28; as critique's starting point, vii, xix; as diagnostic concept, 26–27; dimensions of, 12–14; as domination relation, 22, 224*n*9; emancipation diagnoses, 23; essentialism relied on by, xi–xii; as ethical problem, xxii–xxiii; freedom and, xii, 2, 23, 34–36, 199; as good life theory constituent, 28; heteronomy and, 22, 23, 24, 58–59, 152, 200; history of, 6–10; impotence in, 24; as inauthenticity, 18–21; indifference

and, 149–50, 152; of individual, 217; interpretations of, 134–41; labor and, 11–16; as loss of control, 12–14, 221*n*3; Marx's conception of, 14–16; as meaninglessness, 22; modernity characterized by, 8; normative status of, 128–29; positive freedom as opposite of, 199; praxis as important to diagnosis of, 18; project of reconstructing, 40; reconciliation dependence of, 40; relation of relationlessness as core of, xii; roles and, 72–76; second order, 114; self-realization and, 149–50; in sociality, 31; theories of, 5–10, 37

Alienation critique, *see* Critique

Alienness: appropriation's contrast with, 12; feeling of, 228–29

Ambivalence: of indifference, 141–49; of roles, 80–92; tolerating, 245*n*31

Anthropology: Marx's labor, 14–16; social philosophy foundation, 227*n*16

Antiessentialism: appropriation model, 206; articulation understood through, 162; authenticity conception, 210; personal identity conception, 178–79; self-appropriation and, 187; self-invention and, 187

Antipaternalism, 34

Indifference: alienation and, 149–50, 152; ambivalence of, 141–49; autonomy and, 142–43, 202; desires and, 237n6; division called into question by, 160; domination's relation with, 24; emancipatory potential of, 142; in false life, 242n16; freedom of, 149; freedom's relation with, 141–49; good life question undermined by, xxii, 222n10; as identification loss, 134, 136–41; identity and, 143–45; as independence assertion, 150; loss of self and, 141–49; Perlmann's, 131–35, 140–41, 160, 202, 218; person obliterated by, 242n21; as relations loss, 134–36; self-alienation and, 131–50; self-realization and, 149–50

Indifferent man, 131–35

Individual: alienation of, 217; drama and, 232n8; formation part of, 177–78; life experiments, 209–15; relations and, 218, 219; role formation of, 217; self-relation of outward-directed, 81; society's relation with, 232n8

Individuality: authenticity as creating, 210; developing, 213; meaning of, 210; natural development of, 215; resisting, 182; Tugendhat on, 211; as uniqueness, 211–13

Inhibition of actions, 126–28

Inner citadel, 180–85

Inner core, inauthenticity determined by, 45

Inner essence, authenticity determined by, 157–59

Inner freedom, 146–47

Inner life: independence in, 183; as inner world, 182–83; overview of, 182–83

Institutions, constitution of, 220

Instrumentalism, 93–94

Instrumentalization: meaninglessness intensified into by, 13–14; prohibition against, 224n8

Integration: appropriation involvement, 186; ethical social life as form of, 8; on Internet, 197; otherness influencing, 129; of personality, 122–26; process of, 176–77; self and, 176, 192; unity of self as achievement of, 160

Interests, uniqueness and, 211–13

Internal division, *see* Division

Internet: continuity represented by, 197–98; conventions and, 197–98; experiences on, 193–98; formation on, 194–98; integration on, 197; multiple identities on, 194–98; personality influenced by, 197–98

Interpretation: of alienation, 134–41; appropriation needing, 122; blocking out, 218–19; identification needing, 122; on life, 54–60; self-conception as, 124; social, 218–19

Interpretive sovereignty, 71–72

Intractability (*Unverfügbarkeit*): Frankfurt on, 112; inwardness and, 166–85; of self, 167–79; volitional necessities and, 112

Inwardness, 246n37; Archer's conception of, 246n45; critique of, 180–86; independence as, 184–85; intractability and, 166–85; romantic conceptions of, 246n40

James, Henry, 183–85
James, William, 139–41

Kambartel, Friedrich, 206–7
Keiner Weiß Mehr (Brinkmann), 51
Kierkegaard, Søren, 9
Kusser, Anna, 228n1